GUNSMITHING the AR-15

HOW TO
- Maintain
- Repair
- Accessorize

PATRICK SWEENEY

©2010 Krause Publications, a division of F+W Media, Inc.

Published by

Gun Digest® Books

An imprint of F+W Media, Inc.

700 East State Street • Iola, WI 54990-0001
715-445-2214 • 888-457-2873
www.gundigeststore.com

Our toll-free number to place an order or obtain
a free catalog is (800) 258-0929.

Library of Congress Control Number: 2009937518

ISBN-13: 978-1-4402-0899-7
ISBN-10: 1-4402-0899-9

Designed by Kara Grundman
Edited by Dan Shideler

Printed in the Unites States of America

DEDICATION

First and foremost, and as always, to Felicia. I know I gush over her to the point that some believe her to be mythical, but she's real. And she is a far better writer than I am. She can craft prose to make you weep and laugh, think and rant. Me, I'm just happy if you the reader get a good chuckle now and then, and clear instructions from me on how to do stuff.

However, for this volume I also want to thank those who stand guard: the police officers who work crazy shifts, in bad precincts, who help people and do not get up in front of a camera and puff themselves up. A lot more of those officers are now using the AR than in years past. Also, I want to thank those men and women who are in faraway places, putting themselves at risk so the risk does not come here. There is a well-known line, often attributed to George Orwell, that cover them: "We sleep safe in our beds at night because rough men stand ready to visit violence upon those who would do us harm." While no one has been able to prove he actually said or wrote it, it does neatly capture those men and women.

Thank you, all of you.

ACKNOWLEDGMENTS

This book is a compendium of the tricks and information I've gathered in over 25 years of shooting and wrenching on AR-15s. It is also built from the lesson plans of the classes Jeff Chudwin, Ned Christiansen and I (along with a large cast of assisting law-enforcement instructors) have collected in over 15 years of teaching patrol rifle classes for the North East Multi-Regional Training Authority.

The luxury or working with such knowledgable users is invaluable. Besides the differing points of view and backgrounds, Jeff and Ned have experience in areas I have not. As a Chief of Police, Jeff lives daily with the experiences and issues of supervising people under arms. Police officers on duty do things to firearms (and cars, computers, etc.) that would make you cry.

Ned, in addition to being a top-notch 1911 'smith, and rightfully nicknamed the "Master of Metal," is an NRA classified High Power shooter. He has fired "over the course" many times, and he has learned things from that that I would not know, not having done it. But in talking to him, I gained info.

In the course of ferreting out information, I talked to and pummeled with questions many of the AR manufacturers. Mark Malkowski of Stag was a veritable font of information and provided me with much technical info. Dave Beatty of Sun Devil manufacturing provided me with primo gear, as did Mark LaRue, Dave Dunlap of PRI, Dave Manson, and Bill Filbert of Wolf Ammunition. The luxury of working with the whole crew at DPMS, who were exemplary in their efforts to find info and products and let me shoot unusual ARs.

Mark Westrom and the folks at Armalite actually let me pore over their manufacturing facility, watch and photograph everything, and pose questions that at times may have seemed more existential than practical. And then, knowing who I was and what I was like, the crew at DS Arms did the very same thing, letting me take up a whole day and then some.

I'd also like to thank my customers at the gun shop back in the 1980s, for bringing in their broken and home-assembled ARs. Were it not for their enthusiasm at experimentation and exuberance (and over-estimation) of their own skills and knowledge, I would not have begun this particular path of inquiry. The second group comprise all the fellow AR competitors whose experiences, experimentation and performance greatly enhanced my knowledge base. There is no lesson so inexpensive (and hard to actually learn) as the experience of others. Their experiments, excesses, successes and failures all informed my R&D.

Last, but far from least, is Brownells. Their AR-builder software lets you select all the goodies you want, see what the finished rifle would look like, and then simply hit "order" to have it all on the way. Well, that, and to see if your credit card can take the heat. Spontaneous combustion of plastic is not an unknown phenomenon in Montezuma, Iowa.

TABLE OF CONTENTS

INTRODUCTION

The AR-15/M-16 has been the service rifle of our armed forces for over 45 years. As a record, it is surpassed by only a few firearms: the 1911, for one, from 1911 to 1985; the M2HB, or .50 machinegun, from 1919 to the present. (I can't help but point out both were designed by John Moses Browning.) In most of that time, it has been hounded with a reputation of inaccuracy, unreliability, and lack of power. Well, the power thing may or may not be true, depending on just what your threshold of "enough" power may be. While the reports of "skinnies" taking multiple hits in Somalia is one source (and I am not prepared to argue the veracity of those reports) for the most part the "lack" of "power" in many instances is exaggerated – but one made partially true because of the military selection of the M-855 "green tip" bullet, which most of us are not stuck with.

Here, instead of history (although you'll get a good dollop of that) we are going to study just the selection and assembly of the rifle itself. Why selection? Because simply bolting on parts isn't enough. You have to know which ones, why and which ones, why not.

I learned the AR-15 on my own. I had lost some 3-gun matches while shooting .30 caliber rifles in the prehistoric days of IPSC, and I decided losing sucked. One I lost while using my match-conditioned Garand. It was the old-format Light Rifle Pop and Flop, from the Second Chance shoot. You had to run downrange and set 15 pins on their stands, then run back, load and shoot. Fastest time won. I dropped 15 pins with 16 shots, and came in third. The winner used a Universal Carbine (gack) with a telescoping wire "paratrooper" stock (double-gack) a cheap scope in a side mount (triple-gack) and two 30-round magazines in a "jungle clip." He shot so much he reloaded and still trounced my time. So, I acquired an AR, learned how they worked (I was a gunsmith then) and started building, adding to my collection, and modifying them. Until the AR was up and running, I lost a few club matches, getting my butt handed to me by people not using a "manly" rifle.

In the late 1980s, we had an "assault weapons" scare. Lots of guys were buying lots of parts and trying to put their own rifles together. A lot found it to be too much. I gained a reputation as a guy who could make an AR run and soon had a steady stream of un-working ARs coming in. I got good enough at it that I charged a flat fee: as long as you hadn't drilled or reamed anything, I'd make sure it was put together correctly, and test-fired it to make sure. Busted/modified parts cost you extra. We've had other assault weapons scares since, and although I haven't been at the shop during those, I'd bet much the same thing happened. I hope whoever was there to re-build rifles did as good a job as I did.

A long time later I took an official, certified AR-15/M-16 armorers course and nearly fell asleep during it. While it was informative, I'd rather have another root canal than go through those two days again.

A two or three-day class is both too much and too little time in which to learn all there is to know about the AR-15, either using or fixing. For all of its apparent complexity, stripping the AR-15 to its basic component assemblies can be learned, like the Glock, in half a day. Learning to precisely fit all those parts together when they come in a box takes a at least a couple of days. Learning how to fit them all when some might not be mil-spec, some might be out-of-spec, and have to be custom-fitted – well, that could take a couple of weeks.

I teach AR-15/M-16 armorers classes, along with my good friends Jeff Chudwin and Ned Christiansen. In the class, the instruction sometimes becomes more a stream-of-consciousness than a rigidly followed lesson plan. In the give-and-take of a class, some issues can need more attention than others. If everyone already knows a subject, and a few questions makes that clear, we move on. Also, there is more than can be done in two days.

The classes we taught in the beginning started out as

a means of teaching the use of a relatively new subject: patrol rifle. They then expanded to an instructors class. A few years ago, in response to demand from departments and officers, we started teaching the armorers classes.

We had been so successful in spreading the gospel of the rifle to law enforcement that there were now many departments with rifles. And not enough people who knew how to keep them running.

Worse, they didn't have the knowledge and certification status to properly advise their superiors on the subject. It's one thing to know the Chief is getting bad advice, because you know the subject. It is another thing entirely to be able to tell the Chief, "That's not a good idea, we covered that in the State-certified armorers course. Instead, this works."

It is an inescapable fact of life that an opinion backed by a certificate or title means more than one without, even if both are correct.

This book will contain more information that I or anyone can teach in the time allotted in a two or three-day course. It has more background than classroom time permits to explain or discuss. And some things have been left out, things that we go into in the LEO classes. A departmental armorer will have to work on what the department owns. If that is a rack full of government-supplied M-16A1 rifles, then he/she has to know how to run them. If the Chief/Sheriff/Commissioner decided that what they needed was burst-fire SBRs, then that's what he/she works on.

Yes, some of you will have select-fire or burst-fire rifles. Good for you. Most readers won't, and space I might devote to select-fire issues is space I have to take from something else, something everyone needs or wants. So sorry, you lucky machinegun owners. I'm not being an LE elitist, nor deliberately slighting transferable M-16s. I wish I had one, but the $15,000 price tag is just a bit much to swing.

It is in the nature of a book such as this that I will inevitably cover things that a lot of you will already know. And for even more of you, I will be covering things you already "know." I'm not trying to be a smart-alec here, but there are a lot of things that people "know" that just aren't true. And in the pantheon of things that can hurt you, ignorance is often exceed by things you "know " that aren't true. So, if someone tells you something that contradicts what I've put down, don't automatically assume that one of of us is wrong. We may actually both be right, but in different circumstances. In cases of a conflict, do your homework. Study the situation. If you want to, do an experiment to solve the problem, but do it in a manner that won't cause harm and decreases the likelihood of damaged parts.

Or just do it my way.

A bit of info to stick in the back of your mind, when considering the AR-15: it was not designed as a rifle, per se. That is, it wasn't designed with the prior idea of rifle parts and assemblies in mind. It was designed to be as much of an industrial product as possible. Thus, it has small springs and pins that are common industrial fasteners. Yes, specific to the dimensions of the AR, but not like the gas system retaining nut on an M-14/M1-A. The "industrial" philosophy informed the original design, but from there things have changed a bit.

Also, comparisons to the AK-47 are inevitable. One thing you have to keep in mind when comparing them is that the AK was designed as a tool to be handed to the masses. Without getting too philosophical or political,

the AK was intended to be issued by the ruling party to certain trusted members of the proletariat, who would use it to enforce the decisions of the various Committees. The AR was made as a military rifle, to be sure. But for the most part it is personal property, personally owned and modified according to the customer's wishes. As such, checkbook-driven changes and upgrades have made the AR a modular rifle unlike any other before. You can literally have one lower and in a minute slap a desired upper of any configuration on it and slide a suitable stock on the back. And that's a good thing, because without that aspect this would be an entirely different, and probably not as much fun, book.

An unavoidable aspect of this book is that I won't be teaching you the "ABC" manual method. That is, this isn't the "word" according to Colt, the US Government, or anyone else. First of all, they do not agree on many aspects of the rifle we're wrenching on. Second, I've been to a few manufacturers and government-approved armorers classes.

The best of them were mildly entertaining and adequately informative. The worst were marathon caffeine-fests, where it was a struggle to stay awake. You may not find anything new in this book (*I doubt that. – Editor*) but you sure won't be bored.

Also, there are a lot of things about the AR that are legitimately a matter of personal choice. You want a hot pink AR, knock yourself out. I'm not one to condescend on matters of accessories, choices on gear, optics, etc. There are, however, things that matter. Where it matters, I will be clear. I will not leave you up in the air when it comes to things I feel strongly about. Where it is personal taste, have fun. Where it is something I have a clear opinion on, pay attention. If you do not, or decide you know better, I'm not going to give a moment's attention to complaints. But that's just me, wanting a rifle that works 100% of the time.

Read on, plan your builds, and take things one step at a time. Because the AR-15 is perhaps the most user-buildable and workable rifle ever made.

Chapter One

WHAT AND HOW

First, a bit of information about the organizational method of this book. The AR is composed of systems, just as any complex mechanism is. While I try to work on and explain one at a time, they are all interlinked, and sometimes the discussion of one area or subject laps over into another. That's just the way things are in the AR world.

Second, you can make your AR pretty much anything you want (within the law, of course) but regardless of what you do you risk catching grief from some quarters. If you build a rifle or modify one, and it isn't exactly mil-spec, some will view it as a mongrel. Others will insist your rifle isn't complete until it has a paint job, and others will insist just as vehemently that it must be left basic black. Build what you want, at the price point you can afford, and let the self-proclaimed cognoscenti huff themselves silly.

Besides legal limitations, there may be others. For instance, you may have designed a great new caliber for the AR, but unless you can find a barrel maker who will make one, you're out of luck. The popularity of customizing ARs has reached such heights that Brownells has a section on their web site dedicated to building an AR. You can mix and match, select just the cool additions

(Left) You can make and re-make your AR into whatever you want it to be. This photo used to be the wallpaper on my laptop computer, until on one trip TSA insisted I turn the thing on to prove it worked.

to your rifle you want, and when you have reached perfection, the software already has the part numbers and can place an order for you. I love the guys at Brownells, but in good conscience I have to suggest one additional step: Look at the total before you hit "send." You may just find that your perfect AR is one you cannot afford to customize all in one fell swoop.

I do not do a blow-by-blow description of assembling an AR, as if you opened this book with a box full of loose parts at your elbow. In the course of the book you'll get all that, but it is much more likely that you have an AR and want to enhance, modify or rebuild it. So I cover the rifle subject by subject.

And as a final suggestion in the beginning of your AR education, have an idea of what you want the final result to be before you begin an overhaul. Just bolting things on to "see how it looks" can get expensive and soak up a lot of time. Start with a plan, even if the plan is as simple as "I want something lightweight."

The Basics We All Know

And sometimes don't. These may be obvious, they may seem like I'm nagging you, but we all need to know what's up, and be working from the same page. So, with your forbearance (and with a few humorous things thrown in) I'll get you up to speed.

Here it is, the earliest AR-15 I've ever laid eyes on. This is a pre-1963 Colt-made, Armalite-named select-fire rifle. In the Springfield Armory Museum, Springfield, MA.

Controls and Nomenclature

At the rear of the rifle is the buttstock. They come in fixed and adjustable models. On top are the sights, front and rear. The handguards enclose the barrel, and in front of the front sight housing is the flash hider. Some rifles lack a flash hider, and have only the bare muzzle with its crown. (The barrel underneath the flash hider also has a crown.) On the right side of the lower receiver is a button: the magazine catch or magazine release button. Rifles that are fitted with ambidextrous safeties will have a safety lever or firing selector lever on the right side as well as the left.

On the right side of the upper receiver is the ejection port in front, with its spring-loaded ejection port cover. Behind it, depending on the particular model, may or may not be an ejector lump and forward assist. (Rifle/carbines lacking an ejector lump should be viewed suspiciously by left-handed shooters. The face you save is your own.)

On the left side of the lower is the safety/fire selector. Above and forward of it is the bolt hold-open, a lever that is activated by the magazine. When the magazine is empty the magazine follower presses the hold-open lever up and it blocks the bolt. The rifle stays open after the last shot. (If those parts are working correctly, that is.)

On the front and rear of the lower, up next to the upper receiver, are two large-headed cross pins. They are the takedown pins that hold the upper and lower together.

Safety in Work

The AR-15 uses a large number of small parts in self-contained assemblies. It also uses a large number of small springs for those parts to properly function. Cleaning it requires the use of solvents, brushes and cleaning rods.

It is important that any time you are working on your rifle that you wear safety glasses. A part launched into the ceiling is cause for embarrassment, perhaps even snide comments from your co-workers or fellow shooters. A part launched into your face is painful. Without glasses it could be tragic, and be the cause of the end of your shooting career. Perhaps even other aspects of your life would suffer, as well. Who wants to have a one-eyed dentist drilling on a tooth? Trust me, only in romance novels do women find men with an eye patch sexy.

Four Safety Rules

We all know them, and often we live them. But they still bear repeating:

1) All guns are loaded. That means be polite, mind your manners, and don't point them at others, even while working on them.
2) Keep the muzzle pointed in a safe direction. In an armorers class you may be in tight quarters. Quickly flipping a rifle end-to-end could whack someone in the face with muzzle or stock.
3) Keep your finger off the trigger. Not just to avoid accidental (or negligent) discharges, but also because dropping the hammer on an AR with the two halves apart can damage the receiver.
4) Be sure of your target. Know where it is pointed when you do dry-fire your rifle.

Tools Needed

The AR-15/M-16 is designed, as all good military small arms are, to be taken apart with either the bare hands

Taking it apart and working on the AR is easy, once you know how. Lawfully acquiring an SBR such as this is a bit more involved.

or with the assistance of a loaded cartridge. (In a combat setting, the only two things you can always count on the troops having are rifles and ammunition.)

Field-stripping is enough to keep a rifle working in the field. However, more than field-stripping requires tools. A soldier can take his rifle apart with his bare hands, but he can't clean the bore or scrape the carbon off the bolt with just his bare hands. Neither can you. The basic toolkit is listed in Appendix A. The more advanced toolkit can also be found there.

There are a large number of specialized tools for the AR. Not because working on the AR-15/M-16 always require that specialized tool, but because having said special tool can often make a difficult job easy.

In addition to the basic toolkit, you should have a cleaning rod (one-piece is better than a section rod), patches, brushes, solvents and lubricants.

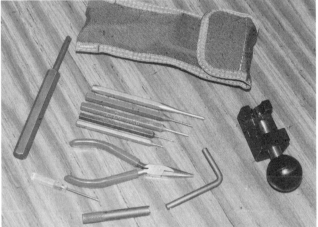

This is the basic toolkit we were handed in the Colt armorers course. With it, you can do pretty much everything but change barrels and stake carrier keys.

A complete armorers tool kit is available from Brownells, in a nearly-unbreakable container that can be sent as luggage or shipped. However, at $1,200 it is more than many shooters need or can justify.

Basic Tools List

Tool	What It's For
Punch, 1/16"	Charging handle
	Forward assist pawl
	A1 & A2 windage drum
Punch, 5/64"	Gas tube retaining pin
Punch, 3/32"	A2 elevation spring pin
	Forward assist assembly
	Front takedown pin assembly,
	auto-sear
Punch, 1/8"	Trigger guard roll pin
	Hammer & trigger pins
Punch, 1/4"	General pin driving
Taper pin starter	Barrel taper pins
Pivot pin install tool	Front pivot pin
M4 stock wrench	Telestock castle nut
Bolt catch pin punch	Bolt catch pin
Allen wrenches,	
3/16", 5/32"	Pistol grip screws, allen head type

The Brownells toolkit is great for departments, for one good reason: it is one item. I talked to Brownells about that, and found an interesting detail of municipal acquisition: If you submit two requisition forms, one for "Armorers kit, AR-15/M-16" with a single line and total, and another with all the parts separately, the one kit will get the nod. Even with both totals being the same! Hence the "one of everything" tool kit. If you want it, get it. But better to get

If you are going to assemble a lot of lowers, you might want an assembly block like this one. However, it can be a bit expensive to use on your one-and-only rifle build.

what you need, when you need it, and build your own kits.

With the basic kit above, you can do most everything you need. As we go through the projects, if you need more, I'll list the tools, and you can decide to get them, or have someone else do the work.

Bench kit and extras

While the standard cleaning and maintenance can be done with your bare hands, or in your lap with tools, there are tasks that cannot be performed without tools. Changing barrels, stocks, assembling sights front and rear are just a few. Ideally, you'll have a solid workbench to work on. The correct height depends on whether you prefer to work standing or sitting. In many instances, it will be what it is. You should have a solid vise mounted securely to the bench. The best setup would be a solid bench, bolted to both the floor and wall, with a 5" or 6" bench vise bolted to it.

Lacking the ability to bolt it to the wall or floor, add weight. You should not be surprised to discover that adding several hundred pounds (or in my case, a ton) of dead weight acts to stabilize a bench. Of course, your bench had better be strong enough to hold the weight, or you'll be starting all over when it breaks.

If you are setting up a workstation, make sure the bench and vise have enough room around them. For instance, if you are installing a new rifle barrel (20-inch) on a receiver, you'll need at least two and a half feet of space from the end of the vise to the closest wall. More would be better, especially if your "skinny jeans" days are behind you. You can assemble a rifle while in a broom closet, but you won't enjoy it much.

Basic Parts Kits

Any selection of parts for future use or need should be considered with two aspects in mind: those that are common to wear or break, and those that are common to get lost. Stocking a spare upper receiver "just in case" is not wise, as they hardly ever break. Well, at least not under normal usage. Remember my mentioning Jeff Chudwin and the experiences of police work? Officers getting involved in fights, taking spills, or just being in automobile wrecks can damage rifles. (Not to mention the officers.) If a departmental rifle does get busted, a spare rifle can be issued until a new receiver arrives. You do not have that luxury. Well, maybe you do. But in that case,

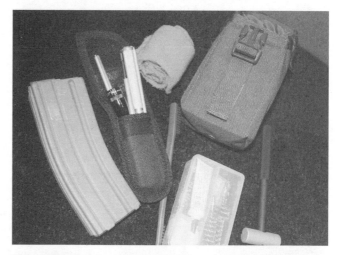

The Brownells toolkit is one item with everything you need. Departments want it because it makes the paperwork easier. You can do as well buying things as you need them.

The GG&G field tool kit and maintenance pouch. Stuff some more goodies in it, and clip it to your rucksack.

if you're going to stock a spare upper "just in case," why not just build it into a complete rifle, "just in case?" Small springs, plungers, etc., that are easily lost in disassembly or armorers work are inexpensive and prudent to stock.

Basically, if it is cheap, small, easily busted/bent, etc. get some and keep some. The more expensive stuff you may have to think about. It is common in some circles to have a spare bolt stuffed in the pistol grip. Think about it: you've got anywhere from $100 to $200 tied up in an assembled, headspaced, test-fired bolt, in your pistol grip. Is that a wise investment?

The CJ Weapons toolkit in a handle. You can do lots of maintenance with this and an extra pouch of spare parts.

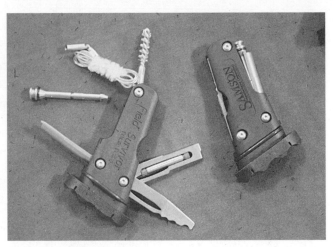

The Samson field survivor kit has a lot of useful tools, and it fits in the pistol grip.

An AR cleaning kit in action.

Field Maintenance

Having spare parts kit or tool kit clipped to your belt or tac vest "just in case" seems to me to be a chancy thing. Granted, if your "beat" is a dusty ridgeline in Afghanistan, having stuff on hand instead of in the vehicle steps, yards or kilometers away is prudent. Then again, I can't help but think of Sam Elliot as Sergeant Major Plumley. He was packing a 1911A1 into a hot LZ, and when asked about taking a rifle, he remarked "If it comes to that, there will be plenty lying around."

If you have the great bad luck to have a busted rifle in a fight, you probably aren't going to fix it in time. You'd best get another one and get back to the business at hand. So, on your belt, the space and weight are better devoted to extra ammo, or a sidearm. But on your rucksack? Now you're thinking.

GG&G makes a toolkit with spares that fits in a web pouch, and is easily attached to your ruck. With it you're set to do a bunch of maintenance. It has a self-deploying cleaning rod, so you have a basic cleaning kit and if you add a few more spares and tools, you can do just about anything that needs doing, in the field.

CJ Weapons makes a tool kit where everything is attached. It is the Swiss Army Knife of AR kits. It also includes a stock wrench, so if your stock comes loose you at least have a way to regularly tighten it until you can get to a bench and staking tools.

Last is the Samson, a tool kit that fits into the pistol grip. I know, I've said on-hand tool kits usually won't help you, but the Samson has a useful addition: a broken case extractor. If your field malfunction clearance doesn't solve the problem, get the case extractor out, drop it in the chamber, cycle the bolt, reload and get back to work. I did just that in a carbine class at Gunsite, except back then I had the case extractor loose in my pocket.

Cleaning Supplies

Use only copper-removing bore solvents in the bore. The various "powder" solvents do little or nothing on copper deposits in the bore, and the copper solvents, combined with a good brushing, wash away powder deposits. Use brass or plastic brushes on the bore of the rifle, not stainless. Buy the correct-sized cleaning patches, 100% cotton. Cotton patches hold solvents better than synthetics.

Using the wrong size "because it's cheap" or cutting down too-big patches is a recipe for hassle or disaster. If too small they won't clean well, and you may lose one in the bore. Too big, and you might wedge one (still secured to the cleaning rod) in the bore, or worse yet it might come off, which can be an expensive error to correct. Ned once had to rebuild a rifle for a shooter. The fellow had been diligently doing the correct barrel break-in procedure on his expensive new barrel. Unbeknownst to him, the sectioned cleaning rod unscrewed and left the cleaning rod tip and patch in the bore. The next shot? Bulged barrel, busted bolt, heartache and expense.

The carbon deposits on the bolt and carrier and in the interior of the upper and lower receivers can be cleaned with any good firearms solvent. Many a gunshop and armorers station uses mineral spirits to hose away scrubbed carbon. Be aware that reclaimed mineral spirits contain a high-enough percentage of kerosene to create an odor. You might well find yourself unwelcome at home due to the odor of mineral spirits.

Lubrication and the AR-15/M-16

The subject of lubricants is vast, and opinions vary. In most situations, as one of the instructors has been known to joke, "sunscreen would probably work for a while." Adherents of one or another brand of lubricant will extol its virtues endlessly. Whatever you use, use it. A dry AR

is a rifle looking to malfunction. Invariably in the patrol rifle and patrol rifle instructor classes taught in NEMRT, we have rifles whose owners thought they had sufficiently lubed them start to malfunction right after lunch of the first full firing day. You don't want so much lube on it that it splatters you and bystanders on every shot. But if, when you touch the carrier through the ejection port, you don't get oil on your fingertip, the carrier (and thus the bolt) is probably too dry. Some have suggested that the best way to keep an AR-15 or M-16 running reliably is to keep it dry, to prevent it from attracting dirt. They are wrong. You need oil to reduce friction, and carry grit and dirt away from the working parts. Running a rifle while it is dry will simply make it malfunction sooner, not later.

Let me repeat that, just in case someone you know is a strenuous advocate of running your gun dry: they are wrong.

So where to lube?

You do not need a 55 gallon drum for a dip-lube, nor do you need a shaving brush to give every surface a nice, even coating of 5W30. But you do need lubricant, and some places matter more than others. By "wet" I mean a visible layer of lubricant on the surface. By "damp" I mean the surface has been clearly oiled, but there is no danger of oil dripping off the part. An automotive example to demonstrate the differences: if you pull the dipstick out of your engine, the part that was in the oil is "dripping." The rest of the stick is "wet." If you wipe it with a cloth or paper towel, the dipstick is now "damp."

Bolt: You want the extractor joints, pivot pin and spring each wet with oil. The locking lugs should be damp, and the bearing band (the slightly raised part behind the cam pin hole) should be wet.

Carrier: The running rails, the raised sections that run the length of the carrier should be wet. The rest of the exterior should be damp. The cam pin slot should be wet, as should the cam pin riding there. The bolt tunnel should be damp.

Trigger mechanism: The bolt, trigger, disconnector and safety should be damp. The pivot pins should be wet.

The rest of the rifle can be damp or dry, as you wish, or as maintenance regulations or climate require. In the course of shooting and cleaning, all the other parts will end up with a very light film of oil. The only way to make them absolutely dry again is with liberal applications of degreasing aerosol. But it isn't needed. Unless you're in an extremely humid climate for long periods of time, the exterior steel isn't going to rust. The plastic and aluminum aren't going to rust even then.

Dry Rifles in the Armory/Rifle Rack

Many service personnel will be familiar with rifles stored in the base armory or depot being stored bone-dry. The reason is not for the longevity of the rifle, nor to ensure it is in a constant state of readiness. It is so the inspecting officer will not get oil on his or her white glove, and as a result conclude the rifles have been stored in an uncleaned condition. I kid you not. Rational? No. Should your rifle or rifles be stored dry? That is something only the

If you are lucky enough to live where you can have a suppressor, then your AR will require even more cleaning and maintenance. Keep the moving parts lubed, and the rifle will be happy.

Muzzle safe, finger off the trigger. Oh, how the world has changed: this is a Ruger!

departmental armorer (in this case: you) can decide. Oiled rifles will attract and hold dust and lint. Dry rifles must be lubed when grabbed for use, or they will not function properly. A rifle stored "just in case" as a backup can be left dry. A rifle racked "just in case" that is loaded or close to it must be properly and fully oiled. And those of you who are reading this who are not departmental armorers, keep your rifles oiled.

Which Oil?

Use whatever firearms-suitable lubricant you have. You can use the expensive stuff, the free stuff, even synthetic motor oil. Just use something. Anything is better than nothing, but avoid grease. In hot weather grease will work, but unless you are diligent about cleaning it out for the cold weather months, it will harden and become stiff in the cold. Also, over time it will collect lint and harden. As much as I love it properly applied on my M1 Garand or M1-A, grease is not good in an AR.

Handling Drills and Habits

When working on any rifle, you should (and must) ascertain that it is unloaded, every time you handle it. You must make this a reflexive habit. As a lifetime habit, this is one of the best to cultivate. You also must be in the habit of controlling the direction of the muzzle. Yes, there will be lots of times when the rifle well-and-truly isn't loaded. But if you let yourself get into bad habits, one day they will jump up and bite you or someone else.

When handled a rifle to work on, your first action must be to ascertain that the weapon you're holding is, indeed, unloaded.

ChamberSafe®

The ChamberSafe is both a training aid and a ready-to-go aid. To use it, remove the magazine (if any). Extract the chambered round (again, if any) and insert the Chambersafe into the chamber. Ease the bolt forward. It is now not possible for there to be a round in the chamber. While good safety habits (and basic good manners) dictate that you should not point the muzzle of your rifle at anyone, in a training setting instructors and students can now handle their firearms during discussions, non-live-fire training, and administrative tasks knowing they are not loaded.

The Chambersafe can also be used in storage racks and as a ready-to-go chamber check. As the Chambersafe blocks only the chamber, a loaded magazine can be inserted and locked into the magazine well. Since the Chambersafe blocks the chamber, the rifle cannot have a live round in the chamber. To load it, however, requires only that the Chambersafe be pulled free and the charging handle cycled.

If you want to have a rifle on hand, ready to go or close to it, this is the way. Now, were I on guard duty in some dusty locale in Afghanistan, would I have a Chambersafe in my M4? Probably not, unless the senior NCO insisted. However, most of us do not live in locations as rough-and-ready as Afghanistan. If you do, I have one piece of advice: move.

Checking Status of Your Rifle

Unless you own one and only one firearm, you can't remember the status they are all in. More than one, you have to check. (Even with just one, regular checks are a good habit to have.)

Bench Check

Remove the magazine, if there is one in the rifle, and extract the chambered round, if any.

Grasp the charging handle and pull it back. Either hold the handle back or lock the bolt open. Look in the chamber. If you lock the bolt back, you can use a light or your fingers to check that the chamber is empty. This check only takes a few seconds and is time well-spent.

Range/Match/Street Check

There should be a magazine in place. The bolt will probably be open, or have a Chambersafe in it. Press the magazine button and release the magazine while holding it. Look at the top of the magazine to ensure there are rounds in it. In the dark, you can feel the front of the magazine opening for the bullet tips. Press the magazine back into place and then try to pull it down. DO NOT PUSH IT IN, LET GO, AND THEN SLAP THE MAGAZINE TO SEAT IT. If you do, it is entirely possible for the magazine to drop free and fall to the ground as you are swinging your hand to slap it. Also, if the bolt is locked open, slapping the magazine can dislodge the top round. When you do then send the bolt forward, it will attempt to chamber both the free round that popped loose, and the one below it, the one still in the magazine. Your attempt at looking cool or "making sure" simply creates a malfunction.

Cobra Technique

You do this one when you expect the rifle to have a round in the chamber. You've loaded for a match, or you

The ChamberSafe chamber blocking device is a great aid to training. It allows a class of shooters to safe their rifles and concentrate on the instructional material.

The Cobra chamber-checking technique, which you can do even in the dark.

are in a potentially lethal force situation, and you want to be sure of your rifle's status.

Do as above. With the magazine checked, inserted and re-locked in place, place your right hand (for right-handed shooters) behind the charging handle with your wrist against the stock. Now cup your hand and draw your fingers back. You will be lifting your hand (with your wrist against the stock) as if you are imitating a cobra ready to strike. You do not pull your arm back. With your wrist against the stock, you will only be able to draw the charging handle back a couple of inches, which is all you want.

With your left hand cupping the handguard directly in front of the receiver, bring your first or second finger around to the ejection port. You can then feel through the port that there is a round on the bolt face, held there by the extractor.

Make sure that what you are feeling is the cartridge, and not the bolt or carrier.

If you draw your right hand back too far you'll extract and eject the chambered round. By drawing it back just enough to feel, but not so far that the round clears the ejection port, you can quietly check the chamber.

Ease the bolt forward, or let go and let it close on its own power. Either way, press the forward assist. NOTE: This is the only time you will ever use the forward assist. Using it to drive home a recalcitrant cartridge on other occasions will simply wedge that round in place, creating a greater problem to fix than you otherwise would have had.

Chapter Two

LOOKS COUNT TOO

We all want a rifle that looks good. The problem is, what looks "good" and what doesn't are social constructs, and not anything else. You can work hard to keep your rifle looking pristine, as if it was just lifted out of the shipping box. Or you can let it get worn bright on the high spots. Your choice.

Surface Finishes and Composition

The upper and lower receiver, and many of the aftermarket railed handguards, are made of anodized aluminum. The only uppers and lowers to be considered for law enforcement use are those made from forgings,

(Left) The idea of an all-black rifle is passé in many circles. Here, two soldiers pause on a patrol to enjoy the shade in Baghdad. U.S. Army photo by Staff Sgt. Bronco Suzuki.

and the aluminum should be the alloy known as 7075-T6. There are uppers made from extrusions, and lowers that are castings. They work fine for competitive applications, but I'm not too keen on them for tactical or defensive use. Extrusions are generally made of 6061 aluminum, also known as "aircraft" aluminum. The 7075 is the alloy and T6 heat-treatment method for the AR-15/M-16 uppers and lowers that are mil-spec. The only surface treatment you should consider for the upper and lower is MIL-A-8625, Type II or Type III, both known as "hard anodizing." They differ from each other in the temperature and electrical charge used to create the anodizing. Anodizing is a surface treatment that creates a hard, porous aluminum oxide finish. The military insists that the porosity of the aluminum oxide surface be sealed with a nickel acetate treatment.

Type III is harder, thicker, smoother and more-resistant to corrosion than Type II.

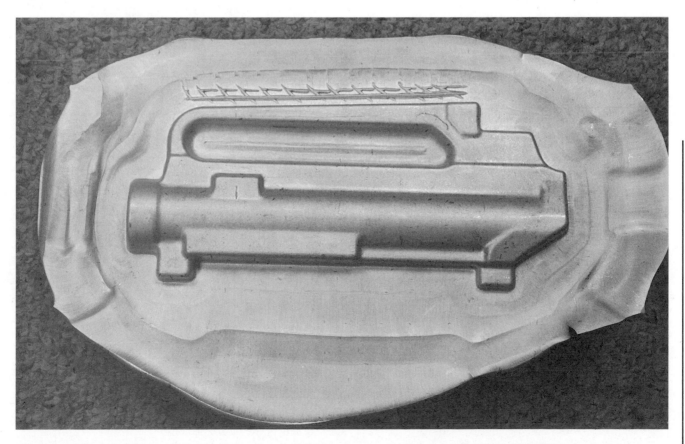

This is a "platter" that has come from the forging machine but has not yet had the excess trimmed off.

This very early M-16 (no A1) has a dove-gray anodized finish. If you want to make an M4 clone, not the color you want. If you want an XM-177, this is it.

The surface of the anodized aluminum is made harder, resistant to corrosion, and somewhat matte in texture by the process. Type III anodizing can only be done in shades of gray and black. If something is anodized a different color than gray or black, it was done with the Type II method of treatment. Type II can be done in black, which is more durable than the colors, but not as durable as Type III. Early-production Colt rifles (there was no other brand but Colt for us civvies before the mid-1980s) were given a gray finish, not black. The anodizing cannot be dyed or darkened once applied and sealed. If you want something other than the black that is there, you have two choices: apply a paint or bake-on finish or send the parts off to U.S. Anodizing, who can re-do the finish for you.

Krylon flat black or ultra-flat black will closely match Type III and does not require the heat of bake-on finishes.

US Anodizing can re-anodize aluminum parts. However, the process can be expensive, and the differing alloys and heat-treatments of the various parts can lead to slightly differing shades of black on them. (Anodizing is clear; it's the dye used to darken and seal the surface that determines the final color.) If having everything match exactly is important, then the bake-on or Krylon approach is the only one that will ensure an absolutely exact match.

Aluminum handguards are more often 6061 alloy. As

The upper and lower on this rifle do not match. If you can't live with it, there are many ways to either make them match, or make them some other color.

they do not need the durability of the upper and lower receivers, they are commonly given a Type I anodizing, which is more than enough. Handguards given a Type II or Type III anodizing will be harder, but the process is more expensive, and the handguards will also be more expensive as a result.

If a rifle must be some color other than flat black, a spray and bake-on finish should be applied over the anodizing. This is much simpler than trying to find a durable anodizing of the desired color.

There are some receivers made of stainless steel, brass

Robar did this AR in a desert camo for me. It is a tough, durable and easy-to-clean finish.

The NP3 Robar does is so slick, it was imperative to stake the castle nut on this AR.

Here is a digital camo pattern from Duracoat.

Once you paint, it will wear and chip, which simply adds to the camouflage of your camo job.

and fiberglass-filled polymer. They are not the standard. They should be avoided for several reasons. As non-standard rifles, they may have dimensional problems that prevent them from being 100% compatible with existing uppers and lowers you might have. If reliable interchangeability is your goal, then get only mil-spec uppers and lowers. Actually, get them all from the same maker. The steel and brass ones will be significantly heavier than standard rifles, which some long-range competitors might like. Me, I'm not too fond of a 17-pound AR-15. And the polymer-receiver rifles have not proven as durable as standard, aluminum-alloy, rifles.

The "furniture," the plastic parts, are generally durable polymer, usually with some fiberglass filling in the mixture to add rigidity and abrasion resistance. While it is possible to repair plastic furniture, it is not cost-effective. A new set of handguards, or a new buttstock, can be acquired for far less than the departmental cost of the armorer's time and materials needed to repair the parts.

Steel on the AR is treated with a black oxide finish. Often called "Parkerizing," the modern black oxide is much more durable than the old gray/green Parkerizing. However, that does not mean the older finish is weak. Decades of use have proven that the older finish, cared for and kept oiled, will last.

Project "Tacticool"

Our first project is something you'll probably do last on your rifle. But some of you will want to have something to do right away, and some of you will already have rifles ready for this project. We're going to either camo it, or make the finish match. Making the finish match involves having your upper and lower, and perhaps your buffer tube and handguards (or not) all the same color. In the past, uppers and lowers could be found in anything from a medium gray to black, to a purplish black or purple/blue. To match everything, you need to detail strip your upper and lower. That is, every single part: pins, springs, etc. must be removed. You need a proper finish material. You can use Krylon. It is fast, reasonably durable, and cheap. It comes in a few colors that matter to us, but it is not as durable as other finishes.

Something like Duracoat, from Steve Lauer, is available in a dizzying number of colors, and they can also supply you with the overlay patterns to do camouflage patterns. However, it requires a spray gun (not an aerosol can) and heat to cure the coating. You do have the added benefit of tweaking the nose of Mayor Bloomberg of NYC, who has made it a personal campaign (among others) to stamp out painted guns.

Or, you can use one of the many Brownells products,

offered in camo colors, which can be baked on.

Whichever you do, start by prepping the surface. If you are going to match the upper and lower, detail strip. If you are going to camo, you can paint the whole thing, but it is best if the base coat is done to a detail-stripped rifle. Use an aerosol degreaser and get the oil off. Then, gently rub the entire surface to be painted with 0000 steel wool. You aren't trying to "sand" or anything; you just want to make sure anything loose gets rubbed off. If, when you're done, you can see any more than a slight amount of burnishing to the original surface, you did more than you needed to. Ease up next time. Degrease again.

Warm the parts with a hair dryer or heat gun set on low. Or just set them out in the noonday sun on a hot day. Once it's warm to the touch (and don't touch with bare, greasy fingers) you're ready to paint. Apply a light and even coat. If you want to match finishes and make them close to original, Krylon Ultra-Flat Black does a good job. Otherwise, use the base color for your camo job. Let dry according to instructions, and apply another coat. You will want two or three light coats. Any more than that and you'll simply be building up a thick layer that will chip under hard use.

If you're doing a camo job, now put the parts or rifle down on a big sheet of cardboard, lay your camo "negative" pattern on, and overspray with the next color. Remember, the last color gets the least coverage, as you add another masking layer for each color. The greater the masking layer, the less of the overspray color you get. I've known guys who made cardboard cutouts vaguely like an AR, and practiced on them until they got the pattern they liked. You can use foliage, grass, straw or even cloth plastic or wire mesh as an overlay. The colors? That depends on where you are and what you want to match. In the southwest, tans will work. In a grassland, light greens. In a forest, something darker; greens or browns. Remember: black stands out in any area.

As an alternative, you can send your rifle off to U.S. Anodizing, who will match the aluminum parts to whatever period color you want. They can also parkerize the steel. Duracoat can coat your rifle in any color and pattern you can dream up. Robbie Barkman of Robar also does durable coatings, and he can add NP3, a nearly indestructible and self-lubricating plating, to the steel parts.

Having painted, you have to reassemble. This is where light coats becomes important. Too heavy a spray and you may find threads bind, parts won't fit, and assemblies become recalcitrant. And this is also the reason a lot of shooters simply spray-paint the assembled rifle (masking the sights to keep them black, of course) with the base coat of the camo job. Your rifle, your choice.

Chapter Three

GETTING THINGS APART

The basic is field-stripping, where you take the rifle apart well enough to clean it. Cleaning is important. Have you seen the movie *Major League*? Charlie Sheen (who pitched in college, by the way) is a rocket launcher-armed pitcher who can't hit the strike zone. He can't see. He gets glasses, very ugly glasses. The coach remarks "It's important to see." One of the other players counters with "It ain't that important."

Stripping to clean is that important.

Field Stripping

In order to safety-check and to clean or begin armorers work, you must be able to field-strip the AR. Place the safety on "SAFE." If there is a magazine present, remove it. Pull the charging handle to the rear and lock the bolt open. The bolt hold-open is the lever on the left side of the upper receiver. Keep the charging handle pulled to the rear. Either pull the wider, serrated paddle part of the bolt hold-open out from the receiver, or press the smaller, lower portion of the bolt hold-open into the receiver body. Ease the bolt forward. Once it stops, you can release pressure on the bolt hold-open. (If you did not pull the charging handle back far enough, the bolt may appear held open, but will snap forward with any slight vibration. Be careful until you have looked at the bolt.)

Press the charging handle forward until it locks in place. Look into the chamber. Use a light if you need to, as an oxidized brass case, or a steel case, may be so dark that you'll overlook it except in bright light. If your finger fits, reach in and check the chamber. (The ejection port is

small, and not many people have fingers small enough to reach. The only method most can use is to reach up from the magazine well.)

With the chamber verified empty, close the bolt. It is best to build correct habits even while doing administrative tasks on the rifle, so close the bolt by pressing or slapping the hold-open lever. The bolt will crash closed. Stop cringing, that is the way it operates when you fire it, so closing the bolt that way is not abuse.

Press the rear takedown pin from the left to the right. Pull it until it stops at its full movement. The upper will hinge away from the lower. (Be careful to control the upper so it doesn't swing up and strike you in the face.)

Pull the charging handle halfway back. Then grasp the carrier and pull it back, down and out of the rifle. Place it on the table. Pull the charging handle back until it stops, then pull it down and out. Press the front pivot pin from the left to the right until it stops. The upper and lower receivers can now be separated.

In the field, or in a range class, this is all you need to do to gain access to the working parts for a quick cleaning. From here, aerosol cleaners and lubricant can clean what needs to be cleaned, lubed and reassembled.

But, since you have it apart right now, let's do a quick inspection and functions check. After all, if you own an AR, or plan to be doing any work on them, these are things you'll be doing on a regular basis. Best to learn how right away.

Operational Checklist

An operational checklist is a process whereby you inspect a rifle for proper fit and mechanical function, without firing it. Any fault you covered in an operational check should be corrected before that rifle can be used in

(Left) Which direction, and how far, are clues. Track them with a new rifle, and if they ever change, you know something is up.

a match, practice or for defense. Right now I'm not going to cover the causes and corrections of the faults found, only the process. Faults uncovered are divided into two groups: those that require immediate correction (or at least correction before use) and faults that can be overlooked in an emergency, where the fault would not impair function sufficient to prevent use as emergency equipment. An example of a fault in the first group would be a rifle lacking sights. There are very few faults that fall into the latter category, as a rifle as emergency equipment is not like a fire extinguisher that only has 87% of its charge. A fault in the second category would be a stock that is present, but loose. Usually, most faults on firearms are an "all or nothing" situation, especially defensive firearms.

Properly done, an Internals/Selector check takes two minutes, and you should get into the habit of doing this check every time you pick up your AR, or any other firearm, for that matter. I know, I know, you did it last week, and the week before, why do it again? Because since the last time you may have been doing some work on your AR, got interrupted, and left it as-is. Having now forgotten, if you don't do a check, you may be depending on an inoperative rifle.

Internals Check

We're already at the field-stripped stage, right? If not, move back up, read and field-strip your rifle.

Inspect the lower.

Make sure the hammer springs are on either side of the trigger pivot, and above the trigger pivot spring. Check to make sure they are intact, and one or both legs are not broken. Look at the hammer and trigger pivot pins, and make sure they are flush to the outside of the lower, and not protruding. A pin that sticks out indicates it is not secured, meaning some spring in there is out of place.

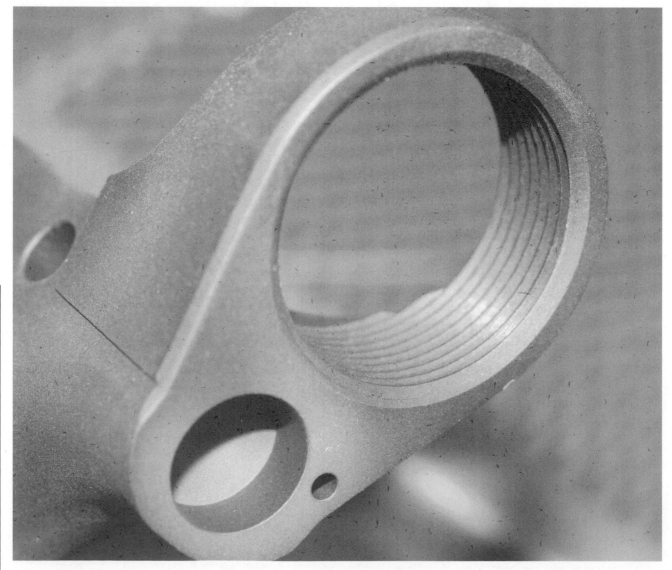

The rear hole is the one where the rear takedown pins plunger and spring go.

Move the selector back and forth from "Safe" to "Fire" (and on to "Auto" or "Burst" if the rifle/carbine in question is a select-fire weapon) and visually inspect the lower to ensure there are no debris, dust, lint, threads from cleaning patches or loose primers present.

Inspect the carrier. Grasp the carrier in one hand and the carrier key in your other hand. Try to move the key. Any movement at all means the rifle must be pulled from service until the key can removed, reinstalled and locked in place.

Inspect the bolt. Are the locking lugs clean and oiled? Any visible chips or cracks in the lugs require the rifle to be pulled from service until the bolt can be replaced. Does the ejector move in and out of the bolt when pressed with a small rod? (It won't move under finger pressure.) Does the extractor flex when pushed? Too much or too little movement requires service on those parts.

Finally, pull the bolt forward in the carrier, and stand the bolt on its head. If the weight of the carrier causes the bolt to collapse towards the tabletop, the gas rings are worn and must be replaced.

Install the bolt back into the rifle and close the action. Close the upper to the lower and press the takedown pins back in place.

Selector Check, SEMI

Lock the bolt back. Inspect the chamber. Once clearly unloaded, press the bolt hold-open lever and allow the bolt to close under its own power. Move the safety to all positions. If it does not move, the problem must be found and corrected.

Press the selector to SAFE. Press the trigger with 10 to 12 pounds of force. The hammer should not fall. If it does, the trigger mechanism is defective, broken or improperly assembled, and the fault must be found and corrected. Release the trigger. Press the selector to FIRE. If the hammer falls when the selector is moved, but before you press the trigger again, again the mechanism is either defective or improperly assembled and must be corrected. The selector function when on SAFE acts by blocking movement of the trigger. If the hammer falls, the selector did not prevent trigger movement, and when it was moved to FIRE the trigger completed that movement, allowing the hammer to fall.

With the selector on FIRE, press the trigger. The hammer should fall. If it does not, it is obviously not ready for issue, use in a match or for defense and must be corrected. If it does, now hold the trigger back. Grasp the charging handle with your other hand and cycle the bolt. Gently release the trigger. You should feel it "click" as the hammer resets

off the disconnector hook and onto the sear nose of the trigger. If there is no click, open the upper receiver. If the hammer is forward, or still caught on the disconnector, the mechanism is either improperly assembled or the parts mistimed. Find out why, and correct it.

If the rifle passes the SAFE and FIRE checks, you must then check for disconnector retention during cycling. Cycle the charging handle to cock the hammer. Press the trigger and allow the hammer to fall. Hold the trigger back. Briskly pull back and release the charging handle, allowing the bolt to close under the full power of the buffer spring. Gently and slowly release the trigger. The hammer should "click" from the disconnector to the trigger sear. If it does not, it must be adjusted. Then leave your finger off the trigger and briskly cycle the charging handle and allow the bolt to crash home at full power. Then dry-fire again. If the hammer has followed the bolt forward, the disconnector is (again) either improperly installed or mis-timed and must be corrected.

All those faults are covered in their own chapters, so read on.

Visual Inspection/Tightness

Inspect the fit of the upper to the lower. While a certain amount of looseness is often customary, and does not hinder proper function, an excessively wobbly fit indicates either serious wear or a dimensional mismatch. Excessively loose upper-to-lower fits can be solved by exchanging uppers until the uppers and lowers you own all fit properly. I have this discussion often in the law enforcement classes: While "mix-and-match" rifles will almost always function properly, remember that the accuracy of a rifle goes with the upper, not the lower, but the felt trigger pull goes with the lower. A matched upper and lower used in a precision marksmanship role must not have the upper and lower swapped with patrol car issue rifles, or the accuracy and/or trigger pull of the precision marksmanship rifle will be lost.

Inspect the stock for tightness. Solid stocks (A1 and A2) should be immovable. Tele-slider stocks will usually have some wobble in the sliding portion, but the buffer tube itself must be tight. Loose A1/A2 stocks or loose tubes in either rifles or carbines must be corrected.

Inspect the barrel for tightness in the upper receiver. An upper with a loose barrel cannot be accurate, and the cause must be found and corrected.

Inspect the front sight for tightness to the barrel.

Inspect the sights to be sure all parts are present and that any paint markings to indicate zero settings have not been disturbed.

Visually inspect the rifle to see if there are any obvious

On the range, it is is more important to figure out why your rifle has just malfunctioned than it is to immediately leap into your field drills. "Why'd this happen?" should be your focus in testing.

signs of having been dropped, abused, altered or parts exchanged. Also, check the serial number to ensure it is the weapon being issued and signed for.

Range Analysis

Range analysis differs from the bench checks you've done, in that you are firing the rifle.

A range checklist is done to ensure that a particular rifle functions perfectly, is zeroed and that all accessories on it are working within accepted limits. A range test-fire session is performed to ensure that corrections, alterations

or repairs have been correctly performed. As an example, a rifle with a worn barrel that does not shoot accurately enough will require a new barrel. Once installed, the new barrel must be test-fired to ensure that not only does it shoot accurately enough, but also that the sights are zeroed and that the rifle performs with sufficient reliability. (The only acceptable standard is 100%.) A new barrel is not like changing the oil in a car. The replacement must be tested.

Function-testing a rifle on the range is not the same as getting a recalcitrant rifle working in a shooting incident. On the street, getting the rifle working quickly, or safely disposing of it and using another weapon, is paramount. At the range, uncovering the origins of the fault is the prime consideration. (That, and safety.) When a rifle malfunctions on the range in a testing session, your immediate response should be to stop all activity. Inspect the rifle and note the condition of all parts, the locations of all controls, and the position and status of the bolt and carrier.

As an aside, as I was writing this chapter I happened to have a link to a video on the internet sent to me. I watched as some poor guy was firing an AR. He had a problem, yanked the charging handle and pulled the trigger. Nothing happened. So he hammered the forward assist. Nothing happened, so he swapped mags, worked the charging handle and hammered on the forward assist some more. I thought to myself: "This cannot end well." Then he pulled the trigger and the rifle disassembled itself. Typically with these events, he was not harmed. But the rifle was trashed. Even if the zombies were pouring over the wall, his problem-solving process was flawed. If you are in a tough situation you may have to get a rifle working again quickly, but on a target range, any problem means you stop shooting and study the situation.

When firing you should note the direction and distance of the empty brass when ejected, as this is important information that can aid the diagnosis.

Officers: In a law enforcement setting, any weapon being "debugged" and serviced should have extensive notes taken on it during the process: ammunition used, to include lot number, firer, magazine type and number if the department gives it one. Direction and distance of empty brass ejection, location and size of group fired, etc. An attitude that is well-known in the law enforcement and other communities is: "If it wasn't written down, it didn't happen." All testing, changes and procedures used must be documented. For you, the non-sworn reader, that isn't a career requirement, but the information gained can be very useful.

Another note: a big-name High Power shooter once wrote that he was checking his shooting log when he realized that his basic zero for long-range shooting on his rifle was now two minutes higher than it had been the season before. While his rifle was still shooting "X" ring accuracy, it clearly had a worn throat. (How is this obvious? When the bullet moves forward, it slows at the impact with the rifling. That increases pressure, and velocity. His bullets were traveling further forward, getting less of a spike, and thus shorted on velocity. Less velocity meant more clicks up to hit the target at distance.) There was no way of telling how much useful life was left in the barrel, when the barrel would quit and stop shooting accurately. Accurate record-keeping allowed him to change

the barrel before accuracy went away.

Most problems can be solved by one of the four problem areas discussed later, and rarely will a rifle need more than attention to the "Big Four":

Weak extractor spring
Lack of lubricant
Loose carrier key
Faulty magazines

Reassembly

The charging handle and carrier-bolt assembly can be installed in the upper before or after you connect the upper and lower receivers with the front take-down pin. If you install them before, insert the charging handle into the upper receiver. Then press it upwards until it stops against the inside. Move it forward and back in the top track until the retention flanges on the charging handle drop into the access slot cut in the track. Then press the charging handle forward halfway. (If it drops, or tries to drop out, you missed the access slot. Try again.)

Take the carrier-bolt assembly. Make sure the bolt is fully forward by snapping your hand forward while holding tightly onto the carrier. The bolt, if not all the way forward, will slap forward to full extension. Insert the gas key into the charging handle recess and press the carrier forward. Once it reaches the charging handle, the carrier will push the charging handle ahead of it. Press the carrier and charging handle fully forward, until the charging handle latch catches on the receiver. (There is a slot machined on the receiver for it to latch onto.)

Close the dust cover door. The charging handle latch, and the dust cover door, have enough retention to keep the carrier in the upper against gravity. However, if you have the rear of the upper receiver pointed down and something jars the upper, the catches may not hold. So while you have the upper off the lower, keep the muzzle level or pointed muzzle-down to keep the parts in.

Place the front takedown lug of the upper in between the flanges of the lower, and press the takedown pin from right to left to secure the upper. Then hinge the lower down until it is closed and press the rear pin across.

Chapter Four

HOW IT WORKS: THE UPPER

The AR is not operated by magic. Little gnomes and fairies do not make the bullets go spitting out the front and empty cases to the side. Lots of other operations will be explained as we go, but as the parts in the upper are the most important, they come first.

Method of Operation and Safety Functions

The AR-15/M16 rifles use a method of actuation known as "direct gas impingement." That is, the gas that is vented out of the barrel (the port is under the front sight casting) is directed through the gas tube back into the receiver. There, it launches the carrier backwards, starting the moving portion of the cycle. Unlike other systems, where the gas pushes on a piston, the gas of the AR is vented directly into the receiver. The advantages of the DI system are light weight and accuracy. The obvious disadvantage is gas residue in the receiver.

Gas System Function

When the chambered round is fired, the bullet leaves the case and travels up the barrel, propelled by the expanding gases. The bullet passes by the gas port, and the expanding gases vent into the gas tube. There is a short time (measured in parts of a thousandth of a second) until the gas reaches the carrier key. While the bullet remains in the bore, it pressurizes the gas system. There is a short time period, from the instant when the bullet passes the gas port until it leaves the muzzle (depending on the length of barrel remaining past the gas port), when pressure builds in the system. Eventually, the bullet leaves the bore, at which time the bullet's exit allows the pressure in the bore to drop to atmospheric pressure. The delay of gas flow from the gas port to the key is called the "gas lag time" and the

time until the bullet leaves and the internal gas pressure drops to atmospheric is the "gas dwell time." The gas port acts as a valve, throttling the gas from the bore to the gas tube and then to the carrier. The larger the port, the sooner, and at higher pressure, the gas reaches the carrier key. Short gas lag time (the usual cause is an overly-large gas port) leads to premature bolt opening, and violent extraction. The longer the barrel is past the gas port, the longer the gas dwells against the key, increasing carrier velocity. (Using a carbine-size port on a rifle-length barrel can cause this.) Increased gas dwell time leads to harsher felt recoil, as the buffer and spring have more energy to deal with.

A moment here to discuss the finer points of gas flow. The assumption of many is that the gas squirts past the bullet base, through the port, and arrives at the carrier faster than the starship *Enterprise*. It does not; it takes a finite amount of time for the gas to travel that distance. Also, the assumption is that the gas arrives in the key with the same pressure as existed at the port. Again, not so. Increasing volume and frictional losses make the pressure in the carrier much less than that of the port bleed pressure. Were it not so, the carrier design would have to be different.

The actual pressure inside the carrier depends on a number of variables, but the biggest ones are gas tube length and the powder being used. Typically, a rifle (20-inch barrel, full-length gas tube) will have a carrier pressure of around 1,000 PSI. A carbine (16-inch barrel, short gas tube) will have pressure in the 1,500 PSI range. Conceptually, gas tube condition must have some effect, but it can't be much. A fouled gas tube will restrict flow, but the tubes seem to be self-cleaning to a pretty effective degree.

Once the gas reaches the carrier key, it passes through

the key into the carrier opening where the bolt lies. There you'll find the carrier gas chamber, and the bolt stem and gas rings. The gas expands into the chamber, with the net effect of pushing the carrier to the rear. (Gas expands evenly, and presses with the same force, on all surfaces of a container. That is why a filled scuba bottle remains at rest. If you break the valve off, however, the gas pressure becomes unequal, and the bottle rockets away, hurling itself through the wall.)

At first glance it might appear that the operational gases have no effect on the bolt. However, in discussing this with some AR manufacturers, it appears that the gas flowing

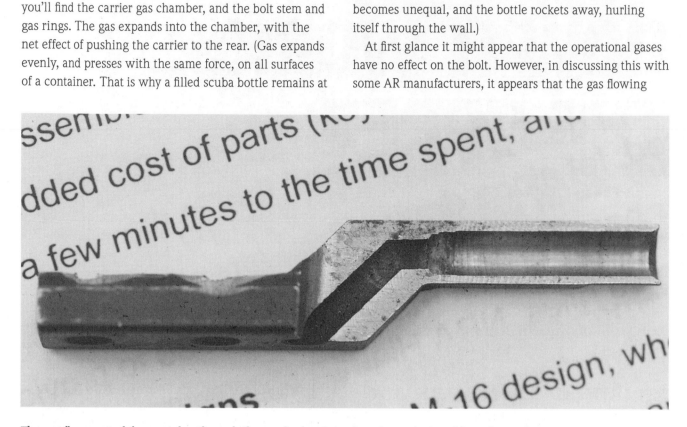

The gas flows out of the gas tube, through the carrier key (seen here in section) and into the carrier.

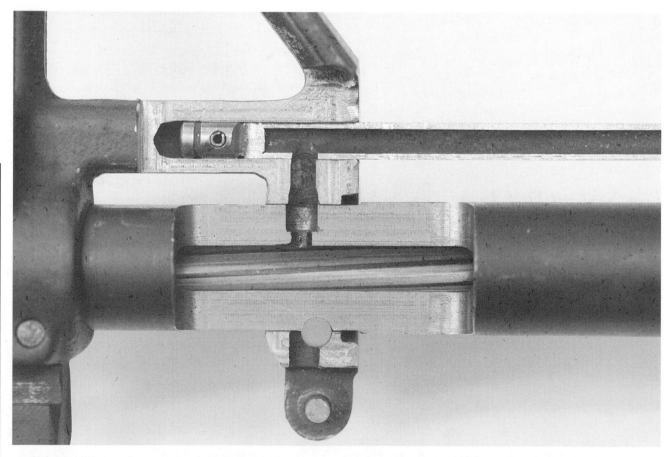

The origins of the gas flow. The gas gets vented out of the barrel, through the front sight housing, and down the tube towards the carrier key.

into the carrier also impinges on the rear of the bolt. As such, it presses the bolt forward, taking some of the force off the locking lugs when the bolt unlocks – enough so that bolt service life is actually increased as a result. (More on this in the section on piston-driven ARs.)

On the side of the carrier are vent holes. Gas will jet out of these holes when the rifle is fired. They are part of the self-limiting nature of the gas system.

The gas presses against the interior of the carrier gas chamber, with more force to the rear of the carrier than forward, until it has overcome the inertia of the carrier's mass, called (as before) the "carrier lag time" and the "carrier dwell time." The sooner, and at higher pressure, the gases reach the carrier, the less the lag time and the less the dwell time. Think of the bolt and carrier as a leaky piston, in a cartridge-operated internal combustion engine.

If the gas key is loose, or the gas rings worn or missing, the system will vent too much gas before it has delivered enough energy to the carrier, and the carrier will not be pushed with enough force to overcome the buffer weight and spring. Delivering more gas (the typical response by the overly-enthusiastic "gunsmith" is to drill the gas port larger) is a poor way to solve those problems. Instead, tightening and securing the gas key, and replacing worn or missing rings, are the proper solutions.

Why is all this important? Because the AR-15/M-16 extractor is small and weakly sprung. The bolt lugs are small and heavily-loaded. Shortening the lag time of the gas and carrier, or increasing the dwell time of the gas in the carrier, causes the bolt and extractor to attempt unlocking and extracting the fired case sooner than designed.

When fired, the case expands to the size and shape of the chamber. The inherent springiness of the brass case allows it to contract from the chamber walls and back towards its original dimension (but not fully) to allow extraction. However, if the chamber pressure is too high (an over-pressure round, or poor-quality reload) the case may have been expanded too much and thus not contract enough to lose its grip on the chamber. If the system is cycled too vigorously, or too soon in the planned timing, the case will not have had time to have contracted from its fired state and it will resist extraction. The friction of case to chamber wall thus may be too great, and the extractor can slip off the rim. Or break part of the rim off. Even if the case is extracted, it may shed particles of brass from the rough treatment it has received. Those particles can build up in the chamber and locking lug recesses and eventually cause the bolt to wedge closed on a chambered round and thus stop functioning.

In the short explanation, that's it: the gas flows, it blows the carrier off the gas tube end, the carrier drags the bolt.

They compress the buffer spring, and once the energy has been completely absorbed, the spring pushes buffer, carrier and bolt back to rest. Unless, of course, you're out of ammo, in which case the magazine locks the bolt open.

The Moving Parts of the Upper

The whole point of the "piston in a rifle" method of operation (indeed, of any self-loading rifle) is to fire a bullet, get the empty case out and a new cartridge in. Here are the mechanics.

Bolt Function

OK, the gas flows, the carrier gets blown off the gas tube, but what exactly is going on there? The bolt rotates, driven by the cam pin riding in its slot in the carrier. The initial rotation creates "primary extraction" where the drag of the bolt on the fired case partially rotates the case, freeing it from the friction of expanding to the chamber size. A good example of a system that lacks primary extraction is any pistol. The barrel drops down from the breechface, but the case is not otherwise broken-free from its grip on the chamber walls. The movement of the slide snatches the fired case straight back out of the chamber without first rotating it slightly to break it free from the chamber walls.

If the .223/5.56 case in the AR-15 chamber is over-expanded due to excessive pressure, or the bolt attempts rotation too soon caused by an improperly-tuned gas system, the case will not have had time to shrink from firing, and the frictional bond will not be broken between case and chamber wall. The result can be merely annoying, as the abraded case leaves brass particles in the chamber and feedway as it is rudely snatched from the chamber, particles which are also splattered on the bolt and carrier, and on the inside of the receiver. At worst, the cases will have the rims bent or broken-through, partially extracted and wandering aimlessly about the upper receiver. Or the extractor will slip off the rim entirely, leaving the fired case in the chamber.

Ejection, Feed, Chamber, Etc., Etc.

The bolt, having pulled the case from the chamber, hands the job off. The spring-loaded ejector hurls the empty out of the receiver. The bolt-carrier assembly, pushing the buffer and spring behind it, finally runs out of steam. The buffer and spring push them back into battery, stripping a round off the magazine, shoving it in the chamber, and the final act of the carrier in its forward travel is to rotate the bolt to the locked position.

That's all there is to it. Now let's take a look at the subassemblies in the upper that allow all of this to happen.

Chapter Five

THE BARREL

An inaccurate rifle is worse than useless. It may lead you to do things you would not do with something known to be less accurate, such as a shotgun. Since accuracy is important, and reliability matters, we're going to spend quite some time on barrels.

Barrels

The barrel of the AR is made to be a simple item to replace. Unlike the barrels of earlier rifle designs, the AR/M-16 barrel does not require headspace reaming (or shouldn't, anyway), barrel wrenches and elaborate timing gauges. The replacement barrel, as it comes out of a package, will have a threaded muzzle (or not; some makers offer the option of "no threads" for jurisdictions that do not permit them) with a flash hider on it. It will have a front sight casting or forging, a barrel nut with handguard retainer, flex spring and retaining clip, and a permanently attached barrel extension.

Good-quality barrels will typically be marked. A common marking would be "C MP 5.56 NATO 1/7" or "SS 5.56." The markings can be as cryptic as a small "C" on the barrel, and some barrels may not be marked at all. (The earliest Colt barrels made for the military, for example, had no markings.) When they exist, they provide information. The first set of markings would be on a Colt

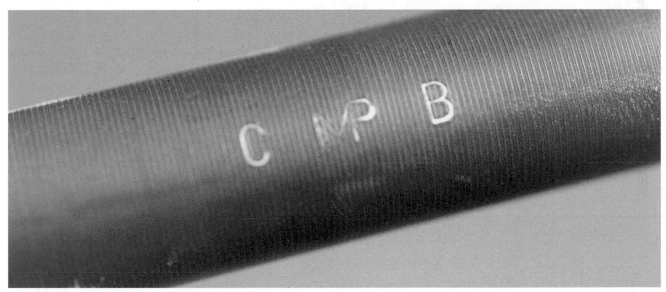

Here is a chrome-lined, magnetic particle inspected barrel from Bushmaster.

If you have one of these, you've got a good barrel. Translation: Colt, magnetic particle inspected, NATO 5.56 chamber, seven-inch twist and heavy.

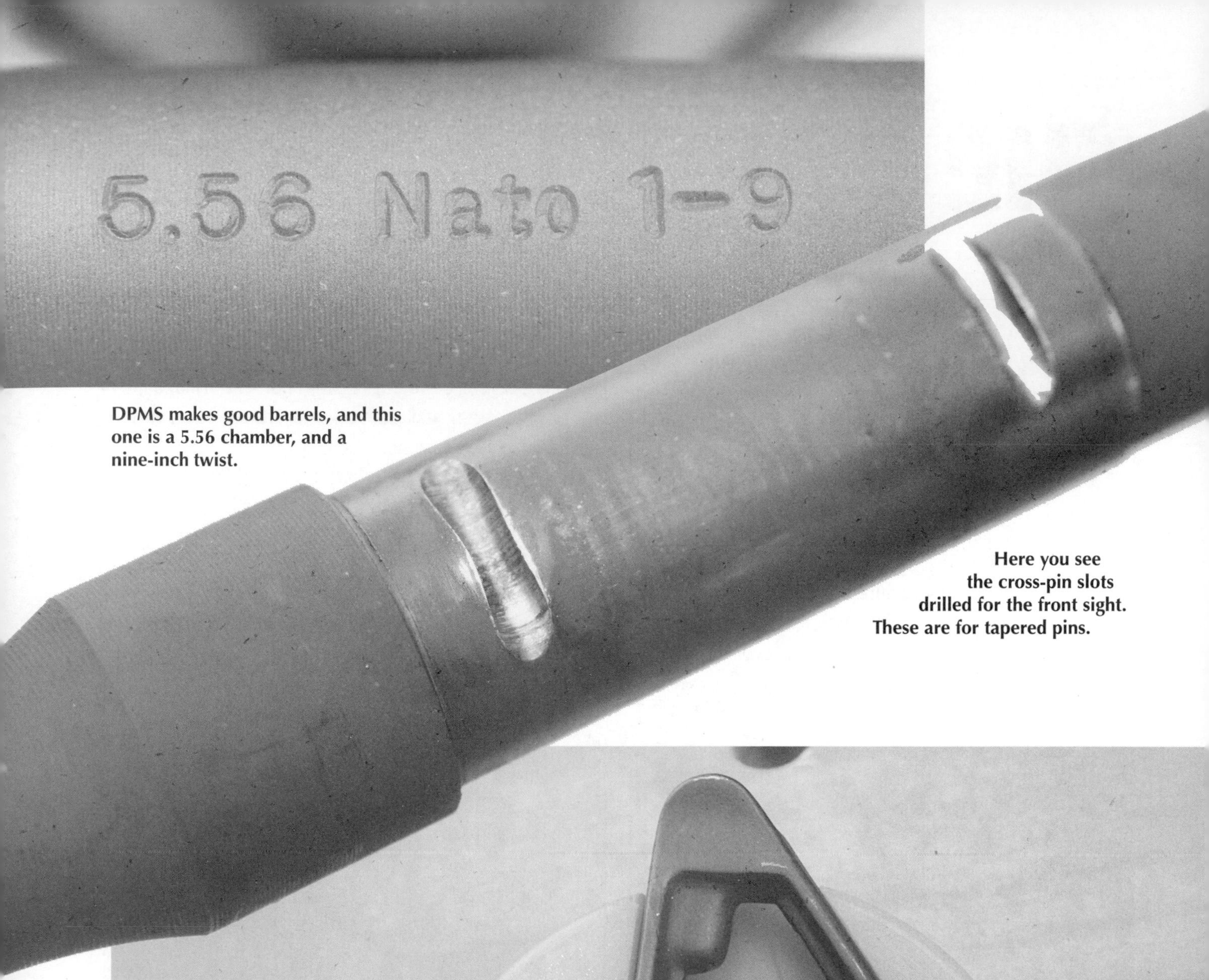

5.56 Nato 1-9

DPMS makes good barrels, and this
one is a 5.56 chamber, and a
nine-inch twist.

Here you see
the cross-pin slots
drilled for the front sight.
These are for tapered pins.

PINS
OUT

BROWNELLS

K&DECKER™

If you ever plan to take a front sight off, you must buy this bench block from Brownells. I'm not kidding; buy it now.

barrel, indicating that the barrel has been magnetic particle inspected, it has a 5.56 NATO chamber, and the twist is one turn in seven inches. (An excellent barrel, by the way.) The second is a common marking on Olympic barrels, and indicates it is stainless steel and has a 5.56 chamber. Different manufacturers use different markings; not all are chrome-lined and not all mark the twist. But many do.

The standard threads on a .223/5.56 flash hider and muzzle will be 1/2X28. That is, a half-inch diameter threaded shank with twenty-eight turns to the inch. (Right-handed turns, all English-unit measurements assume right-handed threading.) Other calibers will have different threads, so that it will not be possible to attach (for example) a 5.56 flash hider on a 9mm barrel. For example, the 9mm barrel standard is 1/2X36.

The front sight casting comes in two heights. The older style has a "deck" height (the front sight flat to barrel center) of 2.275 inches. The newer Colt M4 required a slightly different front sight height to accommodate the flat-top receiver, and the Colt M4 and all mil-spec front sight housings of its type will have a nominal deck height of 2.355 inches, a difference of .080 inch. Colt marks the M4

front sight housing with a barely-visible stamped "F" that can be found on one side or the other of the housing.

Deck height is important. Using an M4 front sight housing (or barrel) on an older receiver will have the front sight too high by some .080 inch. Installing an older barrel on an M4 upper will have the front deck height too low by the same amount. In either instance, zeroing the rifle will be difficult, if it is possible at all.

Front Sight Attachment Methods

The original design uses two tapered pins, driven into reamed tapered holes, which pass through the front sight housing and bearing on shallow grooves reamed into the barrel during the fitting process. This method is rigid, secure and utilizes a minimum of parts, but is easily dismounted when needed. (It is rarely needed, though.) Many later designs use solid or roll pins lacking a taper. These pins are not as secure, and to ensure they stay in place when installed, you should use Loctite. (This is one of the few locations where the use of a thread-

Here is the "dimple" I drilled to create a locking pocket for the set screw. Once aligned, check for center and Loctite it so it won't move. All a lot of work for a barrel that should have been made the right way to begin with.

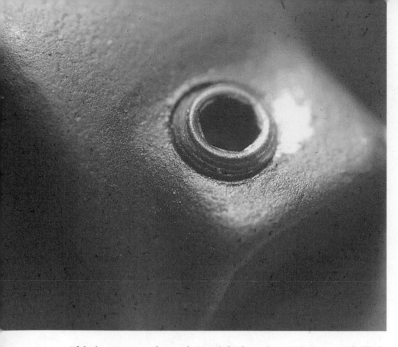

This is a screw-clamp front sight housing. It is recess-drilled, Loctited and painted-in. It won't move, at least not without giving notice.

locking compound is called for on the AR-15/M-16.) Last are the front sight castings or forgings secured with set screws. These fall into two types: the least-secure and the sufficiently secure. The least secure simply use four small set screws in the pin holes of a standard-style front sight housing. The four set screws have very little bearing surface, and front sight housings that use them are prone to slippage. If you have a barrel with a front sight attached this way, you can be sure that sometime in the future it will give you trouble. Why do barrels get made this way? Cost.

The sufficiently secure set-screw housings use more or larger ones, or have a large enough bearing surface on the sight housing to be secure to the barrel. Typically the screws of these do not contact the barrel, but instead constrict the lower legs of the front sight assembly, acting to clamp the front sight housing to the barrel. Again, cost is the driving force. Barrel makers point out, and rightly so, that front sight housings attached in these ways can be adjusted to make the front sight dead vertical, or to match the tilt of the upper receiver. If your rifle is only ever going to be used as a competition rifle, no problem. But one intended for defense must have taper pins instead.

All front sight housings using set screws must be marked once test-fired and found to function properly. Once centered and zeroed, the position of the sight must be positively indicated by means of an electric marking pencil, paint or stake marks. Subsequent inspections of that rifle should include checking the location of the front sight housing. As the front sight housing covers the gas port, and locates the gas tube, any movement of the housing could adversely affect function of the rifle.

The clamp-on front sights are also prone to tipping when struck or can suffer non-vertical installation. If the front sight is not dead-center vertical, the rear sight may not have enough windage correction to zero the rifle. If that is the case you must locate the rear sight to center, loosen the front sight, and gently tipping and test-firing, establish a dead-center vertical for it. Then it has to be locked in place, marked and checked regularly.

Length, Twist, Composition

The minimum legal length for a rifle barrel under federal law is sixteen inches. (16.00 inches is legal, but if any wear occurs, and the barrel becomes 15.99 inches long, it is no longer legal. Thus, most manufacturers make their barrels 16.25 to 16.50 inches long.) Police departments can obtain weapons with shorter barrels, and officers in some states can obtain shorter barrels after receiving federal tax stamp approval. Where allowed under state law, you must receive the proper federal tax stamp before installing an otherwise too-short barrel. Here, there is no distinction between "us" and "them" regardless of which side you may be on: Simply being a law enforcement officer does not mean a personal weapon may have a shorter-than-16-inch barrel without federal approval. Most manufacturers will not sell shorter than 16-inch barrels without proof of an existing tax

If you plan on making an otherwise too-short barrel legally long, you'd better know a good welder.

stamp, except to a department or agency. A permanently-attached muzzle device that creates a longer than 16-inch assembly is allowed by law. "Permanently attached" means to the BATFE one of the following: high-temperature silver solder, welding or a blind pin. An M4 barrel (nominally 14.5 inches) can be made legal by tack-welding on a flash-hider that is long enough. Welding is a process that is understood, while "high temperature" (1125° or higher) silver solder often is not. Soft solder or "lead solder" (an alloy that melts at 600°) is not sufficient, and no chemical thread-locking compound or epoxy is sufficient to meet with BATFE approval.

Barrel length is measured with the bolt closed and locked, by measuring a rod placed down the bore. The distance from the face of the bolt to the furthest extent of the permanently-attached-to-the-barrel object is the barrel length.

While a shorter than 16-inch barrel can be handy, the costs can be great. (Besides the legal or tax costs.) A shorter barrel produces more noise, and that noise is closer to the shooter. The changed gas flow dynamics can result in a less than reliable carbine. A shorter weapon is easier to "sweep" or point the muzzle at others in the immediate vicinity.

Barrel Legalities

The BATFE definition of "permanently attached" does not mention anything about obviousness. If you do make a too-short barrel long enough to be legal, it would be prudent to leave the process obvious. Leave the weld beads "proud" of the surface, or do not paint over the silver solder. Leave the blind pin visible.

As mentioned before, a military 14.5-inch M4 barrel with a Vortex flash hider welded or pinned in place, that is longer than 16 inches, would after the permanent installation and be legal for personal possession by an officer. However, if it isn't clear the attachment is permanent, it could lead to headaches until the barrel is tested. Be prudent, and leave the work obvious, but not ugly.

A number of rifles have been made in the past where the barrel assembly is a section of rifled barrel 11 inches or so in length, with a 5-inch long flash hider welded or silver-soldered to it. The finished assembly is of legal length. The construction method came about in previous assault weapons ban near-panics, when manufacturers found orders outstripping barrel supplies. Barrel blanks come in roughly three-foot lengths. (A "barrel blank" is a steel tube with a rifled bore through it, but which has not yet been lathe-turned to profile it or thread it for installation on a

rifle.) Thus, a manufacturer can make one 20-inch barrel, two 16-inch barrels, or three 11-inch barrels from one blank. By soldering or brazing an inexpensive extension onto each of the three 11-inch sections, a manufacturer could make many more rifles with barrels. While legal, the barrels offer no more velocity than any other 11-inch barrel would, and the "11+5" barrels produce more muzzle flash (despite the longer flash hider) than does a 16-inch barrel with an A1 flash hider installed.

A barrel may be shortened to less than legal length for the installation of such an extension, provided that that individual barrel is not assembled onto any rifle until after the extension is permanently installed. Thus, you may purchase a 14.5-inch M4 barrel, and have a flash hider permanently attached, and you are legally OK as long as the barrel stays un-installed until after the extension is attached (and the finished barrel is over 16 inches long).

However, if you're going to do that, do it as soon after you receive the short barrel as possible. I would not have a stash of 14.5-inch barrels lying around for "when I wear out other barrels" to be made legal-length. There is staying legal, and then there is just tempting Mr. Murphy too much.

Short-Barreled Rifles and Machine guns

If you have a rifle that you acquired or built as an SBR (short-barreled rifle) or a machine gun (M-16), you may have short barrels installed as replacements. Even if the original machine gun (an M-16, M-16A1, etc. you lucky devil) had a 20-inch barrel, the fact that it is a machine gun allows for a shorter barrel. If a barrel longer than 16 inches is installed on a rifle acquired as an SBR, it still remains an SBR under law, until the BATFE has been notified and requested (and has done so) to remove it from the NFA Registry. Pay attention; the BATFE takes this matter very seriously.

A standard rifle MAY NOT have a shorter than 16-inch barrel installed without applying to the BATFE for SBR status, and paying the tax. From their viewpoint, making an SBR without prior approval falls in the same legal area as making it a machine gun.

Barrel length issues on barrels shorter than the legal length are closely controlled, and strictly viewed by the BATFE. Again, being a police officer does not confer special status or privileges in this area.

A question that comes up in classes, and one that bears on those who own SBRs: A department may not simply construct its own SBRs. (Obviously, individuals cannot.) If the department has a properly-acquired SBR, the short-barrelled upper from that rifle may not be installed on a

SBRs cost you, in velocity, in the tax stamp, and in the ammo you consume having a ton of fun.

non-SBR lower. This also applies to non-sworn firearms owners. Yes, the department has ownership of an SBR, but it is the one with the particular serial number logged in inventory as an SBR. The SBR status may not be simply transferred within the department to another receiver. If you have SBR and non-SBR rifles in inventory, do not get the uppers for them mixed up, police officer or not. Inadvertent construction of a prohibited weapon is still construction of a prohibited weapon. (It also is useful to point out to police officers at this time that departmental instructions to mix and match SBR and non-SBR rifles will not allow you to escape federal prosecution, if it comes to that. You, as the informed and responsible officer, must find a way to make the situation clear to superiors who may not know the peculiarities of federal law in this area.)

As an aside, the minimum overall length allowed under Federal law is 26 inches. Due to the buffer tube design of the AR-15/M-16, it is not possible to even get close to the minimum when a 16-inch barrel is installed. Even with a telescoping stock, collapsed to the minimum length it moves, a carbine with a 16-inch barrel will still be about 30-31 inches long.

If a rifle has been registered as an SBR, or is a lawful machine gun, then the 26-inch overall length minimum does not apply. Only semi-automatic, non-SBR rifles and carbines must be over 26 inches in length.

As a final note, if a rifle is or has been lawfully altered to be an SBR, you may not return it to a standard rifle (legally, anyway) simply by installing a longer barrel. As far as the BATFE is concerned, it remains an SBR until you request to have it removed from the SBR list and have received approval. Then it can be considered a standard rifle. If you take an SBR, install a 16+-inch long barrel on it, and lend or sell it, as far as the BATFE is concerned, it is still legally titled as an SBR.

Know what the rules are, and there isn't a problem.

What Should A Barrel Cost?

Barrels are not identical. In any production run, at any barrel maker, barrels will fall into a bell curve. Some few will be bad, and be rejected. Some few will be perfect. However, while bad can usually be seen, perfect cannot. So, if you buy a barrel that was made by "Billy-Bob's Discount Barrel Shop" you will get a functional barrel at a low price. The more expensive barrels? The makers tend to the details of barrel making so that they shove their bell curve "to the right." That is, no bad barrels, all above the Billy-Bob average, and many more perfect ones.

You may be lucky (or your buddy) and end up buying the one perfect barrel from a production lot by Billy-Bob. That doesn't mean the next barrel from him will be perfect, which leads us to Sweeney's Ninth Law: Cheap barrels are a lottery, but too expensive is too expensive. At the moment, you can buy a decent, serviceable barrel for a carbine for $185. And it won't be much of a risk in the lottery, either. You can spend a lot more. If you want an air-gauged, cryo-relieved, match bull barrel for NRA High Power shooting, a Kreiger single-point cut barrel will run some $400, fitted and installed. Trust me, when you're spending the big bucks for the best barrel, you would be smart to let the guy who makes the barrel fit it, headspace it and send it back.

Handgun Barrels

OK, different subject here. Handguns are firearms that have no stock, nor any provision for one. No problem. You can have a handgun with any length barrel you want. However, don't tempt Mr. Murphy. You know him from his motto: "If anything can go wrong, it will. And usually at the least opportune time." You want to show off, you get an AR handgun, and one day while you're just goofing around, you put your 16-inch barreled upper on it. And while you do so, lying there by themselves are your rifle/carbine lower, and your 7-inch barreled handgun upper.

You know, you just know, that if you leave them lying there, that your brother-in-law is going to walk in, go "Hey, that's cool." And slap the two together. Instant violation of the law. No problem, right? You tell him to knock that stuff off, you put things right, and don't worry about it. But your brother-in-law wants to go shooting he remembers that "cool combo" and he borrows your rifle when you aren't home, to go to the range. The next thing you know your sister is on the phone, screaming at you that her brother just got arrested for owning a "sawed-off rifle."

If you own AR handguns and rifles, keep them locked up separately, and keep the unwary away from them.

It may look it, but this is not an SBR. It is simply a carbine with the front sight all the way forward (covered in the gas flow section).

Barrel Twist

Barrel twist is the rate of spiral of the rifling grooves in the bore. The measure is an indication of how many inches of bore it takes for the rifling to complete one revolution. Twist rates are marked by the rate after a numeral one, as in 1/12, 1/9 or 1/7. Longer and heavier bullets need more twist (smaller numbers after the "1/") to be gyroscopically stable and accurate. The first ARs had a twist of 1/14, which was found to not be stable enough under certain circumstances. The earliest regular-issue AR rifles had barrels with a twist of one in 12 inches. These older SP-1, AR-15, and M-16 and M-16A1 rifles can be accurately fired only with bullets of 60 grains or less in weight. M-16A2 and M4 rifles have a twist rate if one turn in seven inches, which is fast enough to stabilize bullets up to 77-80 grains. The 1/9 twist rate is a compromise, which will fire accurately all bullet weights commercially loaded except some of the heaviest, the 75 and 77 grain bullets. (Some 1/9 barrels will shoot those bullets accurately, but not all, and there is no way to tell except by test-firing each barrel with the individual load in question.)

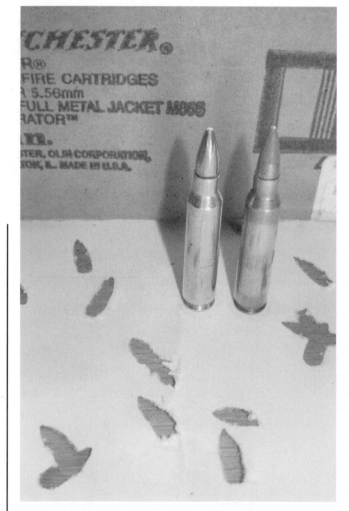

This is what happens if you put M-855 ammo through a 1/12 barrel: bullets sideways at a short distance.

Ammunition must be matched to twist rate to avoid improper combinations. A 1/7 or 1/9 barrel can use any standard cartridge within certain limits:

1) Fast twist and light-weight bullets can be a problem. A 1/7 barrel will shoot 55 FMJ and even 52 grain match hollowpoints well. Some are quite spectacularly accurate while shooting such bullets. There is no need to avoid using 55 grain FMJ, XM-193, W-W white box and similar loadings from Remington, Hornady, Federal et al, in a 1/7 twist barrel. However, you should not go any lower in weight. Avoid the use of "varmint," "blitz," or extremely light-weight bullets. Varmint bullets are designed for use in 1/12 barrels, and the jacket is made as thin as possible to enhance the bullet disintegration when it reaches the intended rodent. A bullet from a Federal XM-193 cartridge, going 3,100 fps, will be spun up to 318,000 rpm in a 1/7 twist barrel. Fire a 40-grain varmint bullet, at a typical 3,800 fps in that same barrel, and it will be spun to over 390,000 rpm. Faster spin and thinner jacket means a greater likelihood of bullet breakup. The result will be a streak of gray smoke headed towards the target, but no bullet strike. That same ultra-light bullet, fired from a 1/12 barrel, will have a rotational rate of "only" 227,000 rpm.

2) The compromise twist rate, 1/9, can be a problem with some of the newer heavyweights. The Mk 262 Mod O or Mk 262 Mod 1 rounds, using either 75 or 77 grain bullets, can be accurate in some 1/9 barrels. Others, not so accurate. While of interest to the non-sworn gun experimenter, such a potential combination can be fraught with peril for the department. Why risk a combination that with wear, poor bore cleaning or just bad luck, might without warning turn into an inaccurate combination? If the department insists on using or issuing the Mk 262 Mod 1 ammunition for its greater effectiveness, (the better of the two) then all rifles in the department, issued or personally-owned, MUST have 1/7 barrels. Otherwise, the 1/9 twist rate works well with any lighter-weight bullet load the department might select.

3) The original twist rate of 1/12. Here, the only selections are 55 grain bullets, such as the XM-193 or the Cor-bon 53 grain DPX. The slow twist will not stabilize anything heavier with the certainty needed in a defensive weapon.

Measuring Twist Rate

If your barrel isn't marked, how can you tell what twist it has? Simple, get a cleaning rod with a swiveling handle. Fit a tight-fitting patch in it, and stuff the rod with patch down the bore. Make sure the patch can go both directions. Push in until it is more than halfway down. Wrap a piece

Especially for defense it is best to use ammo with cannelured bullets. They both ensure reliable feeding and break at the cannelure at high-enough velocity.

of masking tape around the rod, with the ends stuck together, forming a "flag." Attach this flag with the ends straight up, as close to the flash hider as you can. Then slowly pull the rod out, watching the flag rotate. When it comes back up to vertical, stop. Measure the distance from the flash hider to where the flag is now. That's your twist rate.

Composition

All barrels are made of one or another steel alloy. Carbon steel (or blue steel), is a tough alloy that can be heat-treated. (And all good barrels are heat-treated.) It lacks, however, much in the way of corrosion resistance. While carbon steel barrels can be very accurate, any oversight in maintenance can quickly lead to a ruined bore due to corrosion. Stainless steel is steel with sufficient amounts of nickel and chromium added to the alloy to resist corrosion. Stainless steel resists corrosion, but does not prevent it. If the manufacturers were to

add enough of both chromium and nickel to the steel in order to make it truly corrosion resistant, the resulting alloy could not be hardened. Soft alloys are not used in barrels, as they will not stand up to the friction and heat of shooting, regardless of how corrosion-resistant they are.

The military solution is to make the barrel of a very tough carbon steel alloy (known as 4150 in the steel trade) and then plate the interior with chromium for wear and corrosion resistance. As an alloying ingredient, chromium softens steel. However, plated in its hardest form it is harder than the steel it is plated to. Unfortunately, the plating is not even. While only averaging .0002 of an inch thick, it can vary in thickness, and that variance can affect accuracy. The accuracy difference is so small that only long-range target shooters care. But they care passionately, so you may hear that "chromed barrels don't shoot accurately." True, if you're trying to shoot a six-inch or smaller group at 600 yards. For anything else, the difference is negligible, and the corrosion and wear resistance is superb.

4150 vs. 4140? You'll hear a lot of arguing about steel composition. Purists will argue that since the mil-spec is 4150, anything else is a cheap compromise. Harrumph. To the machinist, the difference is a lot more tool wear and cost, using 4150 vs. 4140. To the shooter, almost none. Now, in a military context, where you may have to use an M4 as an impromptu SAW, 4150 is good. It will make the rifle last another five minutes longer, which can matter in combat. The rest of us? No difference.

Hard Chrome or Not?

Where the cost difference is relatively small, and the marginally-greater accuracy of a match carbon steel or stainless steel barrel is not needed, then chrome plating is called for. As a rule of thumb, if the cost difference is less than $100 per barrel, a chrome-plated barrel should be selected.

Chrome bores do have a downside: The chrome is so hard that except for specialized applications, they cannot be reamed or altered.

A bore must be chrome-plated when it is manufactured, if it is to be plated at all. The surface of any steel oxidizes at a known rate. Within a short time period after the barrel has been manufactured, the surface of the bore has oxidized enough that the plating would not bond, were chrome-plating attempted. (The time depends on the climate; hours to days.) Barrels that are to be chrome-plated are done so as soon as possible at the factory after the bore and chamber have been formed. It is not possible to send a barrel back to have it chrome-plated.

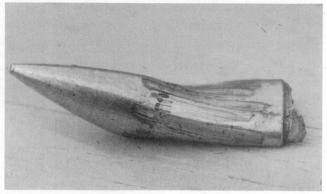

At proper velocity, this is what an AR bullet does terminally: it breaks up. Drop velocity enough, and it fails to break.

At a low enough velocity, this is what you get: a bullet that flattens, curves off-track, and doesn't do its job.

Barrel length is a matter both of the law and of ballistics.

Barrel Length and Velocity

Most hunting bullets operate terminally by upsetting, the classic "mushroom" shape that bullet manufacturers are so fond of showing in advertisements.

The .223/5.56 cartridge (with some exceptions) operates terminally by means of yaw and fragmentation. The bullet cannot be stabilized enough in flight so that it will remain stable in the target. (Some cartridges can be that stable, but not the .223/5.56) As a result, once it has entered an object it begins to yaw, or tip. The 55 grain FMJ bullet, when it reaches horizontal (tipped 90° to the direction of travel), will break in half at the cannelure, the impressed line around its center. The two pieces, and the fragments of the break-up, then continue to travel and as a result increase wound severity. Bullets continually lose velocity as they travel downrange.

If the bullet velocity on impact has fallen enough and is travelling slowly enough such that the stresses on the bullet on impact are not great enough to cause break-up, wound severity drops drastically. (No break-up, only one bullet, no fragments, reduced fluid pressure from impact: all these act together to decrease terminal effectiveness.)

All rifles in general, and the AR-15/M-16 in particular, have a maximum effective range in which the bullet operates terminally as designed. In the law enforcement or defensive situation this is not much of a problem. However, use in Iraq and Afghanistan has demonstrated that the rifle/ammunition/optical sights combination allows soldiers and Marines to strike combatants far beyond the effective terminal range.

Residual pressure in the barrel is what creates velocity. Shortening barrels decreases velocity. The threshold of fragmentation of the 55 grain FMJ bullet is well known and happens around the 2750 fps figure. (Longer/heavier bullets, due to the length of the lever arm working on them on impact, have lower fragmentation velocities.) It is entirely possible, if the barrels used are 10.5 inches or 11.5 inches and the departmental ammunition is not loaded to full 5.56 pressure and velocity, that bullets may never reach sufficient velocity to achieve fragmentation. As velocity is always a decreasing figure from the muzzle out to the target, you have to start with more to end with more.

While short barrels may be handy to carry and use, and "cool" in their aura of rarity and compact looks, they have the potential to severely decrease effectiveness.

Chronograph Testing of Various Ammunition

The following chart is not definitive, only an indication. Two different barrels can deliver ±50 fps velocity at the same length and with the ammunition, and manufacturers may vary the acceptable velocity from one production run of ammo to the next. The only way to be sure the departmental ammunition on hand, or that has just been delivered, is producing the expected or desired velocity is to test it in your rifle or rifles.

Brand	Designation	Weight	11.5" Vel	16" vel	20" vel
Frangible loads:					
Int Cart Corp		42 frang	2799	3098	3215
Int Cart Corp		55 frang	2288	2600	2668
Precision C.C.		55 frang	2594	2939	3022
Standard, 1/12" twist loads:					
NATO		55 FMJ	2689	3004	3073
REM-UMC	L223R	55FMJ		2846	2971
Rem Express	R223R2	55HP		2962	3049
Federal	XM193	55FMJ		3138	3229
PMC	223A	55FMJ		2799	2886
Winchester	Q3131A	55FMJ		3047	3128
Winchester	RA223R	55SP		2828	2986
Federal	AE223	55FMJ	2553	2928	3058
Winchester	USA223R1F	55FMJ		2922	2991
Federal	XM193	55FMJ		3105	3211
Winchester	USA223R1F	55FMJ	2483	2809	3007
Federal	XM193	55FMJ	2667	3052	3187
Cor-bon	22355BK/20	55BalTip		2962	3024
Winchester	Q3131	55FMJ	2718	3117	3204
Winchester	Unk**	55FMJ		3064	3171
Federal	XM193	55FMJ	2648	3111	3244
Rem Express	R223R1	55SP		2958	3048
Winchester	Q3131	55FMJ		3042	3157
Winchester	Q3131	55FMJ		3091	3195
Winchester	USA223R1	55FMJ		2938	3019
Federal***	XM193	55FMJ		3127	3231
REM-UMC	L223R3	55FMJ		2904	2997
Federal***	XM193	55FMJ		3140	3232
PMP	5.56	55FMJ	2542	2876	2897
PMC	223Rem	55FMJ	2676		
Cor-Bon	223Rem	55JHP	2527		
Federal	XM-193	55FMJ	2701		
Federal	223A HiShok	55SP	2517	2790	2857
Winchester	USA223R1F	55FMJ	2470	2767	2843
Loads requiring a faster twist than 1/12":					
Black Hills	Red	60 VMax	2530	2876	2965
Federal	Tactical	62Tactical	2365	2756	2750
Federal	GM223M	69HP	2641	2725	
Winchester	S223M	69HP		2747	2863
Black Hills	Blue	69HP	2357	2659	2758
Black Hills	Blue	68 Match	2322	2625	2731
Black Hills	Blue	77 OTM	2253	2537	2600
Black Hills	Mk 262 Mod 1	77 OTM	2385	2678	2713

*Headstamp with NATO proof/acceptance mark,   **The factory box bore no lot number or no product designations,   ***Unlike other XM193 brown boxes, these were white

The effects of shorter barrels can to some extent be offset. Selecting a load with a higher initial velocity can leave a high muzzle velocity. However, that increase of velocity is "bought" at the cost of increased chamber pressure, muzzle blast and noise. Note also that no loading used in the 11.5-inch barrel exceeded the fragmentation threshold, even at the muzzle. Any consideration of using such short barrels in a law enforcement environment must take that fact into consideration.

.223 vs. 5.56 Chambers

Discussing chamber dimensions requires knowing what the parts are, and what they do. The chamber is a three-dimensional mirror of the cartridge case, but with enough extra room to ensure reliable function. However, the definition of "enough extra" can be what makes the difference between a reliable or an unreliable rifle. As in the story of Goldilocks and the Three Bears, too much and not enough are both bad. The critical chamber dimensions and parts of the chamber are as follows:

A) The neck diameter. The neck diameter must be slightly larger than the case neck itself. When fired, the case of the cartridge expands with the chamber pressure, releasing its grip on the bullet. If the neck is not large enough in diameter, chamber pressure will be greater than desired due to the extra force needed to drive the bullet from the case in the first part of cartridge combustion. The neck also must be larger than the case diameter to ensure that any and all cartridges will fit in the chamber, even when the chamber is fouled from extended firing sessions.

B) The freebore diameter. This is a cylindrical (or in some designs, very slightly tapered) section where the bullet slides forward, before striking the onset angle of the rifling. Freebore exists to allow the bullet to pop out of the case neck (yes, just like a cork) and get started on its way to the rifling. Freebore diameter is smaller than that of the case neck diameter, but larger than that of the bullet being fired. If freebore is too small, excessive fouling will build up quickly. Also, the small variances in bullet diameter become more and more of a problem as freebore

diameter is made smaller. If the freebore is too short, or the bullet starts "touching the lands" (against the rifling) then chamber pressure will again be too high.

Benchrest shooters commonly increase accuracy by loading their ammunition such that the bullet rests against but is not wedged against, the onset of the rifling. It increases accuracy (However, "accuracy" to a benchrest shooter means groups smaller than a tenth of an inch, center-to-center, at 100 yards.) at the cost of only being able to use specialized, hand-crafted ammunition. They also have the chamber reamed such that freebore is as small a diameter as possible. However, benchrest bullets are manufactured to a level of precision that makes regular .224-inch bullet look rough as a cob by comparison. When you order your bullets at .2240" ± .00005" you can afford to have a very tight freebore.

C) The throat angle. This is the taper of the front edge of the rifling. The rifling must have a taper to it, or the bullet at the beginning of its trip will slam into the rifling, stall momentarily, and again cause a sharp increase in pressure. Steeper, closer-to-the-bullet throat angles increase accuracy (not enough to matter in a defensive situation) while increasing chamber pressure.

D) Neck length. This is the distance from the case/chamber shoulder to the end of the neck diameter section. Short necks increase accuracy, until they become too short, and then they greatly increase chamber pressure.

E) Freebore length. This is simply the distance from the end of the neck to the start of the rifling angle. Freebore length that is too short can case "hard chambering" where the bullet is wedged into the leade. Such rifles will occasionally pull the bullet from a case when unloading. Even if they do not, the bullet has been loosened (and even tipped) in the case neck, and will often show decreased performance.

.223 vs. 5.56 Dimensions

The two cartridges are similar, but they are not identical. They differ for good reasons, at least to the users of each, are real, and can be significant. The differences are in the throat, or leade, the combined length of the freebore and throat angle.

In the .223, the leade is shorter, and the angle at which the rifling begins steeper (smaller number). In the 5.56, the length of cylindrical section is longer, and the angle more shallow (larger number). The difference is a matter of intended use. .223 chambers were designed for extreme accuracy. The .223 Remington was designed for use as a target and varmint-shooting cartridge.

The length of the neck (D) matters. The longer the neck

On the left you see the neck of the chamber. In the middle, the throat or freebore. Then you see the ramp of the rifling leade. This is a 5.56 chamber.

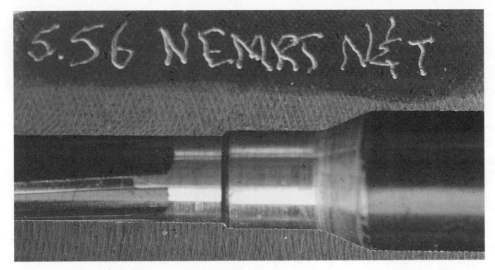

This sectioned barrel shows it all: Under the "N" in NEMRT is the leade, under the "E" is freebore, under the "M & R" is the neck, and under the "N" of N&T is the shoulder, which establishes headspace.

length of the chamber, the farther forward the throat angle (C) starts. In the 5.56, a longer neck section is more forgiving of war-time production ammunition, which may have case necks a little longer than commercial .223 made in peacetime.

The freebore length (E) has an effect on pressure. The longer the bullet goes forward before striking the throat angle, the lower the pressure spike in the beginning of combustion. Also, the longer the "ramp" of the rifling onset, the lower the chamber pressure will be. In the third drawing, F is the angled face of the rifling as it ramps up to full height.

The more-tapered (smaller angle) the throat angle is, the longer the leade, and again, we have lowered pressure.

The fourth drawing shows a magnified view, in cross-section, of the leade. B1 is the freebore diameter. B2 is the full height of the rifling lands, and B3 is the bore diameter, the .2240" that all .223/5.56 rifles aspire to be. As you can see, the steeper the ramp (the larger the angle figure) the greater force required to drive the bullet into the rifling and begin spinning it. The greater that force, the more the bullet "stalls" and thus drives up chamber pressure.

The 5.56 chamber dimensions evolved gradually. The length of the leade, and the shallow onset of rifling is meant to keep chamber pressure from mounting too high when a rifle is hot from firing, hot from the environment, fouled from firing or dirty from lack of maintenance in a military/combat setting. Also, the long leade allows the use of tracer ammunition in the 5.56 cartridge, such ammunition featuring bullets of extreme length for their weight. (Reason also for the 1/7 twist in military weapons.)

Next we see a chart of the comparative dimensions of three chambering reamers in common use (chart provided by a reamer manufacturer). The .223 Remington is a standard set of dimensions used by bolt-action rifle makers and varmint shooters. The 5.56 dimensions are a common

set used by manufacturers in providing 5.56 chambering reamers to barrel makers for ARs. The .223 Wylde is a combination of the two, where target shooters wish to have the accuracy of the .223 and the reliability of the 5.56.

Chamber part	.223 Remington	5.56X45	.223 Wylde
A) Neck diameter	.2510"	.2550"	.2550"
B) Freebore diameter	.2242"	.2265"	.2240"
C) Throat angle	1.5° to 3.1°	1.2° to 2.5°	1.25°
D) Neck length	.2034"	.2200"	2.220"
E) Freebore length	.0680"	.0566"	.0619"

These are representative dimensions, and there are many drawings and reamer dimensions in use. Some custom gunsmiths use these, or variations of these, in rifles depending on their intended use.

Use of 5.56 ammunition in .223 chambers can result in malfunctions. Much 5.56 ammunition is loaded to pressures that allow for the maximum velocity that the cartridge is capable of while remaining safe and reliable when used in 5.56 chambers – and only 5.56 chambers. That is, they take advantage of the pressure-lowering characteristics of the longer, larger and more-open tapered freebore and leade, and in so doing, are loaded to higher pressures to increase velocity. Firing 5.56 ammunition in a .223 chamber, with its shorter leade and steeper rifling onset, can increase the chamber pressure beyond standard design limits. In such instances the cases might lose their

This is a primer anvil, part of the primer that blew out of this rifle and kept it from working. Until we disassembled the rifle and scraped the anvil out, the rifle involved was no more than a club.

primers on firing. A primer loose in the lower can lead to an inoperative rifle. In many instances, the shooter will never notice the difference using 5.56 ammunition in a .223 chamber. But if all the variables stack against the shooter (e.g., if the rifle is hot, the temperature is hot and thus the ammunition hot, if the rifle is fouled and thus the chamber tight and the bore offers more resistance to the bullet, if the cases are at the bottom of the allowable range for softness, etc.), the bolt will scrape brass shavings off the cases and primers, and eventually the rifle will "blow" primers. The extractor may even rip through, or slide off of, the case rim.

OK, we've gotten this far, and you're chomping at the bit. You haven't had a single gunsmithing task to do. Here you go:

Measuring Chambers

When I first heard of the problem, there was no way to measure exactly what leade any particular chamber had. To measure the depth and taper of the rifling, without sectioning the barrel, required measuring tools far beyond the means of any gunsmith. (Obviously, sectioning the barrel to measure the leade is akin to burning the village to save it.) One quick and dirty method is the Stoney Point gauge. It is a modified cartridge case, with a bent rod attached and a sliding wire brace. To use it, you scrub the chamber clean, insert a bullet of your choice in the gauge. Then insert the gauge and push the wire brace forward until the bullet stops. Pull the gauge and bullet out, and you can now measure the maximum length of a loaded cartridge with that particular bullet at the point at which it touches the rifling. However, it does not tell you .223/5.56, except to a more-or-less degree.

The purpose of the gauge is to let a shooter know just how long he can load a particular bullet. In some target competitions, shooters will load the bullet to a known

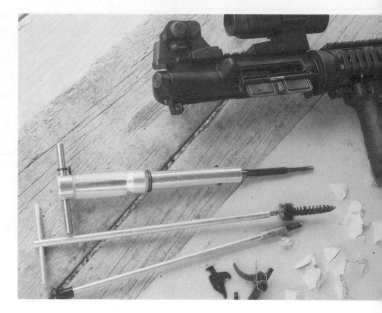

Here we have the tools needed to check for and ensure a 5.56 throat.

distance "off the rifling" so as to maximize accuracy. We have not that luxury, unless we're willing to turn our ARs into single-shot rifles. (Which, for some long-range shooters, is just fine.) Even if we knew that a chamber/leade is .223 instead of 5.56, we had no way of changing it.

Well, that has changed. As usual, it is Ned Christiansen of Michiguns to the rescue. What Ned did was design a measuring-gauge chamber plug. The plug has its neck and leade machined to the dimensions of a 5.56 chamber. The process of determining what your chamber is, is simple:

First, thoroughly scrub your chamber and bore. Any debris or fouling left behind can interfere with an accurate measurement. Take the clean upper and turn it muzzle-down. Insert the handle into the gauge, and drop the gauge into the chamber. You don't have to drop it far. If the gauge goes "clink" and bounces free, or when you turn the receiver over it falls out of its own weight, you have a 5.56 chamber.

If, however, the gauge goes "clunk" and wedges in place, or requires a pull to get it free, you have a .223 chamber.

The gauge does not measure headspace, and tells you nothing about what headspace you might have. It only "reports" on .223 vs. 5.56 leade.

You can, if you have a .223 chamber and you wish to know where it is wedging, mark the end of the gauge with a sharpie, insert it in the chamber and try to turn it. The ink marks will be marred by the contact.

Now, this is a relatively delicate measuring tool. If you abuse it, it will cease to provide you with information on your chambers. Don't let it rattle around in your tool box with all the other tools. Don't force it in. (If you have a .223 chamber, and hammer the gauge in, you could

You have to scrub before measuring, and you need to ream if the throat is short or steep.

damage your chamber or the gauge.) If you have one and only one rifle, buying a special gauge just to measure leade may seem frivolous. But if you have more than one, and you want to know, then acquiring this gauge is a must. (Michiguns: www.m-guns.com)

And if, after testing, you discover that your rifle has a .223 chamber, instead of the desired 5.56 chamber? What then?

Solutions

A temporary solution is to install a DPMS receiver rug. It is a small synthetic insert that fits inside the lower receiver, under and around the trigger. If a primer blows out of a case, the rug at least prevents the primer from wedging under the trigger and stopping the rifle. As useful as the DPMS rug is, there are a lot of other places that blown primer can go to raise hell.

The permanent solution is a 5.56 chamber from the start, made by the barrel maker, or a modified-to-5.56 chamber. Either barrels/rifles ordered from the manufacturer that way, or reamed by you (or the departmental armorer) afterwards to 5.56 specifications will do. Stainless steel barrels are particularly useful here, as they can easily be reamed to 5.56 chamber dimensions, simply by using a 5.56 reamer and not allowing the reamer to cut the chamber shoulder. (Doing so increases headspace, a subject to be covered shortly.) For a chrome-lined barrel, a special reamer that cuts only the leade (which can also be used in

How meticulous is Ned? He marks his reamer to track how many barrels it has reamed, to check on sharpness and wear.

Once reamed to 5.56, this is what your chamber would look like on the inside. (No change in headspace, by the way.)

stainless or carbon steel barrels) will ream the leade and just the leade to 5.56. Yes, the chrome is removed where reamed, but a chrome-lined barrel with a non-chrome 5.56 leade is better than a fully-chromed .223 chambered barrel. This special reamer is available from Michi-guns. The photograph above shows a cross-sectioned chamber, after it has been reamed with a Michiguns 5.56 throat reamer. From right to left; the first part; the chamber body, is dark. Then the chamber shoulder (directly underneath the "N" of N&T). The first cylindrical portion is the neck, under the "MRT". Then the Freebore (under the "E"), and finally, as a lighter bar of steel extending to the left, you see the throat angle. (The angle "F" discussed earlier.)

Headspace

Simply put, headspace is the room between the bolt face when the bolt is closed and locked, and the shoulder portion of the chamber. Too little, and the bolt cannot close on a cartridge. Too much and the case will stretch when fired. Stretched enough, the case will break in two, the forward half will not be extracted, and the rifle will not be able to chamber the next round.

How much is the gap between case and chamber allowed to vary? .006" or "six thousandths" in machine tool trade lingo. How small is that? In the May 2007 NEMRT Basic Patrol Rifle class, one of the rifles stopped working. A close look at the rifle revealed that the "Inspected by" tag that had been loose in the rifle case had worked its way into the chamber. Chambering a round wedged the cartridge in place over the tag, and the extra thickness prevented the bolt from locking. Until the tag was extracted from the chamber, the rifle was inoperative except as an aluminum and plastic club.

Standard copy paper is generally around .007" thick. So, even a small slip of paper can wedge the cartridge in the chamber and not allow the bolt to close and lock. Keep stuff not needed out of your chamber.

Ammunition Selection & Reloaded Ammunition

You, selecting ammunition for defense, have many of the same constraints as a police department, as well as a few areas of freedom. The departmental ammunition should either be factory-new, or (and for training only) commercially-reloaded ammunition. The ammunition should have the same bullet weight and velocity (within manufacturing tolerances) as the duty ammunition issued. That way the muzzle blast, recoil and trajectory (as well as zero) of the training ammunition will match

Know your ammo. The use of cheap or shoddily-reloaded ammo can lead to an expensive repair. On this rifle, the lower and shooter were unharmed, but everything else was scrap.

the duty ammunition. In addition to shooting the training ammunition (usually FMJ, less expensive than duty soft points, tactical or barrier-penetrating loads) the officers should fire some amount of duty ammo to ensure that the rifles do indeed work 100% with it and are zeroed for it.

You, selecting ammunition for defense, should look at the same things: factory ammo, new, in the box. Practice and match ammo can be reloads, but only top-quality, not the lowest-cost stuff at a gun show. And not ammo loaded by someone else.

In the era of suddenly-expensive ammunition, the temptation to use inexpensively-reloaded ammunition can be great. However, unless the reloader is scrupulous in quality inspection and is willing to reject suspect items at any point in the workflow, the ammunition may not be entirely safe to shoot. The result can often be a blown case, which usually means severe damage to the rifle. However, the AR is amazingly protective of the shooter. Even a blown case which destroys the upper (leaving only a few parts salvageable) rarely causes the shooter more than the inconvenience of accounting for a damaged weapon.

Of course, if the Chief authorizes reloads and an AR is consequently destroyed, the department will supply the officer with a new one and the city buys a replacement. You, on the other hand, will have to reach into your pocket to replace the damaged components. So, before you go and "save" $20 on ammo costs, how much is a new upper?

If you have a case separation, sometimes the broken front half of the previous case comes out when you do your malfunction drill. And sometimes it doesn't.

Cleaning the Chamber

Yeah, yeah, yeah, we all own rifles, and we all know how to clean them. Why is Sweeney wasting our time and busting our chops on how to clean the AR? Simple: based on what most people do, and what most "learn" in law enforcement or the military, you spend entirely too much time cleaning the wrong areas.

Cleaning rods, brushes, tips and swabs for rifles come in two thread sizes: the commercial and the military. Commercial-threaded tools have a thread size of 8-32, while military tools have an 8-36 thread. That is, a size 8 thread diameter, and either 32 or 36 threads to each inch of shaft. Obviously, commercial and military tools will not work together. Knowing what size you have is important when ordering replacement supplies. Brownells carries them both, but if you order the wrong stuff, they will only be so willing to replace. Once or twice, sure. After the fifth time, don't expect an exchange.

More barrels are probably worn out either through improper cleaning or neglect, than are worn out through shooting. Cleaning the barrel requires cleaning two different areas via two different methods: the bore and the chamber. Always clean the chamber first.

Use a chamber brush and a short section of cleaning rod. The best kind of rod is one just long enough for the brush to reach the chamber, with a "T" handle on the end. Screw the chamber brush into the "T" rod. The chamber brush is a bronze or nylon bristle brush, with a "collar" of stainless (for the bronze) or nylon bristles of larger diameter than the chamber-sized section. A little cleaning solvent will decrease the friction of the brush, and the force needed, but cleaning solvent is not necessary for the chamber. Insert the brush into the chamber, and press it all the way in as you turn the rod. The stainless steel bristles are intended to clean the locking-lug recesses of the barrel, so you are fully into the chamber when the collar bottoms out against the rear of the chamber. The brush, when you pull it out, will have the front end of it crushed by the neck and shoulder of the chamber. That indicates you have achieved full insertion. You want to be scrubbing the neck and leade of the chamber, as well as the shoulder.

Once the brush is in all the way, turn through two full rotations in the same direction you've been rotating as you inserted it. Then, pull the brush back out while still turning it that same direction. Which way doesn't matter, as long as each brush is only rotated in a single direction when used or re-used. The best way is clockwise. It is easy for right-handed shooters to do (with apologies to left-handers) and it acts to tighten the brush on the rod. The bristles will have been bent in cleaning, both the small

With a few tools, you can properly clean and thus keep your AR running for as long as you have ammo.

Shown without the receiver, this is the proper way to use a chamber brush. Get the "collar" down into the locking lugs and turn.

ones in scrubbing against the chamber walls and the large ones in the locking lug recesses. If you simply pull the brush out you will flex the bristles in a different direction and eventually break them. By turning as you remove the rod, you extend the life of the brush. You remember the bag tag we discussed earlier? Broken-off bristles getting lodged in the chamber, and wedging a cartridge in place when you later go to load the rifle is not the way to win matches, impress your friends, or save your hide.

In extreme cases (or because you're the thorough type) after scrubbing you can exchange the chamber brush for a cotton mop from Brownells shaped like the chamber brush and swab out any residual powder residue and solvent left in the chamber and locking lug recesses.

Scrub the chamber first. If you clean the bore first, when you clean the chamber you may dislodge gunk down into the bore that you just spent so much time cleaning.

Cleaning the Bore

Each round fired deposits powder residue and microscopic amounts of jacket material in the bore. Over time they can build up to the point of decreasing accuracy. Sufficiently large amounts of powder residue can also decrease reliability. Since it is difficult to actually observe the bore, some traditional or customary cleaning methods can approach voodoo in their methodology and supposed effect.

Simply put, you are scrubbing the deposits out, aided by chemicals that soften or dissolve the powder and jacket material. That scrubbing can harm the bore more than the bullets themselves would. Bore brushes should be either nylon or bronze, never stainless steel. While some barrel manufacturers do not take a position on brush material, some do, and uniformly the position of those manufacturers is; no stainless brushes. The stainless brush bristles are too hard, they feel, and can wear the bore.

An additional source of wear is the rod itself, particularly the sectioned rod joined by means of threaded ends. If pushed through the bore, the rod flexes, and the not-quite-perfect match of the joints bring the exposed edges of each joint to bear against the bore, scraping it. Jointed aluminum rods are worse than steel ones, as the aluminum is soft enough that grit can embed itself in the rod surface. The aluminum rod, pushed through a bore, soon becomes an abrasive stick.

In a pinch, jointed rods and even aluminum rods can be used. A clean rifle that works reliably can mean more in an emergency than the (theoretically estimated) few hundred rounds of service life scrubbed from the bore by the use of such rods.

There are two ways to run a brush and rod through the bore: the push and the pull method. For the push method, you are best to have a single-piece rod. No joints. Coated is better than non-coated. You also need a rod guide. The rod guide is a cylinder that rests inside the upper receiver, with a bore-diameter hole through it from end to end. The rod guide supports the cleaning rod, preventing rod flex. Without it, the rod will flex as you push, and the flex will cause the rod to rub against the bore at one of the two critical-to-accuracy places in the bore: the leade. (The other is the crown, at the muzzle.) The rod guide essentially moves the flex back to the rear of the receiver, where it doesn't matter at all.

The pull method is one learned from some members of the USMC. It allows cleaning with jointed rods without risk of cleaning wear to the barrel. Here, you drop the rod un-brush end first (without the handle, obviously) down the bore from the chamber end of the barrel. The brush will catch in the bore, and keep the rod from falling to the ground. Then, you grasp the rod and pull the brush through the bore and out of the muzzle. Since the rod is being pulled, it can't flex, and you thus do not need a rod guide. (Be sure and screw together enough rod sections so the rod protrudes from the muzzle, otherwise it will be difficult to pull it out once it gets stuck.)

The pull method, while useful in an emergency, has two downsides: it is messier, and it is a bit hazardous to bystanders. Pulling the brush or patched rod out of the bore will spray a fine mist of solvent in the air. Also, there will be some spray from your hand swinging as the rod comes free, throwing a trail of solvent at the floor or wall. In the field, that is not problem. Indoors, it could be a big problem. The other hazard also comes from your hand swinging free. It takes a bit more elbow room to hold the upper with one hand while you pull the rod free with the other. If someone happens to walk into the room just as you pull a brush free, they may catch your elbow in the ribs or the rod in the face. Indoors, use a bench or cleaning cradle, a one-piece rod, and clean by pushing. In the field, when you lack those items, clean by pulling.

The cleaning process of getting and keeping a bore clean is where the various methods that are championed vary. Some advocate cleaning methods of precise numbers of strokes, using this or that cleaning solvent, and repeating the steps a certain number of times. I will avoid all the bore-cleaning cant and sidestep controversy, except to inject some of my own. The simple facts are these: modern cleaning solvents react to copper. When the bore solvent selected does not show a color change after a clean patch with some of the solvent on it is drawn through the barrel, there is no jacket material remaining in the bore. Do not bother with powder solvents; they do nothing to copper. The copper solvents will work on powder residue. When you get to the point that you do not see copper residue reactions on the patch, stop using copper/bore solvent, run a dry patch down and then an oiled patch down the bore. You're done.

Lessons Learned

In the process of learning the extra stuff that comes with keeping a bunch of random ARs running in law enforcement classes, I learned a lot. One important one was: have a loaner, because darned few of the officers attending the class will have brought one. And those that do will have reliable rifles. So, I quickly learned to bring a loaner. I selected a reliable, zeroed carbine of mine, and had it ready. I told each officer the same thing: "Don't change the zero. If you have a malfunction, I want to see it. Don't clean anything." That rifle kept working through several years of classes, and all I did to it was give the chamber brush a twist before each class. Period. I didn't even bother oiling it for a couple of years.

That rifle still works (I've since moved on to other loaners) and it still works reliably. It doesn't shoot much better than 1.5 MOA, but then, it didn't do that when the bore was clean, either. Forget scrubbing the frakking gas tube until it is clean, get to the important parts: the chamber, bolt, etc.

Removing a Barrel from the Upper

You don't remove the barrel from the upper receiver unless/until it is to be exchanged for a replacement barrel or you are installing a railed forearm and wish to salvage the delta ring assembly. The process is simple, but it does require tools. You'll need a drift punch for the gas tube retaining pin, an upper receiver fixture or barrel clamps, a vise in which to clamp them, and a barrel nut wrench. Additional, useful tools are the Brownells front sight holding fixture, a handguard removal tool, a gas tube wrench and penetrating oil.

Barrel nut wrenches come in two types: the military wrench, which is a flat plate with three posts in it, and one of the many multi-toothed wrenches. If at all possible, avoid using the military wrench. The big "advantage" it possesses is that a mil-wrench has a square hole where you can attach a torque wrench. However, the torque wrench

Once the barrel nut is free, you can simply (or with great effort, they're all different) pull the barrel out.

is over-rated for barrel installation. The mil-wrench tends to pull away from the receiver with the slightest off-angle force applied to it. Thus the mil-wrench ends up needing three hands to use it: two to hold the torque wrench and pull it, and one to keep the mil-wrench in place against the barrel nut.

Unlike the mil-wrench, which tends to pull away from the barrel nut, the multi-segment wrenches (as with all things gunsmithing available from Brownells) will stay in place on the barrel nut. At least as long as you maintain wrench tension more or less directly in line with the wrench handle and along the rotational axis of the nut. If you pull the wrench too far toward the muzzle, or push it toward the receiver, it will slip off. It is, however, a lot more forgiving than the mil-wrench in that regard.

To remove the barrel: Remove the handguards. Remove the gas tube retaining pin. If removed carefully and not lost, the pin can be used again. It is, however, easily lost. If you plan to replace barrels, lay in a supply of gas tube pins. They are inexpensive and do not take up much space in storage. Remove the gas tube. If the rifle has been heavily used, the gas tube may be secured in place by powder deposits and require muscle to remove. The MOACKS tool, or the Brown tool, can give you more purchase and leverage than pliers will. They also will not mar the tube, as pliers will.

Clamp the upper receiver or barrel in your vise. Either use the aluminum barrel blocks (less effective) or the synthetic upper receiver fixture (much more effective). If the barrel nut is really tight, the barrel will probably turn inside the aluminum blocks. In such a case you must gain greater traction, and use rosin, Loctite or other methods. (If the barrel is worn enough to require replacement,

Here I have a receiver set up to show barrel removal. I've taken the delta ring and other stuff off so you can see the barrel nut. Make sure the receiver is securely clamped before you go and lean on the wrench.

damage to its exterior hardly matters.) The upper fixture clamping block set is much more effective, but even it has limits. When using the upper receiver block on an obstinate barrel, you must use the internal support. If you do not, you risk pinching the upper receiver slot, and your charging handle will not freely move afterwards.

Place your barrel nut wrench on the barrel nut, and turn the nut to loosen it. It may require great force. It may require more force than you can (or may be willing to) bring to bear. The military specifications call for barrel nuts to be torqued to 35-45 foot-pounds. However, it is customary (as you'll soon learn) to use more force. We have seen barrels whose nuts would not move even when the torque applied to the barrel nut exceeded 80 foot-pounds. In such cases it will be necessary to apply penetrating oil to the threads and wait. Waits of days or weeks may be needed. In extreme cases we have had to use a mill and cut the barrel nut thin enough that it could be broken and then removed.

Once the nut is loosened, spin it off and pull the barrel forward out of the receiver, or the receiver backward off the barrel. It is meant to be a tight fit, and many thousands of rounds worth of powder residue may have worked into the joint so it may take some effort. If it is solidly wedged in place, resist the temptation to use a mallet to tap it off. Soak the joint with penetrating oil for a day or week and try again.

Once the barrel is out, scrub the receiver clean and prep for the new barrel installation.

New Barrel Accuracy Considerations

Rifle accuracy depends on a number of variables. The bore itself must be straight, with a twist rate appropriate for the bullets being fired. The ammunition must be of good enough quality for accurate firing. The muzzle must be concentric. And the barrel should not be under undue tension.

Barrels are straightened at several steps along the way in the factory as part of the manufacturing process. Top-quality, match and mil-spec barrels are not allowed to require more than a minimal amount of straightening to pass QC. Cheap barrels may have been straightened (some severely) in several operations during the manufacturing process. All barrels have the potential to fire accurately, even those that have been straightened excessively. However, straightening induces stresses in the barrel. As the barrel heats up from firing, the stresses act unevenly on the barrel and can cause changes in the point-of-impact

or in group size. The only way to prevent this problem is to not buy the cheapest barrel available. The quality of cheap barrels is much higher today than they were in the past, but the cost of installing and discovering a poor barrel by test-firing it, then replacing and testing its replacement, will be greater than having simply bought a good barrel to start with.

Cryogenic (immersion or chilling in substances of extreme cold, as in liquid nitrogen, etc.) treatments on barrels can relax the induced stresses of machining and straightening and increase the accuracy of barrels. However, the cost of cryo-treating a barrel is high enough that doing the cryo treatment on all barrels to increase accuracy is not warranted. If you're building an NRA High Power rifle and you are intending to make High Master this coming season, the cost of cryo is worth it. If your AR shooting is confined to blasting tin cans at the quarry with your buddies, cryo is wasted.

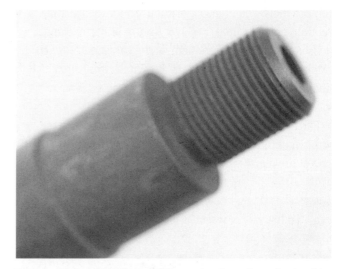

Factory-threaded barrels will have the threads parkerized, along with the rest of the barrel.

Turning the muzzle to the correct diameter is more a matter of setup and feed rates than anything involved. Still, get a machinist to do it if you can.

The barrel crown will have been lathe-turned by the barrel maker, and is almost never a source of accuracy problems unless it has been damaged. One of the great services a flash hider provides besides hiding flash is to protect the crown. Without a flash hider, a crown banged against a hard object can easily become damaged. Even damage too small to be seen with the naked eye can have a harmful effect on accuracy.

If you have barrels that are in "post-ban" configuration, that is, without flash hiders, you can and should have them threaded for flash hiders. (Where state law allows, that is. Some jurisdictions won't let you. My suggestion: move.) The operation is a simple one for any good machine shop. Simply remove the barrel, make arrangements with a local machine shop, and have the muzzles turned down and threaded ½"X28 tpi. The threaded shank need only be .625 inch long. A good machinist can do it in no more time than they'd spend on his/her lunch break. If you go this route, provide the machinist with a spare flash hider. That way he can make sure that the ½"X28 threads he is cutting will actually fit the threads cut in the flash hider. (Yes, ½"X28 means the same thing anywhere you go in the Western world, but it is easy to provide him with a flash hider to check the fit, and it is such a hassle to return because "the flash hider just won't screw on.")

Machining a muzzle to take a flash hider is a piece of cake for any competent machinist. The hard part is getting the barrel out of the rifle in a form he/she can stuff into the lathe.

Keep the barrel off of stuff. It may not decrease accuracy, but if you don't rest the barrel on stuff, you won't have to worry.

If you undertake this operation yourself, here are the steps: First, you need a lathe big enough to accept the butt-end of the barrel. A lathe with a headstock clearance of 1-1/2 inches is enough. Clamp the barrel as close to the front sight as possible. You can, if you wish, remove the front sight and then you can clamp the barrel directly behind the area you'll be machining, decreasing flexion of the barrel. Use a cutoff tool to cut the new shoulder, 0.625 inch behind the muzzle. This cut should be to create a slot with a bottom that is .490 inch in diameter. Now, make multiple passes with your left-hand smooth face cutting tool until the muzzle shank is .500 inch in diameter. If you have a threading tool, cool. Thread the end 28 tpi. If not, you'll have to change to a 60 degree cutting tool and set the thread-cutting feed of your lathe to 28 tpi. Change to a slower feed rate, and take multiple passes, cutting the threads.

If you have a ½"-28 die, you can use that to clean up the threads once you get close enough. Otherwise, use a clean and new flash hider as a gauge. Keep taking passes on the threads, cutting deeper and deeper, until the flash hider screws on smoothly but without wobble.

Take the opportunity to use the Brownells crowning tool as well. While each barrel is in the lathe, use the .224" pilot and the 11° crown cutter to clean up the crown. Simply have the machinist lubricate the pilot and cutter with a good cutting oil, and hand-insert the cutter into the muzzle as the lathe is turning.

Once back home, clean the barrel and re-install it in the upper. And then install your desired flash hider. Test-fire and ascertain zero. Threading the muzzle end of the barrel should not change the zero of a rifle. However, you have had to remove the barrel from the upper receiver to thread it, and that can change the zero.

Chance objects bearing on the barrel when the rifle is fired are viewed as creating potential accuracy loss. However, testing has shown that the effect is limited, if it happens at all. Again, the problem is one of scale: in long-range target shooting, or in a military context of firing at 300+ yard distant opponents, anything that changes point of impact can be a problem. However, at urban distances and most LEO engagements, even resting the barrel on a wooden fence, windowsill or post has made no discernible change of point-of-impact at 25 yards.

However, there is the potential that some rifles might react more strongly to such pressure, so it is still prudent advice to give: keep the barrel off of things while shooting.

There is no correlation between barrel length and accuracy, by the way.

Any time you install a new barrel, clean the bore before shooting. Good barrel makers ship barrels with the bore lubricated with a protective coat of oil, grease or other material. That coating may have gathered dust, grit or other abrasives since it left the factory. Clean those out before running bullets down the bore.

Feed Ramps

The barrel extension of the AR-15/M-16 barrel has a pair of ramps machined into it. These ramps correspond to the location of the rounds as they feed off of each side of the magazine. They guide the cartridge up from the magazine, over the locking lug recesses, and into the chamber. The ramps (or the lack thereof) can be the cause of some malfunctions, mostly due to ammunition. Bullets that are not sufficiently crimped, or do not have a cannelure, have been pushed back into the case by impacting the feed ramp. This malfunction occurs mostly with reloads. If you reload your ammo, the reloading process must use cannelured bullets and have the case mouth crimped into the cannelure.

On AR-15, M-16, M-16A1 and M-16A2 rifles, and carbines before the M4, the feed ramps are machined only in the barrel extension, and the ramp does not extend down into the aluminum of the upper receiver.

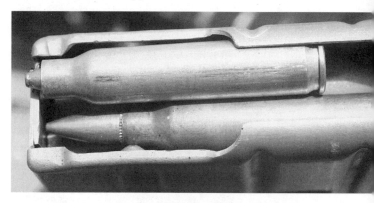

Why do feed ramps matter? Because if your rifle has bad ramps, then this is the likely result.

The barrel extensions are machined for the ramps before the barrel is installed. Here you see some M4-type ramps.

Here is a cross-sectioned barrel, giving us a better look at feed ramps.

In the course of developing the M4, Colt found that the dynamics of full-auto fire, especially with M-855 5.56, created a situation where the carbine would sometimes not feed reliably. To solve the problem, Colt changed the angle of the feed ramp and extended it down into the aluminum of the upper receiver. Barrels so manufactured can be identified by the ramps: on a non-M4 ramped barrel, the cut for the ramps extends only to the edge of the barrel extension. The barrel extension circumference is a smooth circle. A barrel with M4 ramps cut will have the ramps extending past the extension rim, and at the ramps the barrel extension will have a saw-tooth like profile.

Colt upper receivers machined for the M4 will be so marked. Colt alone makes them marked, and they stamp an "M4" on the front of the receiver, above the gas tube

Here you see the feed ramps, machined into the barrel extension and the receiver. Be sure you match barrel ramp type to receiver type, or there will be problems.

hole. Other makers may or may not make an M4-like upper. Theirs will not be marked. (The designation "M4" is a Colt trademark.) However, you can look at the inside of the upper receiver, where the barrel extension tunnel comes into the carrier track. If the upper is made for a non-M4 barrel, the edge will be circular. If it was made for an M4 barrel, the lower edge will have two notches, corresponding to the ramps cut on the barrel.

Colt feels that only the M4 needs the ramps. They do not cut the ramps on rifle barrels, only carbine barrels.

You must not mix the types. An M4 barrel, installed in a non-M4 upper, is not a problem. (At least not for feeding. The front sight, however, may not be the correct height.) The ramps on the barrel extension will be set back a bit from the lower edge of the receiver, but the rifle/carbine most likely will feed properly. However, a non-M4 barrel, installed in an M4 upper, is trouble. The lower edge of the receiver will have the cuts, but the barrel extension won't. As a result, there will be little pockets in the receiver, with an overhang from the barrel extension. If a bullet tip catches there, the rifle will immediately stop.

Always inspect feed ramps, on both upper and barrel, before combining them on assembly.

I ran into the problem of short-ramp feeding problems back in the 1980s. What I did then was to chuck a carbide end cutter into my dremel tool, and reaching from underneath the stripped receiver, cut the ramps down so they were low enough to "carry up" a cartridge that fed nose-down. It worked then, and it works today. However, you will run into AR snobs. They will look at a rifle with dremeled feed ramps as some sort of butchery. (Well, in the wrong hands, it can be.) If your rifle or carbine needs it, do it. If not, don't. Do it carefully, precisely, and as little as possible. And then don't let the snobs look in there.

Barrel Installation Tools and Parts List

You will need, obviously, the new barrel. Installation must be done on a bench, with a vise. You'll need the tools you needed when you took off the old barrel: a barrel wrench, upper receiver blocks, and lubricating oil. You'll need a new gas tube and gas tube retaining pin, plus the drift punch and hammer to remove/install. Useful additions are a barrel nut timing gauge and headspace gauges. The barrel should come with a new barrel nut already installed. If not, you'll have to remove the front sight assembly on your new barrel to install a barrel nut. (Buying a barrel without the barrel nut is false economy. The money you save is not worth the hassle you have to go through to install it.) You can use barrel clamps instead of a receiver block, but the barrel clamp is more likely to slip at high torque, leading to either an old barrel not coming off, or a new barrel not tightened enough.

New Barrel Installation

A new barrel installation usually happens when the old barrel has been worn from use, or damaged from some mishap. New barrels usually come with a choice of flash hider threads or not, and often a flash hider installed, and a front sight housing already in place The front sight housing will also retain the front handguard plate. (If the new barrel is to have some types of free-float railed handguards on it, you may have to remove the front sight housing in order to remove the handguard plate.) It also will come with its own barrel nut. The only parts to be used from the old barrel will be the gas tube and tube retaining pin, (if you're cheap) the handguards, and the handguard delta ring, spring and clip. If those will be re-used, use a pair of reverse pliers to expand the delta ring clip. Once it is free, then the spring and delta ring can be removed from the old barrel nut. Install them on the new barrel. Delta ring first, then spring, then the retaining clip. The clip goes into the slot turned into the rear exterior of the barrel nut.

If the new barrel comes with a new bolt (a wise choice on a high-mileage barrel) check to make sure it is properly headspaced. Yes, the manufacturer says it is, but check anyway. Using the old bolt in a new barrel can be done, but unless the service life of the old bolt is known precisely, it is best to get a new bolt with each new barrel. It is possible to use a bolt in two successive barrels, but not past 10,000 rounds. If the round-count is unknown, use a new bolt. (Again, do the math: a new bolt is $125. The 10,000 rounds it took to require a new bolt cost not less than $2,000. Man up and buy a new frakkin' bolt, for god's sake.)

Discard the old gas tube. The gas tube is subject to wear where it fits the carrier key, and a lack of gas seal is one of the largest causes of malfunctions in the Stoner system. If the old gas tube pin is so loose that it can be pressed out by hand, discard it as well. Install a new gas tube with a new barrel. Both are cheap, so spend the extra few dollars and do it right.

Building on a Bare Receiver

If you are building a receiver from parts, you must install the dust cover door before installing the barrel. The sights and forward assist can go on any time, but installing the dust cover door after the barrel can be a frustrating

A bare receiver can take any barrel you install, but it can't be more than it is. This is an original Colt upper, without forward assist and ejector lump. It is perfect for a retro project, not an M4-gery.

experience. Before putting the barrel on, it is a snap to install the dustcover door. Building on a bare upper is a common experience for the individual AR owner. After all, assembling just the "right" parts is as much fun as the resulting upper. Or at least, to some it is.

Fit to Upper

Scrub the upper clean, regardless of whether it's new or old. Remove any debris or locking compound that may be on the receiver threads. Wipe the barrel extension clean, and check the fit of the barrel to the receiver. It should be a snug fit, requiring some muscle to insert the barrel into the receiver. If it is loose, the rifle may never reach its accuracy potential. Press the barrel in until the locating pin rests in the slot in the receiver. With the barrel hand-seated in the upper receiver, spin the barrel nut on a few threads, just to keep the barrel from falling out. Now look down the upper receiver and barrel as if you were aiming. Does the front sight appear to be straight to the rear sight? If the front sight is tilted, either the barrel locating pin is probably installed incorrectly, and should be returned to the manufacturer/dealer it came from. Or, the problem may be the upper receiver. If the indexing slot is cut in the wrong place, that upper will never have another barrel index properly on it. Check several other barrels in that upper before you send a barrel back with a nastygram, complaining of low-quality barrel manufacture.

If the front sight appears vertical, then unscrew the barrel nut and remove the barrel.

Upper Receiver Fixture

To install a barrel you have to hold the receiver. There is no one known who is strong enough to hold a receiver in his bare hands while you wrench on the barrel nut and successfully tighten it. You need a holding fixture. The clamshell receiver fixture is a great asset to installing barrels. The big drawback to the barrel clamp method is the lack of gripping force. Even with the biggest vise

When you buy a receiver fixture, get the new one, the one that works with both flat-top and A1 uppers. And never use the fixture without inserting the internal support bar.

Buy these blocks, and get the ones that accept both uppers. Do not mess around with barrel blocks, unless there is no other way to swap barrels.

pulled as tightly as possible, the barrel is not fully locked in place. At the upper end of the torque needed to tighten the barrel nut, the barrel may start to rotate within the barrel blocks. Once it does, you cannot apply any more torque to tighten the nut. If the nut is not in alignment, your barrel installation can't be finished. With the upper fixture you are clamping a square part (the fixture) and there can be no rotation.

Insert the center support bar into the receiver. Without it you risk pinching the upper rib of the receiver when you tighten the vise. Since it has already been installed, close the dust cover door. Close the fixture around the upper. Brownells now makes a fixture that works with both A1/A2 uppers and M4 uppers. If you don't have blocks yet, buy that one. If you already have a set for one type, get the dual-use one, too.

If you are using barrel blocks, place the blocks on the barrel and the blocks and barrel into your vise. The blocks have two different diameter grooves in them. Use the groove that most closely corresponds with the diameter of your barrel. Place the blocks on a parallel section of barrel, and not bearing on a tapered section. Once the blocks are in the jaws tighten the vise as much as possible. It is not possible to damage the steel barrel, squeezing it between two aluminum blocks, so the more you tighten the better.

Slide the receiver onto the barrel extension. Use a soft

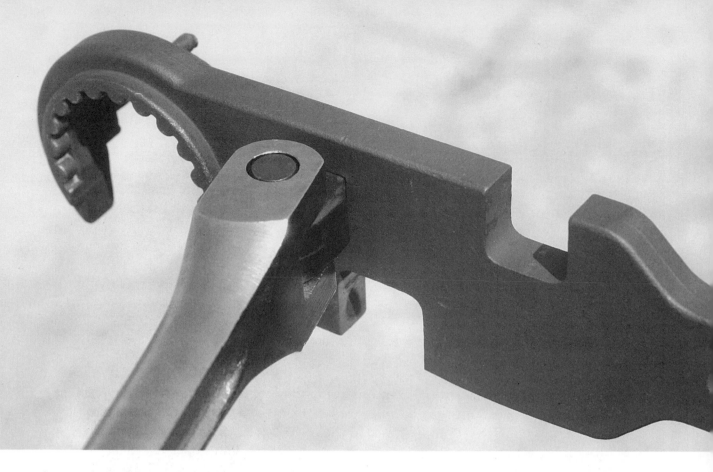

You don't need a torque wrench, but if you have one, use it. You can learn interesting and useful info. Either way, done right, your barrel is on to stay.

piece of wood, or the heel of your hand, to seat it firmly in place. Some advocate the use of an anti-seize compound to keep the barrel nut from "freezing" (locking) onto the receiver, preventing future barrel changes. Still others advocate the use of Loctite to keep the nut from coming loose. (These competing schools of thought obviously cannot be reconciled.) We simply use a bit of oil to allow the threads to slide, and not bind, when you screw the barrel nut on. (If you want the full technical description of thread-tightening, it is at the end of the barrel installation section.) Tension will keep the nut in place, if installed correctly. Spin the barrel nut tight by hand to hold things in place while you get your wrench out.

Get whichever barrel nut wrench you have.

Barrel Nut Torque Methods and Checks

Install the wrench on the nut and tighten the nut. The military specifications call for the nut to be tightened to 35-45 foot-pounds, which a strong man can almost manage with his bare hands, let alone with the leverage of a wrench. Once tight, loosen the nut. Tighten and loosen again. The thread surfaces and their finishes, on both the steel and aluminum threads will have high and low spots

as unavoidable aspects of the manufacturing process. The duplicate tightening burnishes the high spots and eases the final, third, tightening. Tighten the barrel nut until the top-most notch in the barrel nut lines up perfectly with the gas tube clearance hole in the upper receiver. How many foot-pounds does it take? It depends on each barrel and receiver combination. Tighten until the notch lines up. If you cannot muster enough force, you'll have to loosen the nut and start over (see below).

If you have one, you can use an alignment gauge to check the nut location. This gauge fits into the gas tube of the carrier. You then slide the carrier (without bolt but with the gauge inside the gas tube) into the upper until the gauge pokes out through the gas port hole. You then check the nut alignment to the gauge. If you lack a gas tube clearance gauge, a #16 drill bit is the same diameter and serves the same purpose. However, tens of thousands of rifles are barreled each year using only the installer's eye as an alignment gauge, and they work fine. While the gas tube bearing lightly on the barrel nut flange may be unsightly to someone who is concerned about every detail, it does not impair function as long as the gas tube is in line with the carrier key and not bent out of alignment by the contact with the barrel nut.

Occasionally, a barrel nut simply cannot be tightened enough to make one of the barrel nut slots line up properly.

The upper receiver/barrel nut threads are 1.25"X18. With twenty notches to the nut, and the nut stopped halfway between one and another notch, the choices are: loosen the nut and leave it alone, or fit the nut and receiver. If the backed-off half-a-notch nut is still well over the 35 ft-lb torque figure, then it can be left looser and the barrel is done being installed. However, the usual result of loosening the nut to gain clearance is the nut is then not tight enough to stay put. Firing will further loosen it, and accuracy will suffer. To allow the nut to be drawn-down enough, the front face of the receiver must be dressed down or shimmed up. A full rotation of the barrel nut moves the nut .055 inch toward the receiver. (The technical result of 18 turns in one inch.) The distance the nut turns to go from a tooth directly in line with the gas tube hole, and a notch centered on the hole, is 1/40th of that, since we have to go half of a notch, and there are 20 on the nut. Thus, the amount you need to remove to draw the nut half a notch tighter is .0013".

We're assuming you've already done the "tighten and loosen twice" method before attempting to bring the nut in line. The .001+" you need to remove is less than the thickness of the anodizing treatment of the aluminum surface. Remove the barrel. Clamp the empty receiver vertically in your vise. With a large, sharp clean file of a medium to fine cut, take several passes across the barrel opening using light to moderate pressure. All you will have done is burnish (brighten) the face of the receiver. Make sure your filing is done across the entire ring of the receiver. If you leave a high spot, the barrel nut will stop on the high spot, negating your efforts. Attempt re-installation of the barrel. You'll find the nut turns a bit farther. There is no fast or easy way to do this. If you file off too much you will be right back where you started from, and probably close to breaking through the hard anodized surface. Repeat the steps until you can firmly torque the barrel nut with the top notch lined up with the gas tube hole.

The receiver face can also be adjusted with a receiver lapping tool. The steel bar of the tool rides inside the receiver, and fine or ultra-fine lapping compound on the protruding lip of the tool laps the front face of the receiver. As with the file, you must do this in stages and "sneak up" on the adjustments, or you will go past your desired lapping amount, and be back where you started. However, filing the receiver face is now old-school, and not needed. (But explained here if you need a barrel fitted "right now" and can't wait for the ordered shims to arrive.)

If your barrel nut simply won't turn up correctly, the front face of the receiver is the place you have to gently file or shim. You'll have people tell you to use Loctite on these threads. Ignore them.

Shimming

Randall Rausch of AR15 Barrels makes .001" thick shims to fit under the barrel nut. A .001" shim shifts the barrel nut one-third of a notch in its rotation. So, if the barrel nut (looking at it from the muzzle end) has the offending barrel nut notch on the left side of the gas tube hole but blocking it, add one shim. If the barrel nut notch is in the way on the right side, add two shims. Simple parts to use, but not something you can make on your own.

Technical Info for the Curious

The modern threaded fastener is a highly-refined object. It should be; we've spent over two centuries perfecting it. The way a bolt works is simple: the threads of the bolt and the hole it is threaded into flex against each other when they are tightened. Until the bolt bottoms out, there is no flex, just friction. Once it bottoms out (or the head contacts the top surface) the threads then bend, and act as spring-loaded tensioners. How tight can you tighten a bolt? The national boards that determine such stuff figure that when a material has been flexed to 80% of its yield strength, it is maxed-out. Done. Tight. There to stay. More force or a higher percentage of tension, and you risk breaking something. Less, and it risks loosening. Obviously, a harder bolt can be tightened to more pressure (measured in inch-pounds or foot-pounds) than a softer one.

However, friction also plays a part. Let's say you use a torque wrench, and you set it at "50 ft/lb," which just happens to be the rated 80% yield of the bolt we're using for our demo. The wrench won't stop until it has reached "50", then it will click to release. Now, let's assume you are tightening a dry bolt on dry threads. Friction will build more quickly, and you will reach 50 ft/lb of combined friction and tension before the bolt reaches its 80% yield target. You'll stop too soon. Now, let's plate the bolt and hole with the world's greatest super-lubricant. The threads will slide with less friction, and you could, theoretically, break the bolt head off before you reach 50 ft/lb. Friction would be so lessened that you would not be torquing the wrench until the bolt head bottomed out.

The specs can be so exacting that in some applications (e.g., racing engines and some aerospace applications) the manufacturer will not only specify the torque limit but also the lubricant you must use.

Anti-seize and Loctite both act as lubricants (at least until the Loctite sets and locks things up). If you use too slippery a lube, you can over-tighten. Without lube, you can under-tighten. I had a personal example of a low-friction surface causing problems. I had Robbie Barkman of Robar coat and plate an AR of mine. He plated the steel parts with NP3, a super-low-friction nickel coating with Teflon impregnation. As a result, I could not tighten the telestock castle nut tight enough to get it to stay. It worked lose, despite strenuous exertions with a wrench. I finally staked the nut in place, to keep it from working loose.

Once a fastener is properly tight, friction keeps the threads binding to each other. If the flex load of bending threads is high enough, it successfully resists friction. If, however, the tension is less, or the friction less, a threaded fastener can work loose.

So, for our barrel nut: Light oil, tighten three times, leave it alone and the barrel nut will stay until you want it off.

A reminder: It is important to get the barrel nut properly aligned. Not just for the gas tube, but for the handguards

and everything on them. The regular handguards lock into and gain their alignment from the barrel nut. If the nut is not right, the handguards will be twisted, as they try to fit between the barrel nut at the back and the front handguard plate, which aligns and locks-in the handguards.

A railed handguard that is on a mis-aligned barrel nut will have a top rail that is not lined up with the top rail of the upper receiver. Also, any vertical pistol grip will be off-vertical.

Get it straight at the start and you'll never need to bother with it again.

Gas Port

When the bullet passes down the barrel, eventually it travels past the gas port. At this location the propellant gases are vented out of the barrel. They travel up the port and into the front sight housing. From there they then travel down the gas tube to the carrier key. All this takes less than a thousandth of a second. It is important for the system to deliver the correct (within limits) amount of gas, at the correct pressure, and maintain that pressure for a short but important period of time. Lacking gas flow, the rifle will not function reliably as an autoloader. It may not function at all. The gas port under the front sight housing is the subject of a great deal of urban myth. A great many problems, usually with the root cause of a parts gun being "assembled" by an unskilled gunsmith, evidence themselves with a failure to eject or a bolt that does not cycle fully. The immediate and "obvious" problem, to far too many untrained or partially trained "gunsmiths," is that the gas port is too smal, and not delivering sufficient gas to the system. The obvious "solution" is to drill the port larger. Manufacturers go to great effort to ensure that the barrel they ship has the correct-size gas port drilled in it.

Gas port diameters differ in size depending on the barrel length and diameter. Also, they differ depending on the length of barrel past the gas port. However, it is a rare barrel where the manufacturer has not drilled the gas port to the correct size. It is also rare that changing the length of the barrel requires a change in gas port size.

One situation where the gas port "obviously" must be enlarged is when a 20-inch barrel on a rifle is cut down to 16.5 inches to make it a carbine-length weapon. The loss of four inches or so of barrel, and the resultant decrease in gas dwell time, would "obviously" lead to the conclusion that the system will lack gas, and fail to function as a result. Experience has shown this mostly not to be the case. The common situation is a LESSO 1033 M-16A1, with the 20-inch barrel shortened to 16.5 inches but with the front

Even a short distance of barrel past the gas port is enough to provide gas for the system.

sight location not moved. The LESSO program was great for the police departments that took advantage of it while it was happening. A police department could, once they filled out the right paperwork, receive four M-16A1 rifles from the government. For $39 per rifle, the cost of postage. Yes, they were mailed. These were still government property, and while the department could alter them, they could not sell, trade or otherwise dispose of them.

Back to the discussion of gas dynamics.

The short section of barrel protruding past the front sight of a shortened M-16A1 would seem to indicate that the gas port must be enlarged. Until recently, not so. To check this when we were first undertaking the task, a test rifle was left out in the cold (17°F) overnight along with ammunition. Test-firing the next morning resulted in it functioning 100%. The ejected brass shows no signs of sluggish or near-short stroking in cycling. However, one of the state instructors recently encountered a rifle that did require a larger gas port after the barrel had been shortened. So it would be prudent to test a rifle before and after having the barrel shortened.

The best test for a rifle being subjected to barrel shortening (within legal limits, of course) would be to set aside several hundred rounds of practice ammunition. Fire several magazines and plot the location (direction and distance) of the empty brass group. Shorten the barrel and test-fire again. Typically, the location, distance and angle of the ejected brass group will not change. If the direction changes radically, then the timing of ejection has obviously changed. However, if the distance does not change, then the vigor of ejection has obviously not changed.

The situation where a change would most likely be warranted, and which you certainly should test, is in installing an altered barrel on an SBR. If the original rifle was a 10.5- or 11.5-inch carbine, and you are cutting down a 16.5-inch barrel to fit and conform to the desired original barrel length, it is possible you may need to change the gas port. (Possibly, but not certainly. Test!) The 16.5-inch barrel, due to the long section of barrel past the gas port, may have a smaller-than-SBR gas port. The smaller port throttles back the gas dwell time and pressure. If the smaller-port barrel is shortened, it is possible that the port

With a new barrel, it is prudent to fit a new gas tube. Here, the tube is lined up on the front sight housing, ready for its roll pin. (Yes, in some installs it is necessary to fit the gas tube to the front sight housing first.)

is now too small. Again, possible but not certain. In many years of AR-15/M-16 work, and the shortening of many 20-inch barrels to 16.5 inches, only one has needed the gas port opened. That particular one was a "Frankengun" (made from parts from multiple sources, home-built and looking like it) and until the port was opened it operated sluggishly. Once opened (barely) it worked fine. However, the rest of the rifles so shortened have not needed extra gas port work.

Gas ports are subject to erosion. As the base of the bullet passes the port, the gases jet past the edges of copper and steel and slam into the opposite wall of the port. The jet of gas erodes the edges of the port, in both directions. Usually, a barrel has lost accuracy through other wear (erosion in the throat or leade, damaged crown, improper cleaning) before port erosion becomes a problem, but occasionally a barrel will lose accuracy or begin to show sluggish function due to gas port erosion. The only solution is a new barrel.

Gas Tube Installation and Alignment

Gas tubes must be the appropriate length of the barrel and gas system lengths. There are three lengths, two traditional and one new: shorty, or M4 length; full-size or 20-inch barrel length; and the new mid-length. Regardless of how long the barrel itself may be, those are the lengths of the tubes and gas systems. The gas tube extends from the receiver to the front sight. It is mechanically possible to have a barrel more than 20 inches in length, with the front sight located where an M4 would be. You would use a shorty, or M4 gas tube on that barrel.

A similar arrangement comes from Bushmaster, called the "Dissipator." It has a 16-inch barrel with a shorty gas tube but rifle-length handguards.

The gas tube has an open and closed end. The open end goes into the receiver. To install, thread the open end through the top-most notch in the barrel nut and into the receiver. Push it back until the closed end clears the

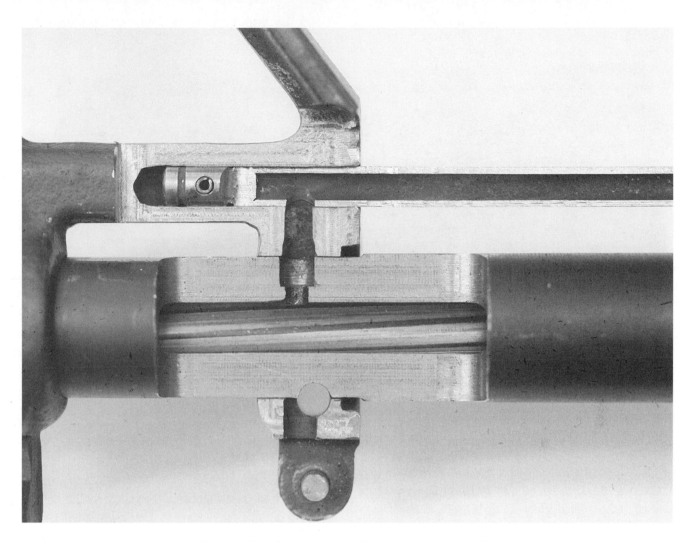

Here you can see the relationship between the barrel, front sight housing and the gas tube. Note that the gas tube has a hole only on one side. Upside-down, it doesn't work.

While you don't need a wrench or MOACKS to wrestle with the gas tube, they do make things easier.

front sight housing. Press the gas tube over in line with the front sight housing, and rotate the tube to bring it in line with the gas tube tunnel in the front sight housing. The gas tube has an intentional dog-leg in it. Do not try to "straighten" the gas tube. The gas port hole in the tube (on the front sight housing end) goes on the bottom. The correct orientation of the gas tube is gas port down from the upper receiver, towards the barrel. It is possible, with much effort, to install the gas tube upside-down. As there is only one gas access port in the front sight end of the tube, the rifle will not receive gas down the tube (the port will be pointing the wrong way) and thus not cycle. (Yes, I've seen it done that way, and no, I won't tell you who did it, except for Not Me.)

Press the closed end of the gas tube into the front sight housing. Look through the retaining pin hole and you will see the end of the tube pass by. Push the tube until the retaining pin hole of the gas tube lines up. Place the barrel in the Brownells barrel fixture, hold the retaining pin with a small pair of needle nose pliers, and tap the retaining pin into place. A dab of black paint will cover both ends

Each time the gas tube and carrier key interact, they rub. The gas tube wears faster.

of the pin, and disclose any later attempts at removal. To make insertion easier, use the MOACKS or Brown gas tube wrench. Also, a large safety pin tip is useful in squirming the gas tube in correct alignment, once you see the pin hole.

In wrestling with the gas tube it may have become slightly bent. Check alignment by removing the bolt from the carrier. Slide the carrier into the upper, and ease it forward over the gas tube. If there is no change in resistance, or just the slightest hesitation as the gas tube slides into the key, the alignment is correct. If you can feel the gas tube flexing to match the key, but it goes together, you will still have to adjust the tube. If the key will not slide over the tube at all, and the barrel nut is not centered, then the nut must be tightened before you can call the job "done." You must remove the gas tube and tighten the nut until the topmost notch is lined up perfectly.

If the barrel nut is properly centered but the gas tube will not easily slide over the carrier key, then the tube itself is slightly bent or kinked. Gas tubes that slightly rub or fail to enter the key can be bent to fit. First, see which way the gas tube flexes as the key rides over it. If it will not enter the key at all, it will be visibly out of alignment and you can see which way it needs to go to fit. Take a large screwdriver and gently bend the tube in the direction it flexes when it tries to fit into the carrier key. Check the fit. Repeat until the resistance eases.

Gas Tube Wear

Even with the best alignment, the gas tube will rub when it slides into the carrier key. Eventually, it will be rubbed oval. The better the fit, the less the wear, but sooner or later it will happen. If you start to experience short-stroking on a high-mileage rifle, and everything else checks out, look at the gas tube. The only way to properly check is to remove it. Slap a micrometer or dial calipers on the raised portion of the end. If it is more than a couple thousandths out-of-round, or a couple thousandths smaller in diameter than brand-new tube, install the new tube.

Of course, on a rifle with that much shooting through it, the barrel is probably gone. Unless, of course, you got cheap when you re-barreled and re-used the old gas tube.

Sight Alignment

Check sight alignment again. It should be vertical. If you have one, a sight alignment gauge (a long steel bar) is useful. However, the gauge is only a guide and you need a handled upper to use it. For best effect you should have checked the alignment of the old barrel before removing it. A particular rifle may actually be vertical when it appears to the eye to be tilted. If the new front sight lines up the same as the old one did, then the rifle is probably going to shoot to the same point of impact as the old, or very close to it, regardless of how tilted the front sight might look.

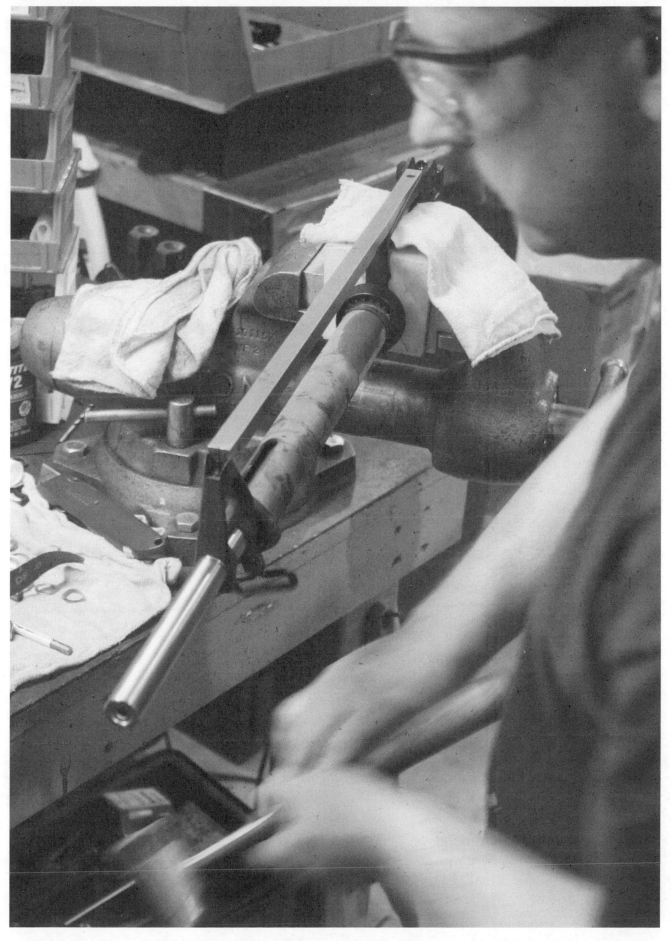

A sight alignment bar is useful, but you can check alignment by eye and range-test to be sure.

SIGHTS

Sights are one of the two items that separate rifles from shotguns. Many shotguns now have rifle-type sights, even optics. The second difference is a rifled bore, but rifles are still more accurate than rifled-bore shotguns. (Some will point out that there are now shotguns with both rifle sights and rifled bores. True, but such shotguns give up much of the versatility shotguns possess: the ability to use a wider variety of ammunition.)

The front sight of the AR was designed to be adjusted by means of a bullet tip. However, while design intent and field manuals say one thing, actual practice says another. Quite often the flange on the front sight post will be as large as the recess drilled for it. The front sight may not turn easily. The notches cut into the flange will be small. The end result is that a bullet tip won't fit. In some cases not even the front sight adjustment tools offered by Brownells and others will fit, or not fit well. One attempted method is to use dental picks to move the sight. However, they are too small and too hard. The hardened pick-tip can break off, making things worse and marring the rifle.

The best way to adjust the front sight is with a "sight wire" or "armorers saxophone." This is perhaps the first tool you'll make yourself for your AR work. To make one,

take a section of coat hanger wire six to eight inches long. File the sight end flat and square. Bend the flat-end end of it into a small loop: it need have no more than half an inch clearance in the loop, and half an inch downwards stem. Then bend the other end in a large loop: three inches length straight down, and then a loop for your fingers.

The saxophone is simple: you use it to depress and hold down the front sight retainer. Once the retainer is down, there is much less friction on the sight, and it takes less force to move it. Then you use the dental pick to rotate the front sight post.

Front Sight Housing

The AR-15/M-16 uses a cast, forged or milled front sight housing that contains the front sight post and its spring and plunger and secures the gas tube over the gas port in the barrel. The housing secures to the barrel by a pair of hoops, drilled and reamed for the diameter of the barrel to which they are fitted. Barrels generally come from suppliers with a front sight housing already attached. There are, however, two heights of the "original" style front sight housing. The first dates from the origins of the AR-15; the second was developed by Colt in the 1990s. When Colt designed and tested the M4 and A4 flat-top uppers, they found they had to make the top deck of the M4 upper a certain minimum thickness in order to ensure structural integrity of the new

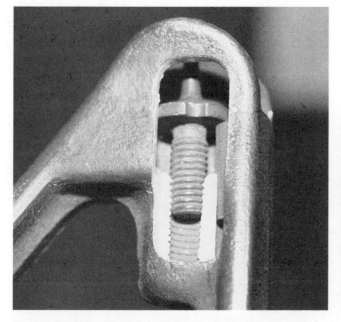

Here you can see the front sight post and its threads. On a brand-new barrel, it is worth the time to use a tap and clean the threads out before you try to force the sight in.

Here is a clamp-on front sight housing. They work well, but I'm not as fond of them as I am of the pinned-on ones.

design. A thickness greater than they could get by simply milling off the handle and installing a rail. Combined with the detachable carry handle, that put the rear sight of the new M4 .080 inch higher above the bore line than on the fixed-handle rifles and carbines. So Colt raised the location of the front sight on the housing. (I will be kind at this point, and charitably point out that had Colt simply lowered the detachable carry handle design they had, they could have easily accounted for the .080 inch and not put us in this fix.)

Colt front sight housings of the flat-top kind can be identified by means of a faint capitol "F" stamped on the housing. The only difference between the two (original and M4) is the location at which the top deck of the front sight is milled, so Colt can still have one front sight housing forging for both sizes. Once a batch has been machined for M4 barrels, they are stamped with the F.

Installing an F-marked sight housing onto a barrel going into a fixed-handle upper will have the front sight too high by .080 inch. Installing a non-F marked front sight on an M4 upper will have the front sight too low by .080 inch and both instances the bullet will impact far from the sights. Correcting the point of aim/point of impact problem by adjusting the front sight creates other problems: if raised enough, the front sight is as high as or higher than the protective wings. It will be prone to damage. If lowered, the front blade becomes so low compared to the protective wings that a shooter may not see it, and use one of the wings as an aiming point instead

Flat-top uppers must get F-marked barrels, and non-M4 uppers get un-F-marked barrels. Keeping them separate is not difficult: only mil-spec manufacturers make F-marked barrels. A Colt, FN, LMT or CMT/Stag barrel, made for a flat-top, is certain to be the correct height. All others are probably the old-height front sights.

Also, if you are building a rifle, or if you are fussing over one to make it as "perfect" as possible, it's time to do a bit of work. Use a dial calipers and measure the distance from the "horns" of the protective ears and the tip of the front sight. You also should mark the sight itself, with a Sharpie or paint, to make sure you have the sight back exactly where it was (assuming it is already zeroed. If not, close enough is close enough).

Unscrew the sight and remove it from the housing. Remove the spring and plunger. Use an 8X36 bottoming tap to clean the threads in the front sight housing. Oil the sight, spring, plunger and housing, and reassemble. Use your measurements and/or paint marker to get the sight back to exactly where it was before. You'll find that sight adjustments will be a lot easier. I do this a normal routine on new barrels, before I even install them on a receiver.

Types
Front sights, fixed

The front sight of the AR system is a rotating post, using a spring-loaded plunger engaging notches on the sight to keep it in place. You give your rifle or carbine a "basic zero" on the range vertically by turning the front sight up or down in the housing, until the point of aim and the point of impact are on the same level. (Or whatever offset you desire; see the zeroing chapter, later.) Rotating the sight down (clockwise) into the housing causes the point of impact of the bullet to move up. Moving the sight up out of the housing moves the bullet impact down on the target. (Sights are typically "factory set" by rotating the post until the adjustment shelf is level with the sight cut deck. This is called the "mechanical zero.")

Regardless of the method of mounting, front sight blades come in two types: A1 and A2. The A1 sight has five locating notches in the flange of the body. The front sight post is a tapered cylinder. In target shooting, the tapered cylinder was found to be wanting: the apparent zero could change, depending on the lighting conditions. So when the M-16A1 was upgraded to the A2, the front sight post was changed as well. The A2 front sight blade/post is rectangular, and has only four locating notches, each aligned so a flat face of the post rectangle is facing the shooter. Why? A round post will reflect light off the side of the post such that sunlight coming from odd angles could make the post appear narrower than it actually is. Aiming with a visuallly narrower front sight will cause the point of impact to shift. (Your eye sees the sight differently, your brain aims it differently, and the bullet is directed to a different spot from the one you expected.) While observable, the aiming error matters almost entirely as a "problem" in competitive marksmanship shooting. While shooting at 500 or 600 yards, the A1 post and its optical illusion would cost a competitor points in a match. In a real-life situation, across a parking lot, the worst it could do is cause a shot aimed at a particular shirt button to hit the right side instead of the left side of the button. (And a small button, at that.) The only real difference is in the amount of shift any sight change creates. At only four settings per revolution, the A2 sight moves the bullet farther for each notch of correction you make, than the A1 would, with its five notches.

If you are happy with an A1 front sight, there is no real reason to change it to an A2 sight.

Night Sights

Night sight posts are built with two flanges. The bottom flange (the spring-loaded plunger captures both, to keep them from rotating) moves the sight up and down to establish the basic zero. The upper flange simply rotates the sight post until the radioactive insert faces the shooter. If you are adjusting a night sight for point of aim, and do not press the plunger down far enough to release the lower flange, or you will simply spin the post and not change point of impact. Having seen this done in various classes, I can tell you it is a frustrating experience. The shooter will turn and turn and turn the front sight, but the zero never changes.

Once a particular rifle has had its basic zero established, it can be useful to keep records of the settings. Now, if you own but one rifle, no big deal. But once you own two or more, do you remember what the zero is, how many rounds you fired, and when you scrubbed the bore last? An inventory card can keep track of rounds fired, maintenance done, and on the card you can note the height of the front sight above the barrel or the front sight post deck, when zeroed. (This, in addition to "painting-in" the sights.) If the front sight on your rifle becomes damaged, a new one can be installed to within a few thousandths to the recorded setting, making the re-zero process much faster. If not, then screw the new one in to the mechanical zero. Then start range-zero work.

Sight Movements, Front

The amount each notch moves the bullet, at various yardages, can matter. The difference each click/notch makes:

	25 yards	100 yards	200 yards	300 yards
A1 rifle	.25"	.00"	2.00"	3.00"
A2 rifle	.308"	1.23"	2.47"	3.70"
A1 carbine	.345"	1.37"	2.75"	4.13"
A2 carbine	.430"	1.72"	3.44"	5.16"

Where sight adjustments matter is in correcting bullet impact and establishing a zero at the 25 yard line. It is important to get the 25 yard zero established as precisely as possible, regardless of which zero system you use: 25, 42, or 100 yard. You can see that if you are off by one notch of sight setting at 25 yards with an A2 carbine, your bullet strike at 300 yards will be off by over five inches. Granted, five inches at 300 yards isn't much, and you'll probably never shoot that far outside of a training session or competition. But the attitude of "close enough" adds up over time, and with distance. Throw in a gentle breeze and your intended hit could be off the target, 10 inches from where you were aiming.

Tracking distance

To keep track of the drop at distances, M-Guns.com offers stick-on trajectory charts ("Ballistickers") that you

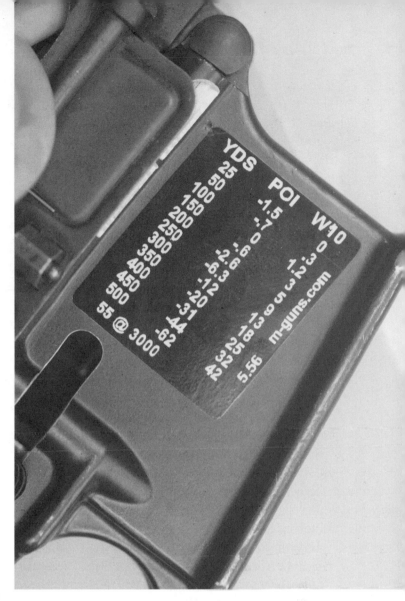

The M-guns Balllisticker is a good way to keep track of trajectory.

can fasten to your rifle. While it might not be something you'd use when firing the length of a vehicle, or across a small parking lot in a defensive scenario, it can be useful if you ever need to fire at a distance. Find a useful location on your rifle. Degrease, peel off the back, stick it on, and you're good to go.

Front Sights, Folding

Front sights that fold come in two heights (leaving aside for the moment those that are built as an integral part of the gas block). One design/height is meant to ride on the top of the rail built into the gas block. To fit, the gas block has to be machined with a Mil-1913 (also known as a "Picatinny") rail on the top. The block clamps onto the barrel and holds the gas tube and the sight clamps to the block, and it folds out of the line of sight of the optics. The second design/height is meant to clamp on to the top rail of a railed handguard. The top rail of the gas block is generally (there is not yet a standard dimension for the gas

A folding front sight, like this combo sight-gas block from GG&G, can make for a very compact rifle.

Installation

Front Posts

The front sight post is threaded into the front sight housing and retained by a spring and plunger at the front. To turn the post, depress the plunger and rotate the post. To remove, rotate counter-clockwise until the post, plunger and spring come free. To install a new/replacement post, clean the threads of the new sight and lubricate the threads of the front sight housing, plunger hole, spring and plunger. (When installing a sight in a brand-new housing, it is useful to use a "bottoming" 8X36 tap in the front sight housing to clean the threads of any hardened oil or grease, grit or metal-finish residue before inserting the sight.)

Press the spring and plunger in place. Insert the front sight post into a sight adjustment tool, and using the tool as a screwdriver, engage the sight threads. Then push the plunger down until it is out of the way and screw the sight down until it is flush with the top deck of the sight housing. Release the plunger, and let it catch in a notch in the sight flange.

block rail height) not as high from the center of the bore as is the rail on a handguard. Thus, the gas-block sights are taller and the handguard sights are shorter. If a gas-block sight is installed on a handguard, the rifle will strike very low, beyond the correction range of the sight adjustments. Conversely, if a handguard sight is installed on a gas block, the rifle will hit very high.

The nominal height of a rail-installed folding front sight is 1.45 inches from the portion that bears against the rail, and the tip of the front sight.

The nominal height of most gas-block folding front sights is 1.60 inches.

Unfortunately there is no accepted marking system by which the two sizes can be sorted. If the sight is out of the manufacturer's packaging, then the only ways to determine if they are the correct height is to either measure them, bore-sight them, or test-fire for zero. With .150 inch difference between them, a mix-up will be quickly spotted, as the alteration of point of impact/point of aim at 25 yards will be on the order of 8.75 inches. Be sure which you have! It is best to get the front and rear from the same manufacturer, and make clear the application you have intended for it.

Why the folding front sight? Two classes of users insist on them. One, in an airborne application, the desire is to make the rifle/carbine as compact as possible, with as few protuberances as possible. When jumping from perfectly good government aircraft, the fewer things that can get hung up on equipment or poke holes in personnel the better. The second group finds the view of a front sight, through their optical sighting system on their rifles, cluttering and confusing. A folding sight clears the line of sight of the optics.

In both instances, the CDI factor of a folding front sight is very high. (CDI: Chicks Dig It. An all too common male fantasy.)

The front sight post, in its revealed glory.

Once installed to the top deck, then proceed to range-fire and zero as normally. Or, if you're replacing an existing sight, begin (as explained earlier) by measuring the distance down from the sight ears to the top of the front sight before removing the old sight. Then install the new sight to as close as that measurement as possible.

Alignment

The front sight must be vertical to the bore of the rifle as it is aimed, or the rear sight will not have enough adjustment to correct the point of aim/point of impact disparity. While the front sight is the offender in this regard, the effect will be seen in the rear sight. The typical mis-aligned front sight problem will show up when the rear sight has to be moved entirely to one side or the other to zero the rifle. In some cases it may not be possible to zero the rifle, as the rear sight in such cases lacks sufficient adjustment to correct for the mis-aligned front sight.

Gross sight mis-alignment can be a problem, and solutions differ according to the manner in which the front sight is fixed to the barrel. If the front sight is fixed in place with cross pins, straight or tapered, the fix is costly and elaborate. Better to return the barrel (or rifle, if purchased already assembled) to the manufacturer with a description of the problem and have them repair or replace it. (Before returning a replacement barrel, try another barrel in the same upper. It is rare, but occasionally an upper manufacturer in the old days would have a mis-cut locating notch in the upper and would "tilt" the barrel installed in that upper to adjust for it. Such uppers will require a new barrel fitted with a clamp-on front sight housing, which can then be counter-tilted to match the upper alignment notch.)

The problem typically arises with front sight housings using clamping screws instead of cross pins. The solution is simple, but tedious: move the rear sight to the center of the settings. Loosen the front sight and correct the alignment by eye. Tighten the front screws just enough to withstand firing, and fire for zero. Repeat until the rifle is zeroed within a few inches at 100 yards (or less than an inch at 25). If the front sight housing is clamped on with two compressions screws (a method used by Armalite in Geneseo, Illionois), then the only way to secure the front sight once it is centered is to apply wicking Loctite to the joint between housing and barrel. Simply using Loctite on the screws themselves is unlikely to solve the problem on a barrel that has already slipped.

Clamp-screw front sights on barrels should be initially aligned by means of a sight bar, a steel or aluminum rod that fits into the groove of the carry handle, and indicates where the front sight should be. However, the bar is only a

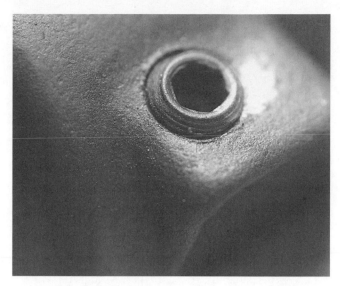

Loctite alone will not keep this screw in place. It takes more than that.

guide. The channel in the handle may not be machined to absolute precision. And rifles using a folding rear sight will have no groove in which to place the sight bar. Setting it by eye and then test-firing is the only way to be absolutely sure.

There are two methods of securing the front sight that use four clamping screws, one in each taper pin opening: the easy and the permanent. To do the easy one, remove each front screw one at a time (on a properly-aligned and zeroed rifle), apply Loctite, and tighten each back in place. Once the four screws are secured, the front sight will be more resistant to movement in the future – "more resistant," but not really secure.

The permanent fix is to remove the screws one by one, and using a narrow marking punch, mark the barrel where each screw bears on it. Or sacrifice the screws by tightening them just short of mangling them, and thus leaving marks on the barrel. Then remove the front sight housing. Use a drill press to dimple the barrel directly on each marked location. The dimples will each provide a shoulder to lock the screws in place. You will have to repeat the range portion of the basic zero, adjusting the sight to get it centered. Once it is centered, then you perform the one-screw-at-a-time Loctite procedure. (Wicking Loctite between the barrel and front sight housing would be good insurance.)

For both methods, once the Loctite is cured, paint over the screws. Use an unobtrusive but non-matching color to show they have been "painted-in." The paint will discourage unauthorized meddling with the screws and disclose when or if any meddling has occurred.

Back in an earlier age, when we were going through the first "assault weapons" panic in the 1980s, I was fixing a lot of ARs. We (there were several of us as at the gun club who were viewed as more than competent AR-mechanics) encountered far too many barrels with tilted front sight housings. One of the guys made a fixture that clamped on the barrel. We'd take a tilted-sight rifle, clamp on the fixture, remove the crosspins, and test-fire. The fixture had adjustment screws, and we could tilt the sight housing until it was hitting center on the 100 yard backstop. We'd then re-drill the pin holes and install new, larger pins.

Luckily, the barrel makers got a lot better, and we stopped having a need for the fixture.

Rear Sights

Rear sights come in two fixed types: A1 and A2, with bolt-on Back-Up Iron Sights (BUIS) following the two types and adding a third: folding. (The Army term is BIS (Back-up Iron Sight) instead of BUIS.)

The A1 is a simple flip-blade rear with two apertures. The two are meant as the "close" and "distant" aiming apertures. For personal defense or law enforcement use, with engagements rare beyond 100 yards, a long-range setting is superfluous. Windage (bullet strike side-to-side) on the A1 is adjusted by means of a circular plate on the side of the carry handle. The plate is moved by either inserting the tip of a bullet or other object into the hole with the retaining plunger, pressing the plunger down out of engagement, and then turning the plate. It cannot be done with the bare hands. The A1 sight will be found on M-16, M-16A1, the AR-15s in the Colt SP-1 series, and the Canadian C7 uppers. The A2 is the "target" sight, with click adjustments by means of a windage knob, and range adjustments by means of a knurled wheel under the sight tower. The A2 will be found on M-16A2, A3, A4 rifles and M4 carbines.

Of the two, the A1 is considered a bit more durable (although, in years of AR gunsmithing, I have yet to see a truly broken A2 sight) but the big advantage is in adjustment. Or rather, the lack of it. If you zero your A1 sights, and use paint to mark them, no one can screw with your sight settings unless they have a sight tool in hand. That is why we recommend the A1 sights to law enforcement.

Some BUIS offer a click-adjustable rear sight, windage and elevation, while others offer only windage. With the popularity of flat-top upper receivers, which lack a rear sight altogether, rifles are often seen with a BUIS bolted on the top rail. Curiously, all too many photos from Iraq and Afghanistan show M4 carbines with optics of some kind and no rear iron sight.

A1
The Original Style

The A1 sight is adjustable for windage, and has an "L" shaped sight aperture post that can be rotated from the short-range (unmarked) to the long-range (marked with an "L") for range adjustments. The difference is achieved by the sight aperture manufacturer drilling the two aperture holes on different "planes." The long-range aperture is a small amount higher (measured from the windage screw) than the short-range sight is. By placing the aperture higher, the designers force the shooter to lower the rear of the rifle (relative to the front sight) and thus achieve a higher arc or trajectory on the bullet launch. The difference matters for military use, where targets may be usefully engaged hundreds of yards removed. In the self-defense or law enforcement setting, a long shot is likely to be across a small parking lot.

Jeff Cooper, when asked why gunfights tend to be held at "conversational" distances, commented that you often don't find out you need to shoot someone until after you've talked to them. It is only in the military context (and not always then) that you can shoot some people "on sight."

For hard-use rifles that will have only iron sights the A1 is preferred, as it has fewer parts and is less likely to be mis-adjusted after the weapon has been zeroed. To assemble from a bare receiver, place the sight spring in the recess in the upper receiver. Press the sight aperture down on the spring, and enter the sight screw from the left side. (Orient the sight so that when the long-range aperture is up, the L stamped on it is visible to the shooter.) Rotate the screw so it captures the sight body, and continue rotating it until it

This A1 rear sight is plenty good enough to get you hits at normal distances.

enters the right-hand wing of the carry handle. Press the screw across, and keep the sight aperture body off of the right hand wing. Turn the sight screw until the sight is centered between the carry handle ears.

Lay the receiver on the left side. Oil the sight plate spring hole, insert the spring and the detent ball. Turn the screw so the hole through it is parallel to the axis of the bore. Press the plate down on the end of the screw, and note the location of the retaining pin hole of the plate. Adjust the screw so the hole in the plate, when the plate is pressed down over one of the detent holes, lines up with the hole through the screw. Use your 1/8" punch as a slave pin to hold the plate to the screw while pressed down on the plunger. The best direction to insert is from the muzzle. That gives you room to work on the sight from the rear, where there are no receiver parts in the way.

Now hold the sight retaining pin with needlenose pliers, and tap the pin to start it in. Once it is on place well enough to stay on its own, set aside the needlenose pliers, and use a drift punch and hammer to drive the pin flush to the plate. In so-doing, you'll knock the slave pin-1/8" punch out of the sight.

Once the sight has been assembled, check the rotation of the assembly. Turning the plate should make the rear sight move left or right across the rear of the carry handle.

To replace or change a rear sight; drift out the roll pin, remove the plate, detent and then turn the screw to release the old sight. Then assemble as if from a bare receiver.

A2

The A2 sight came about mostly due to the Marine Corps need for marksmanship. The A1 sights, while entirely adequate for close-range use (in a military context, "close range" can be out to 300 meters) was a crude tool for longer-range use. As the Corps routinely fired to 500 meters for qualification, a better iron sight was needed. (The changes were done in the early 1980s, when the suggestion of optics for the solution would have been literally laughed at.)

It is not only click-adjustable for windage, but also for elevation as well. While the basic zero is done, as with the A1, with the front sight, once the zero has been established, all range corrections are made with the rear sight.

The sight assembly of the A2 is similar to that of the A1, in that it uses a windage screw and retaining plate, with spring and plunger in detents on the retaining plate. Where it differs is in the plate, and the aperture body. The plate is finger-adjustable for windage. Unlike the A1, where you need use a bullet tip or tool to unlock and rotate the plate,

This is an A2 rear sight, which gives you plenty of adjustments for target shooting.

the A2 windage knob can be moved by the fingers. Indeed, it is meant to be moved by finger pressure. In a competitive environment, where the wind might push a bullet a known distance across a target at a known range, "clicks" to adjust for the wind are useful. In combat, not so much.

1) Rear sight assembly
2) Index spring
3) Rear sight ball
4) Rear sight, A2
5) Windage screw
6) Rear sight spring
7) Rear sight base/housing
8) Windage knob pin
9) Windage knob

The A2 aperture body also differs from the A1. On the A1, the two apertures are on different planes. Changing from one to the other also changes point-of-impact on a

The parts of the A2 sight assembly, out of the upper receiver.

target. (Raising it.) On the A2, the apertures are different sizes, but as much as modern manufacturing tolerances allow, they are on the same plane. The group sizes will change, due to the human eye being able to aim more precisely with the small aperture than with the large. But the center of the group should not shift on the target.

In order to make the A2 rear sight adjustable, the sight has to have many more parts. The assembly is not significantly less robust than the A1, but sometimes the easy adjustment can be too much of a good thing.

A2 Sight Assembly

Unless damaged, there won't be much need to assemble an A2 sight. Uppers come already assembled, as do BUIS. However, knowing the parts involved, and how to replace them if they become damaged, is necessary if any rifles or carbines you own have A2 rear sights and they end up needing work.

Assembling the A2 sight body is the same process as installing sights on the A1 receiver, except there is less to hold onto. One difference between them is in the detent and ball for the windage knob. On the A1, the spring goes into the carry handle. On the A2, the spring goes into the windage knob.

Assembling the completed sight body into the upper receiver of the A2 is more involved. Place the A2 upper upright on the bench. Place the elevation detent spring and elevation detent in their tunnel. Place the elevation wheel upper and lower together, and slide them into the rectangular slot from the side. Press the detent down to clear the wheel. Be sure to place the wheels with the detent holes down, and the upper wheel so the numbers can be read upright.

Leave it standing for the moment. Pick up the rear sight assembly, and insert the tensioner spring and ball into the sight housing. Hold the detent in place and insert the threaded end of the sight housing into the elevation wheel. Without losing either of the detents, turn the wheel to capture, and draw down, the sight housing. Once the housing has been caught, the elevation detent and spring will not escape. Once the housing has been drawn down enough that the tensioner ball is trapped behind the wing of the carry handle, it cannot escape. Turn the elevation wheel until it bottoms out. Then bring it back up three clicks. This is the "mechanical zero." The dimensions of the sight have been calculated for the sight to start "three clicks up" and all adjustments are made from there.

Now rotate just the upper half of the elevation wheel. It will turn without moving the lower half. Rotate it until the "3/8" (on rifles) or the "3/6" (on carbines) lines up with the index mark centered on the left side. Use a 1/16" allen

wrench to install the index screw. Once the index screw is in place, turning the wheel turns both the upper and lower halves, and also changes the elevation of the rear sight.

The last step is the one requiring a special tool. Lay the receiver on its side. (The left is usually easier.) Push the spring in from underneath, and use the special slotted sight tool (available from Brownells, #080-000-079) and compress the spring. Place the roll pin in the hole and tap it into place. If you lack a vise or fixture to hold the upper (we almost all do) this is the time to ask for an assistant to hold the receiver in place (and keep the spring compressed) while you drift in the roll pin. In a pinch you can use a closely-fitting screwdriver to compress the spring. However, as with all such expedients, if something goes wrong you end up losing parts, scratching the rifle or stabbing yourself with the screwdriver. If you're going to do this more than once or twice, invest in the proper tool.

The big advantage of the A2 is its adjustability. However, that advantage brings with it many more parts, and the possibility of mischief. Bored, idle or unknowing "friends" can spin the windage knob back and forth.

One way to make the A2 less prone to inadvertent adjustments is to either acquire a locking windage knob (available from Rock River), or drill and tap the knob. To drill and tap the knob you have to remove it from the upper. Then, drill from the rear, between two of the

Once you've zeroed your rifle, "paint in" the sights so you can tell if someone has been monkeying with them

plunger detent depressions but on the arc between them. If you use one of the depressions as your drilling point, the screw will eventually (if you do this to enough rifles) happen to fall right on the plunger when the rifle is zeroed. Then the locking screw will be depressing the plunger as it locks in place. It gets the job done, but isn't the best solution. Drill in-between instead.

You can also "paint-in" the sight knobs. If the paint is disturbed, you know your "buddies" have been at play again.

BUIS

Back Up Iron Sights are necessary when optics are used. While modern optics are quite durable, even the best will quit before iron sights do. The market for BUIS is a competitive one, and there are many manufacturers. Detailed descriptions and photographs of just BUIS could probably fill a book of this size. And be out of date in a year.

There are two types: non-folding and folding.

Non-Folding

Colt M4 Handle

The earliest BUIS is the detachable carry handle. While it is a means of getting iron sights on a rifle, it negates the top rail, where you'd mount optics. As a "back up" it would be in your gear bag, not really accessible in an emergency. It uses two knobs and a rail to clamp to the upper. Once properly tightened it cannot be removed with the bare hands. The rear of the sight assembly should be installed flush with the rear of the upper rail.

Assembling it is the same as the A2 sight on a complete receiver. I've seen photos in Iraq of troopers with the handle bolted to a rail on the forearm. They don't have room for it, the laser, optics, etc. on top, and don't want to/aren't allowed to lose it. So they bolt it to the handguard.

LMT

The Lewis Machine & Tool sight looks like a carry handle with the handle part cut off. They apparently had one of the secret-squirrel units approach them for a more-durable BUIS. One of the guys had a carry handle he'd attacked with a hack saw. "Can you do something like that?" The LMT engineer reached into his desk and pulled one out that had been professionally machined. "How's this?" And the job was done. The LMT design opens the top rail for access to optics, while maintaining all the adjustments of the A2 sight, and is plenty durable. The LMT uses a single knob, and should also be located to the rear of the upper, flush with the rail. As with the Colt M4, when the LMT is properly installed it cannot be removed with the bare hands.

The LMT BUIS, bolted in the proper location: rear of the receiver, but not overhanging.

Rock River

Rock River did much the same thing with their BUIS, with some differences in machining approach and cosmetic touches. Again, an ultra-durable rear sight.

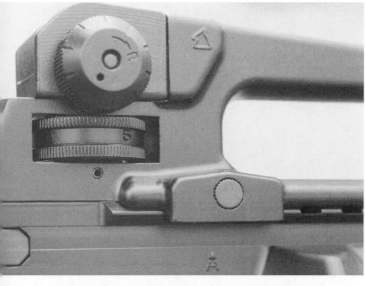

The Colt carry handle on the M4 is its own BUIS, sort of. It just makes it tough to mount optics and BUIS.

Here is a Rock River rear sight, snugged up behind an EOTech.

LaRue

The LaRue uses rear sight parts that are smaller than those of the A2, Colt or LMT, but the housing is a sturdy rectangular block. It takes one rail's worth less of space on the top of the upper than many other BUIS do. It is solid, and with the lever mount, relatively quick to remove. Unlike the previous two, the LaRue can be removed with the bare hands, using their lever mount.

Midwest

Midwest Industries also makes a non-folding BUIS that is compact, and doesn't take up much rail space. It does not have a quick-detach option, however.

Folding

Folding sights all secure to the upper by means of a clamping screw and bevel plate. Since they fold, there is no need to have them quickly removable. The US Army Airborne requirement for folding sights, front or rear, is that they lock in the upright position. As a folded or halfway-folded sight is of little use, it is a wise choice. Another approach, used by the A.R.M.S. company, is to spring-load the sight into the "up" position. Folding BUIS should be located on the rail of the upper such that when folded the sight comes to the rear of the receiver, and does not hang over the edge. If located so it overhangs, it may get caught on equipment, and damaged. If located forward of that position, the sight will not work properly as a sight, and aiming will be difficult.

GG&G MAD

The lowest-sitting on the upper when folded and most compact is the GG&G MAD. The Multiple Aperture Device has four apertures of two sizes. The apertures are on the same plane so changing between them does not change your zero. The device folds flat, and you can have either-size aperture selected while the sight is folded. It locks upright, and you have to press the locking button to fold it down. Folded down it is out of the line of sight of your optics.

Brownells makes a similar sight, which also folds flat.

The GG&G MAD, a flat-folding sight that offers a pair of apertures.

A2 Folder

This is made as a folding sight that has a housing similar to that of the A2. Made by GG&G, Midwest Industries and others. The sight has large and small apertures, but most will only allow you to fold the sight with the large aperture selected.

The A2-style folding BUIS is popular in some circles. Me, I figure I need irons in case my optics quit, not because I want windage adjustments. But I'm a curmudgeon.

Troy

Troy sights fold flatter than most. The sight is compact, and Troy is working on a design that allows the selection of either aperture when folded. At the present, only the large aperture can be selected and the sight folded. If you try to leave the small aperture selected, the sight won't fold flat. A minor aspect of an excellent design.

A.R.M.S.

The #40 or #40L sights are compact, and use few parts compatible with the mil-spec sights. They do, however, fit in well with ARMS rails and railed handguards, and are excellent sights.

The A.R.M.S. #40 and #40L (this is the 40) are compact but adjustable rear sights you would be well-pleased with.

Matec

Matec at last check had an open-ended contract with the government to deliver their sights 20,000 units at a time. Many of the photographs of BUIS in Iraq or Afghanistan will be of Matec sights. The US Army training manual for M-16 and M4 shows the Matec as <u>the</u> BIS for small arms use. Unlike many folding sights, the Matec has a range adjustment feature. Using an eccentric cam, the sight raises or lowers according to the figure you select on the left side. Like the A2, it can easily be adjusted by your "friends." Unlike the A2, it is easily re-set back to the correct range.

Again, it bears repeating: All folding BUIS have to be installed so that when folded they do not hang over the rear of the upper. Otherwise, you're going to get it hooked on something one day, and the outcomes will all be bad: sight damaged, rifle yanked out of your hands, muzzle pointed someplace along with an A.D. You get no choice; life mixes them up for you and presents you with a bad outcome.

Some prefer bright orange, others want a more subdued color. Whatever you do, don't use something so subdued that you can't figure out if it has been painted or not.

The color of the paint is not important, except that black, dark blue and dark gray might not be good ideas on a black rifle. The dabs are so small that bright orange is not likely to give away your position. Light blue also works. Apply the paint heavily enough to create a drop, but not so large that its weight and size make it easy to chip it off the rifle.

If your rifle when zeroed has the rear sight significantly off center, mark its zeroed and sighted-in centerpoint with paint, a marker or a scribe. Otherwise, someone will look at it, think "That's been cranked off-center" and "adjust" it back to where they think it ought to be, despite the presence of the painted-in indications.

The Matec is the current military BUIS, and Matec makes them by the tens of thousands.

Rear Sight Checks

Fixed BUIS should be checked to make sure the locking knob's are tight. All sights, once the rifle has been zeroed, should be "painted-in." The process involves applying a dab of paint to the rifle, across the clamping knob and the receiver. When the paint dries, it acts as a visual indication of the knob's desired location. If the paint is broken or the paint lines do not line up, the knob has become loose or the zero has been changed.

Chapter Seven

HANDGUARDS

Handguards are necessary to protect your hands from the heat generated by firing. Also, on a hot summer day, steel or aluminum can become too hot to touch, while plastic will remain cool. That has not kept a few movie makers from using ARs (or M-16s) lacking handguards as "cool" "modern" firearms. I'm not sure if it says more about their lack of imagination or their lack of a props budget. Handguards are also, in the modern era, a place to hang "stuff." With a large enough "stuff" budget, you can double the weight of an AR by bolting things onto the available rail-estate.

Types: Length

There are three lengths of handguards, the same as the gas systems they cover: rifle, carbine, and the new and non-standard length called "mid-length."

In those lengths, handguards come in a variety of styles. The original method was to fabricate handguards of a plastic and secure them around the barrel. Later, a one-piece tubular handguard that screwed on in place of the barrel nut was developed. Later still, we have "railed" handguards. Typically made of aluminum, they are circular, rectangular, or six or eight-sided and have cooling slots milled in them. They have either sections of M-1913 rails machined into or bolted onto them, as locations to place extra gear. Commonly, the gear attached are lights, lasers, vertical handguards, bipods or optical sights. Railed handguards can be quite expensive. Replacing a new barrel on a rifle, where the old one is worn, can run $300 to $500. (Some barrels can be had cheaper, but as with so many things, you have to remember the two-sided coin of economic law: You get what you pay for, and you pay for what you get.) Railed handguards can run that much or more. When the cost of the extra gear is added, the project cost of upgrading to a better barrel without restraint in the purchase of goodies can end up with the barrel having been the least-expensive part of the upgrade.

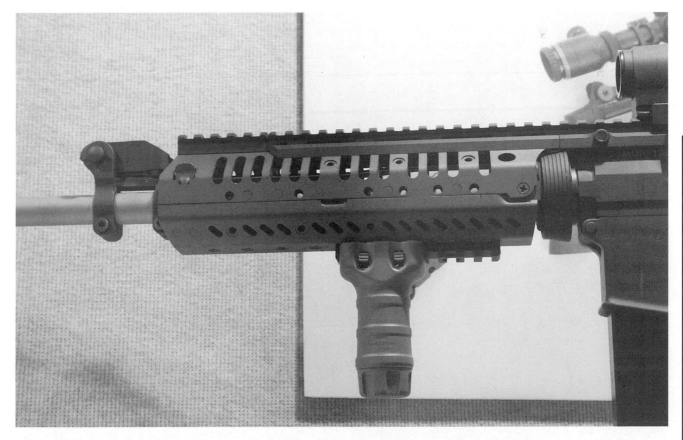

Vltor makes the CASV handguard system, a lightweight, durable and M-203 compatible handguards.

Standard handguards are held on the barrel by means of a sheet steel cup at the front, called the "handguard retainer," and the spring-loaded cap at the rear, called the "delta ring" or "slip ring." To remove the handguards, press the delta ring rearwards, toward the receiver, to uncover the rear lip of the handguards. Then pivot one and then the other handguard away from the barrel. The spring powering the delta ring is strong, to keep the handguards in place and rattle-free. Depending on the fit of a set of handguards to a rifle, it may be necessary to have two people performing this operation, one compressing the delta ring and the other prying the handguards away. You can also use a special tool that hooks on the magazine well and then pries the delta ring down.

Rifle handguards are those that go on rifles with 20-inch barrels: AR-15 and M16 and 16A1. They can be found in two styles. The original, A1 style handguards were triangular in cross-section and noticeably tapered from the receiver to the front sight housing. The plastic they are made from is not particularly durable, and it is common to see tabs of the sections that create the air vent holes broken off. The triangular handguards are made as pairs, a right and a left, and if one is broken beyond repair it must be replaced with one of the same side, right or left. Handguards are so common, and inexpensive, that repairing them is not usually worth the effort.

As part of the development work on the M-16A2 done in the early 1980s, the handguard design was changed. The A2 handguards are circular and ribbed, with a slight taper from back to front, less-so than the taper of the A1 handguards. The A2 halves are identical and install as uppers and lowers. If one is broken, any other A2 handguard will do as a replacement, as they are not made as upper and lower pairs. Like the A1, the A2 handguards have a heat shield in them, a stainless steel liner that deflects heat from the handguards. Unfortunately, it protects the shooters hand by reflecting the heat back to the barrel, decreasing its service life. However, the effect on the barrel is minimal, and the comfort for the shooter in hot climates or heavy firing is greatly improved.

The handguards fit into the handguard retainer, which is itself trapped on the barrel by the front sight housing. A1 retainers are triangular, while A2 retainers are circular. A1 handguards will fit and stay only in A1 retainers. If an A1 handguard set is installed on a barrel that has an A2 retainer, they will not be supported or even retained at the front. They will at the very least rattle, and they may come out. However, A2 handguards are shaped on the front to fit into either-shape retainer. A barrel with an A1 retainer may have A2 handguards fitted, and once installed the A1 design of the front retainer might not even be noticed. While some A2 front caps are circular, all USGI caps are

The A2 handguards are round, identical, and provide a good support.

This LaRue railed handguard provides plenty of room for extra gear. Perhaps too much.

notched at the bottom to provide clearance for the M-203 grenade launcher.

One popular alteration of LESO 1033 rifles is to replace the A1 handguards with A2 handguards.

Short handguards fit on carbines, those that have the front sight housing moved rearward, and typically have 16-inch or shorter barrels. (The location of the gas port, and thus the front sight housing, determines the length of handguards a rifle takes.) The earlier handguards, called "CAR" or "Shorty" handguards, are the same diameter as the forward portion of the A2 handguards, round and ribbed. They have a single heat shield in them. The later M4 handguards are larger in diameter, and oval in cross-section, with the greater thickness up-and-down. In sustained fire, or with repeated full-auto fire, the old handguards became too hot even with one heat shield, so the M4 handguards were made larger, tougher, and have two layers of heat shield, with an air space between them. DPMS takes a different approach with their "Glacier Guards." Instead of a stainless heat shield (or two of them) inside, the Glacier Guards are made out of a polymer with a low heat transfer rate. To aid in insulating your hands, the inside of the guards have thick ribs cast of the same material. The handguards are so thick-walled, and the polymer transfers heat so slowly, that you will be melting your barrel before you notice the heat.

The dimensions of the delta ring and handguard retainer were not changed, so any carbine that takes CAR handguards can have M4 handguards installed, and vice-versa. Also, the delta ring assembly and handguard retaining plates are the same for all rifles and carbines. A parts kit of delta ring parts will fit any rifle. A2 retaining plates, while they fit all handguards, do not fit all rifles. The barrel is machined so the diameter of the barrel directly behind the front sight housing is slightly larger than it is

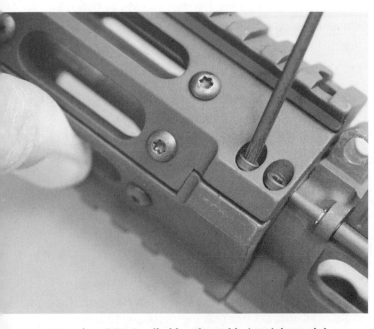

Here is a GG&G railed handguard being tightened down onto the barrel nut.

where the front sight housing is attached. The retaining plate is trapped between that larger portion, and the front sight housing. The barrel hole in the plate must be the correct size for the barrel, or it doesn't work. The old M16A1 barrels were of a much smaller diameter (0.625 inch) than later M-16A2 or M4 barrels (0.750 inch), and retaining plates for the older barrels won't fit newer barrels.

However, replacement barrels customarily come with a front sight housing and retaining plate already attached, so there is no need to fit those old parts to a new barrel.

Mid-length gas system barrels are a new thing. Some shooters feel that the gas system of the M4 or other "shorties" places the gas port too close to the chamber, and the resulting gas pressure curve leads to an unreliable weapon with harsh recoil and cycling dynamics. By moving the gas port away from the chamber, they make the carbine (the barrels with mid-length gas systems are typically left 16 inches long) cycle more like and feel more like a rifle, with its 20-inch barrel and longer gas tube.

The "standard" length for a mid-length gas system is standard only for those manufacturers making them. Colt and FN are not making mid-length gas system rifles. If a mid-length gas system rifle is found to be desirable, be sure to order handguards and a gas tube along with the new barrel. Only by acquiring them together, from the manufacturer of the barrel, can you be absolutely sure they will fit.

Oddities: the Dissipator

There are a small group of carbines known as Dissipators. They have rifle-length handguards but carbine-length barrels. Underneath the handguards is a carbine length gas tube. The front sight housing is only that, as the gas tube does not reach it. Instead, the gas tube is attached to its own, low-profile gas block, underneath the handguards. The idea was to have a carbine-length rifle, but not have the problems of a too-short distance between gas port and muzzle.

Types: Railed Handguards

The big advantage to tubular or railed handguards is that the handguard now no longer bears on the barrel. A free-floated barrel quite often demonstrates greater accuracy than one with objects pressing against it, even objects that are other parts of the rifle.

While barrel contact, even with the handguards, can decrease accuracy, it is not as much of a problem for point of impact as many think. Again, the main problem arises from NRA High Power, with its focus on and requirements of long range target shooting. There, in a solid prone

position with a tight sling, the shooter may find the point of impact changes due to tension on the barrel. Now, before you give up the idea of a sling for shooting support, keep in mind the forces involved: the NRA High Power shooter is going to have a sling pulled so tightly that his (or her) fingertips are turning blue by the end of the shooting string. The point of impact change may only be a few inches. (It may be more, but there is no way of predicting, and a lack of accurate prediction is anathema to long-distance shooting.) The larger barrel diameter of the A2 rifles (and thus added weight) comes about from the same problem. However, that change in point of impact must be kept in context. Prone, slung shooting is done at 300, and 500 or 600 yards. At the distances involved, having the point of impact shift a couple of inches will cause them to lose points.

Engaging a suspect across a parking lot, the law enforcement officer is not likely to have a sling that tight. Even if they do, the relative differences are instructive: an amount of sling tension that will cause a point-of-impact change of five inches at 600 yards will only change the point-of-impact across a 75-yard wide parking lot by 0.83 inch. On the 600 yard line, what would have been a perfect center-X shot becomes an 8-point shot. Across the parking lot, the bullet was shifted from one side of a wide button to another, and that only if the sling is uncomfortably tight. For the homeowner, the distance from the bedroom door to the front entrance surely will not be 75 yards. (What kind of a house would that be?) At 50 feet, the same sling tension that produces a bullet shift of five inches sat 600 yards will change the point of impact by a mere tenth of an inch.

High Power shooters avoid the sling problem by free-floating the barrel. Those who shoot in the Service Rifle category use a special free-float handguard that appears to be a standard A2 handguard set. Inside, however, is a steel tube, and forward of the barrel nut nothing touches the barrel but the gas tube.

Railed Handguards: Installation

Railed handguards come in three types: handguard replacements, which do not free-float the barrel; handguards that clamp over the barrel nut; and handguards that replace the barrel nut. The latter two do free-float the barrel, generally a good thing for accuracy. The replacement handguards are installed simply by removing the old handguards and installing the new, as if the new were simply just another set of handguards. As an inexpensive means of getting rails on a rifle, they get the job done. They do not free-float the barrel, but for almost all shooters, free-floating is not needed.

Spin on the barrel nut, but make sure the handguard cap stays loose and turns freely. Tighten the barrel nut.

Now turn the handguard cap to pull the handguard down to the receiver.

The handguard has locating pins, these go into the holes you used to wrench the barrel nut tight.

Once it's hand-tight, use a strap wrench to tighten the handguard cap. When tight, run a bead of marking paint around the edge to indicate if it ever works loose.

Handguards that clamp over the barrel nut usually need the nut removed. Some don't, but most do. You can use a dremel tool with a cutoff wheel and cut the delta ring, spring and retainer in two. If you do this, be sure to wear the full panoply of protective gear: safety glasses, hearing protection and a breathing mask. Cut-off wheels are fiberglass disks impregnated with abrasive. They throw off a lot of fine dust, which you do not want to breathe. They can break, and catching a piece of one in the face is disconcerting at the least, and could be injurious. A full face shield would be better than simply protective glasses, but the glasses are an absolute minimum. And the dremel tool operates at between 5,000 and 10,000 rpm while you hold it and peer closely to see what you're cutting. The

motor and cutting noise will damage your hearing if you don't wear some sort of protection.

The fast way is to remove the old handguards and cut the delta ring, spring and retainer on each side.

If you wish, you can instead salvage the delta ring and parts by removing them. To do so you will have to remove the barrel, as we've discussed. To make re-installation easier, use a china marking pencil or silver Sharpie to mark the top notch of the barrel nut. That way you'll know which one of the notches should be top-center when the nut is re-tightened. Once the barrel is off, use a pair of reversing pliers (you squeeze the handle and the jaws open) to spread the retainer on the rear of the barrel nut. Once you have the retainer off you can remove the spring

And the prize goes to…. Yes, you can put too much stuff on a gun.

and delta ring from the rear as well. Re-install the barrel, torque the nut up, re-install the gas tube and then install your railed handguard.

The handguards that replace the barrel nut require you to strip the barrel down to its essence: a rifled tube. In addition to removing the barrel from the upper, and the delta ring assembly, you'll have to remove the front sight housing. You have to take the barrel nut off, and it comes off forward. Theoretically you could cut the barrel nut off without removing the front sight, but the barrel nut is very hard. And you still have to get the new handguard on, and its upper receiver attachment point will bear a remarkable resemblance to….a barrel nut. There's no way around it, if you want a handguard that replaces the barrel nut, you'll have to remove the front sight assembly (order your Brownells front sight fixture now, and not after the

new handguard has arrived) and strip the barrel down to a cylinder.

Other Handguards: Installation
LaRue

Mark LaRue makes cool stuff. His handguards, in addition to having lots of rails and being nearly indestructible, have a locking feature. You see, the use of vertical foregrips has caused a problem in some circles: with the handguard securely clamped to the barrel nut, the VFG acts as a barrel wrench. In a tense situation, a barrel nut can actually be unscrewed from force on the grip.

To install, remove the barrel and take off the delta ring and parts. Take off the front sight (with gas tube attached) and remove the barrel nut. Press the barrel back into the receiver.

Hold the "keeper" (the gizmo that prevents rotation) against the receiver, notch towards the back, while slipping the handguard nut over the barrel, and then hand-spin the new barrel nut on. The barrel nut will hold the barrel in but allows the handguard nut to rotate. Tighten the barrel nut as you would any other barrel nut: twice, then a third time to align the gas tube hole.

Put the spacer, with its studs toward the receiver, in the handguard, with the rails aligned at 12, 3, 6 and 9 o'clock. Slide the handguard down to the handguard nut, and hand-turn the handguard nut to catch the threads on the handguard. Hand-tighten and check alignment.

Once you have things lined up, use a strap wrench to tighten the handguard nut. Tighten it as much as you can, and align the screw holes through the keeper with the threaded holes in the spacer. Once it all lines up, put some Loctite (the handguard kit includes blue) on the keeper screw threads and tighten the screws. Then, re-install the front sight, with gas tube attached (it is much easier that way) and re-zero.

PRI

PRI makes a carbon-fiber forearm with rails on it. The carbon-fiber offers two advantages: it is lighter than steel or aluminum, and it is a very poor conductor of heat. Installing it is easy, but you'll again have to yank the barrel off your rifle and remove all the other attachments, as above.

Slide the forearm nut, then the barrel nut on the barrel. Tighten the barrel nut as you would any other, twice, then a third time and align the gas tube hole. Curiously, PRI is very precise: tighten to 40 ft-lbs, and if you must tighten more to line up the gas tube hole, do not go past 65 ft-lbs.

The PRI forearm has the indexing studs built into the forearm, so slide the forearm on, hand-tighten the forearm nut to catch the threads, and guide the studs into the locating holes in the barrel nut. Once it is lined up, tighten. (PRI recommends installing the front sight and gas tube assembly at the same time you slide the forearm on and letting the forearm keep the gas tube under control. You can do it either way.)

PRI makes a wrench to tighten the forearm nut, but you can use your handy-dandy strap wrench, too. Tighten as much as you can. Loctite would be too much, but running a paint pen around the edge, to lock the threads and indicate movement, is a good idea.

Here is the result of using the Brownells alignment fixture: receiver and handguard rails in perfect alignment, ready for a scope.

Chapter Eight

FLASH HIDERS AND MUZZLE BRAKES

And for pete's sake, it is muzzle <u>brake</u> and not muzzle <u>break</u>. It's called that because it puts the brakes on recoil. Also called compensators or simply comps, they reduce recoil and muzzle jump and help keep the sights on the target. They do not, however, do so without cost.

The .223/5.56 cartridge is a high-density, high-intensity cartridge. That is, the powder charge fills much of the case, and the operating pressure of the cartridge is at the operational maximum of the system. Not all cartridges – the 7.62X39 is one example – are run at "full throttle."

The result of these .223/5.56 characteristics is that the AR (or any other rifle in .223/5.56) with a barrel less than 20 inches will exhibit flash. (Even the 20-inch barrels will exhibit flash with some loads.) Depending on the type of powder used, sometimes they produce a lot of flash. Flash inhibitors are chemical coatings on the powder granules that decrease the amount (and shift the spectrum) of the light produced by the hot gases as they exit the muzzle. Inexpensive loadings will probably not use flash inhibitors. Current mil-specs apparently do not require flash inhibitors for powder in mil-spec ammunition. The military depends

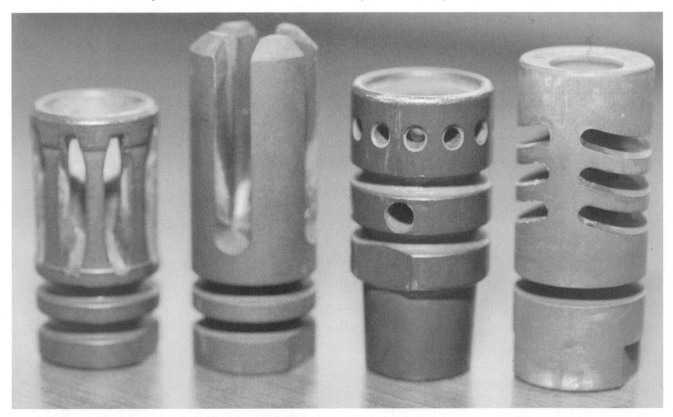

Left to right, a pair of flash hiders and a pair of compensators/brakes.

on the flash hider, or a suppressor, to keep flash under control. However, military ammunition often shows little flash even when the rifle does not have a flash hider. The worst common combination for flash are 16-inch barrels lacking a flash hider and inexpensive .223 loadings. The flash can be anything from a grapefruit-sized flash to a fireball the size of a bushel basket.

Flash hiders decrease the flash from even the worst combinations by disrupting the flow of gases from the muzzle. The expanding gases on a bare muzzle expand in a globe, roughly speaking. The surface stays hot enough to be incandescent, supported by and heated by the interior gas "bubble." The flash you see is not "unburnt powder" but the incandescent (heated into the visible spectrum of light) surface of the expanding gas bubble. The flash hider, breaking up the flow of gases, mixes cool outside air into the bubble and cools the gas rapidly enough to diminish or prevent incandescence. However, the heat is still released, and even the most effective flash hider does little to decrease the flash seen by night vision optics.

A1 vs. A2

The A1 is the standard "birdcage" from Vietnam-era rifles. While it isn't "cool" any more at least to some, it does a very good job of reducing muzzle flash. There is no reason to remove A1 flash hiders simply to install A2 flash hiders. The major drawback of the A1 is that it has slots on the bottom of the body. Thus it jets gases in all directions, including downwards, through those slots. In a dusty environment, while shooting prone, it can kick up dust clouds. Except for that particular situation, there is nothing wrong with the A1.

The A2 is called a "compensator" by the government. Theoretically, it is. The bottom of the flash hider body is closed (no slots there), so no gases can jet downwards. However, calling the A2 a compensator, to dampen the felt recoil of the AR, is like saying opening your car's door and pressing your shoe against the pavement is a braking system. It can work, but at most speeds you aren't going to notice much decrease in your vehicle's velocity. In most shooting situations you aren't going to notice much, if any, decrease in muzzle movement due to the A2 flash hider.

That said, if you change the variables a bit, you can produce surprising results. I have an A2 flash hider on my .308 IRA-10 (Iron Ridge Arms, with an Armalite upper). Give the A2 enough gas to work with (and the .308 does that) and it actually works to keep the muzzle from jumping up in recoil. The only problem is that there is no way to produce a similar volume of gas in a 5.56 rifle. There is, however, a way to increase the leverage of the

flash hider. The inside of the A1 or A2 is a cone. If you bore out the A2 flash hider cylindrically, you change the gas flow dynamics. The gases have a better lever to push against. This approach has several significant drawbacks: First, it reduces muzzle rise but not rearward kick. To reduce the rearward component of recoil, you need a blast plate inside the flash hider or muzzle brake.

Second, the correct internal diameter to produce just enough but not too much depends on the barrel length and the powder used. What works on a 20-inch barrel doesn't work all that well on a 16-inch and vice-versa.

Last, the lack of slots on the A2 makes cutting the steel difficult. If you simply clamp the flash hider in a vise or lathe, and try to use a drill to bore it out, it will cut off-center. You have to use an end-mill in a lathe, or a boring bit, to do the job right. That's a lot of work to reduce some, but not all, of the recoil.

Seeing Flash

The light we see by is called the visible spectrum. Within those wavelengths, light is observable. However, just below the visible range is the near infra-red, and below that the infra-red sections of the spectrum. As they

Yes, suppressors are fun. Yes, they do dampen recoil. They don't do it as well as dedicated brakes do. However, they really stomp the snot out of IR flash (if that matters to you).

are just out of the visible range, we cannot see them. However, night vision gear is very sensitive to near-IR and IR frequencies. Even the best flash hiders show a lot of flash to night vision gear. The only way to eliminate the IR flash component is with a suppressor.

Vortex, Phantom

The Vortex is a refined flash hider, where the tines are proportioned to create the greatest turbulence of the muzzle gases and thus the greatest flash reduction. It is possible, with the right ammunition, to have flash eliminated when using a Vortex, at least in the visible light spectrum. It is the most effective flash hider available short of a suppressor. However, it has drawbacks. The open times can catch on brush, fencing material, and even slash the linings of carrying cases. According to some suppressor manufacturers, it cannot be used with a slip-over style suppressor. The tines apparently flex under the impact of the muzzle blast, and that flexing will create problems with a suppressor. However, Smith Enterprises, the maker, states that it can be used with a suppressor.

An aside: If your shooting needs require a flash hider that is suppressor-capable, you will have to work out the details with the flash hider and suppressor makers. Generally, the companies that make suppressors also make a flash hider that acts as a mount for their "can." It would be best to use their flash hider and suppressor. The Phantom (there are several designs) reduces the flex and the slight hazard of open tines by closing the ends. It does slightly decrease the effectiveness of the flash reduction of the Vortex.

Noveske "Krink"

The Krinkov flash hider was developed from the Soviet AKS-74U, which for reasons unknown is referred to here in the United States as the "Krinkov." Chambered in 5.45X39, the AKS-74U has a radically shortened barrel, only 8.25 inches long. To delay gas release from the muzzle in order to provide enough gas to cycle the action, the flash hider was made as a large can with a reversed cone in it. The result is gas flow to the AKS but also an altered muzzle blast. The Noveske KX-3 is derived from and improves on the flash hider from the 74U and reduces the muzzle blast to the shooter as well as those next to him. Interestingly, it also increases the noise to those downrange. The BATFE has classified it as a flash hider and not a suppressor, so it does not require any federal paperwork or tax stamp. Installation is simple: screw it on and lock it in place with a washer or locking compound. As a flash hider for someone using it for home defense, the Noveske is the best. It eliminates flash, it reduces muzzle blast to the shooter and family members, and increases it to the offenders. A win-win-win scenario.

Muzzle Brakes

A muzzle brake reduces felt recoil by re-directing the gases at the muzzle. The most effective reduce the recoil of the .223/5.56 rifle or carbine to a level comparable to a non-braked .22LR. However, that reduction comes at a cost. The cost is simple: Noise and blast. It can be hazardous to stand near an effective muzzle brake. The most effective comps are large, and the blast from them will scour the paint off of an adjacent wall in a few shots. Anyone standing next to the muzzle would be subjected to the same blast of gas, powder particles and occasional flecks of jacket material. A muzzle brake is contra-indicated for law enforcement work, especially for officers who will be in a team environment. The blast is great enough to deafen or blind a bystander.

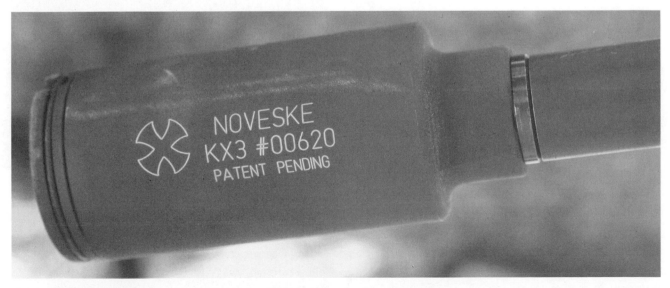

The Noveske flash hider does a really good job of hiding flash, plus it re-directs blast.

We used to regularly have students show up in classes with brake-equipped rifles. Others on the firing line quickly found the side-blast objectionable. The result was that the owners of the comp-equipped rifles found themselves on the firing line with extra elbow room, as the other students tried to stand a bit farther away to avoid the hot jets of particle-laden gases.

One approach to a combo muzzle brake is the Troy Industries "medieval" brake. It is a flash hider with a closed end (except for the bullet clearance) and the closed end is also capable of being used as an impact device. As a brake it is not as effective as a competition-designed brake, but it does work better than an open-ended flash hider.

Brakes for All Hands

A quick rule to remember: the better a brake dampens recoil, the worse it does with flash, and the more obnoxious it is to be around.

Sweeney Brake

I designed and made a batch of brakes in the early days of 3-gunning, with the idea of producing one that was simple, easy to fabricate, and reasonably effective. It worked but not as well as later designs. As I was a gunsmith, and not a manufacturer, I didn't follow up on the idea, but later changes in competition would have made it a good idea: the USPSA allows muzzle brakes in rifle Limited, provided they are not more than one inch in diameter, or three inches long.

As my design used common one-inch rod stock, I'd have been golden.

The Sweeney comp, a dead-simple and effective brake. A business opportunity passed over.

Miculek/Cooley

Two designers, same idea, pretty much identical results. A multi-baffle design, it has the different slots at different widths, and the rear one "shaded" to allow you to "clock" the comp. "Clocking" is tilting the comp to also diminish the sideways component of recoil.

The Miculek/Cooley comp. They look similar, they both work well, and once out of the package (or on a rifle) I can't tell them apart.

Wakal Comp

Known in the Brownells catalog as the F2 comp, this is an enlarged multi-port comp with the ports designed to most-effectively strip gas and re-direct it. It is effective, noisy, and like all comps will not make you friends on the firing line.

McArthur Comp

The winner and still champion: the most obnoxious compensator ever made. It is nearly soda-can in size, and is sculptural in design. It has multiple ports, slots, an internal cone, and were it not a firearms part, many would want one just to have a machined thing of beauty. The McArthur comp comes to us from Bruce McArthur, a long-time bowling pin shooter and owner of Flint 'n Frizzen gun shop.

Left to right, the Sweeney, a no-name, McArthur and Wakal F2.

It is so effective that it became the default brake at Second Chance, on the LRPF. If you had one, and good follow-through, you could see your hits on the steel bowling pins, at 50 yards, through your scope. It so effectively re-channels gases, that I've seen one shredding paint off of a wall that the shooter happened to be standing next to.

Suppressors as Comps

Some who are enamored of "cans" or "mufflers," as sound suppressors are sometimes known, like to say they are the best muzzle brakes, for they handle all the gas. I've shot rifles with and without suppressors, and with and without the best muzzle brakes. I think the suppressor guys need to get out more, as the best "can" is not nearly as effective in dampening recoil as the best brakes. Of course, the coolness factor of a suppressor is off the scale, but if you want to dampen recoil in a 3-gun match, use a brake, not a can.

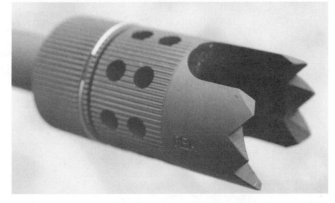

Suppressors work reasonably well as muzzle brakes.

LMT Rebar Cutter

In addition to the normal flash hiders, LMT makes a rebar cutter. As a large, steel unit it hides flash reasonably well. What it does as well is to let you (under certain circumstances) cut rebar. It is a big, toothy thing, with two rounded notches cut into it. Why a rebar cutter? Apparently, over in the sandbox, they make buildings with rebar. (I know, it startled me, too: they have building codes there?) Blast a hole in a wall and the rebar is still there. So, rather than use power saws and torches (they both take time) LMT developed the rebar cutter.

The LMT rebar cutter. Use it right, or there will be problems.

In the interests of scientific inquiry, your intrepid author is testing the rebar cutter. With M-855, success!

Now, it will only cut rebar up to the size of the grooves. Too big, no go. Also, you have to use M-855 steel-tipped ammo. Ball, JHPs, etc., just won't cut it, and yes, that was a pun.

Do you need this? God, I hope not. Is using it risky? You betcha. Do I want the weight on the end of my barrel, unless I really need it? Not a chance. Is it cool? Very.

Installation

Installation of any of these is simple. If your barrel is threaded (the standard thread for the .223/5.56 barrel is 1/2X28) you simply unthread whatever is there and screw on the new one. However, things are rarely as simple as that. The flash hider is one of the few locations on the AR where Loctite is validly called for. NRA High Power shooters, having spent as much as $500-600 just for a barrel before it is even installed, are loathe to mess with its perfection by leaning on a crescent wrench to tighten their flash hiders in place. They often simply "clock" the hider onto the barrel hand-tight and then Loctite or J-B Weld it in place.

Removing a frozen or seized old flash hider may require applications of heat from a propane torch, long soaking sessions in penetrating oil, or even cutting tools. If simply clamping the barrel in barrel blocks and applying a large crescent wrench doesn't remove the old flash hider, look to see if there is a set screw. (I once spent an entire evening trying to remove a flash hider that had a cleverly-hidden set

Suppressors (and flash hiders and brakes) do not decrease accuracy. At least, not when they are properly made.

screw installed on it.) A flash hider that is locked on with epoxy, Loctite or other locking compounds can be loosened by the careful application of heat. A propane torch can heat enough to destroy the compound without harming the barrel. Most epoxies or locking compounds degrade at a temperature of 425° while the barrel steel does not begin to show even the visible effects of heat (color change) below 600°F. Clamp the barrel in a vise, degrease the flash hider and barrel. Then apply heat, to the flash hider only – not to the barrel itself. When you get to the epoxy/locking compound's maximum temperature, the joint between barrel and flash hider will begin smoking. Stop and let it cool. Apply penetrating oil. Then use the wrench to turn the flash hider off. Even though the compound has been destroyed, the "ashes" of it will still bind the threads, so you won't be able to simply spin off the flash hider. You'll have to muscle it off.

In extreme cases you may have to cut the flash hider off. The best way to do this is with a lathe or milling machine, but a dremel tool and cutoff wheels will do. For the latter, again: wear safety glasses (the wheels break), hearing protection (the 10,000 rpm motor is very loud, and your head will be near it), and a breathing mask. (The cutting

A flash hider that has been permanently installed may require a lathe, a machinist and an afternoon.

wheel is a fiberglass disk with abrasive cutting compounds in it. As it cuts, it throws large amounts of dust up. You do not want to breathe the dust.)

Cut parallel to the axis of the bore, and directly to the counter-clockwise side (left) of one of the wrench flats. Carefully cut until you are down to the beginning of the threads cut in the flash hider. Once you see the threads begin to emerge in the bottom of the groove you are cutting, work your groove as close to the barrel shoulder as possible. Once you have cut as much as you can, the weakened flash hider should flex enough when you next use the crescent wrench to break the grip of the threads. In extreme cases a nut-breaker may be necessary to break the flash hider in two.

Washers

Installing a new flash hider requires a washer. Here your choices are three: a "peel" washer, a compression washer or a split washer. Older rifles will have a peel washer on them; new ones, a compression or split washer. The peel washer is a set of metal foil washers glued together. The compression washer is a double cone, and you compress it by tightening the flash hider against it to generate the tension needed to keep the flash hider in place. The split washer uses the spring tension of the split to lock the flash hider on. Insert whichever washer you have, and turn the flash hider until it stops. The peel and split washers have no orientation, but the compression washer requires that the open end be against the flash hider. (You must have a washer of some kind, or the flash hider will not stay in place. At least not without Loctite, which brings problems later when you attempt to remove the flash hider.) If you're lucky, the flash hider stops "clocked" – that is, the slots of the A2 are up and the non-slot portion is down. A1, Vortex and Phantom flash hiders obviously don't have a "clock" setting. However, more often than not, the A2 will not stop correctly positioned.

Unless you're going to Loctite your flash hider on, you'll need a washer to keep it in place.

With peel washers, you simply peel off as many layers of the foil as you need to in order to bring the flash hider vertical. With the split or compression washers, life is not so easy. If the threads of the flash hider and the barrel are both correctly clocked, they should tighten up with the A2 vertical. If not, you must remove metal from some place to bring the A2 up to vertical. If it spins past vertical, you need to use a thicker washer. (This is where a supply of peel washers can come in very handy.)

A2 flash hiders are not surface-hardened. An A2 that doesn't turn up to vertical (it stops short) can be adjusted by filing its back surface with a large file to allow it to rotate more. You do not need to remove very much steel. At 28 threads to the inch, you need only remove .009 inch of steel to allow the flash hider to gain another quarter-turn of rotation. File evenly, so you remove steel without tilting the rear surface of the flash hider. (A fully-equipped gunsmithing shop could cut the flash hider back by the desired amount on a lathe. The irony of it is that in the time spent setting the part up in a lathe, measuring cutting, and removing it, an experienced gunsmith with a vise and a file could have filed, tried, filed some more, tried again, and fitted the flash hider and be done. Sometimes power is not as much help as it would seem to be.)

Vortex and Phantom installations are not so easy. They are surface-hardened and thus too hard for filing, and you will not have any luck altering them. For these you must have a supply of peel washers and high-grade Loctite or access to a lathe and carbide-edged cutting tools for it. But then, the orientation of the slots doesn't matter, so "clocking" these really doesn't matter.

Clocking

As mentioned earlier, clocking is tipping the flash hider or muzzle brake to dampen the lateral movement of recoil. Generally, for right-handed shooters it is tipped to the right, and to the left for southpaws. How much you tip the comp depends on a host of variables: the load you are using, as in which powder, how much, bullet weight, etc. The weight of the rifle and length of the barrel. Heavier rifles will need less tip than lighter ones, and longer barrels less than shorter ones. Also, your style enters into it. The more square your shooting stance, the less tip you'll need, and if you shoot bladed NRA-style offhand, you'll need a lot of tip.

Clocking is a set-and-try, adjust-as-you-go process, and you cannot simply declare, "Oh, ten degrees will do nicely." Set it up, test-fire and see what happens.

Chapter Nine

CALIBERS OF THE AR-15/M-16

The AR-15 was designed for and around the .223 cartridge. However, as with all other rifle designs, a cartridge that comes close enough in size to the original intent can usually be "shoe-horned" in. However, while it is possible, it may not be wise or economically viable. Some calibers fit well in the AR, and others are not so happy. The following overview of calibers is meant to give you the basic info on what does and doesn't work.

Standard: .223/5.56X45

The government recognizes only the 5.56, and only a few loadings of it. However, as civilians we have the option of many more. Where the DoD-accepted loadings feature no soft-points and few hollow-points (and those only because they are more accurate, not because they are designed to expand), law enforcement and personal defense allows for many more options (state law permitting, in some locales).

Rare: the .222 Remington

No, not a typo, there is a caliber named .222 Remington. It was one of the first specifically-designed for target and varmint shooting cartridge introduced after WWII. Colt made a small production batch of ARs in this caliber back in the late 1970s/early 1980s for export, to a country (we've heard both Italy and France as destinations) where military calibers are not allowed to civilian shooters. As

(Left) The pistol caliber carbine allows you to shoot in USPSA handgun matches, running and gunning, and have a blast. The 9mm round won't damage the club's steel targets.

per prudent manufacturing process, Colt made more than they needed. When the contract was shipped and accepted, they dumped the excess rifles on their wholesalers, who did their best to sell them.

Now, what does it take to convert a .222 to a .223? A new barrel. However, a Colt, marked and barreled ".222" is probably worth a lot to a collector. You might be better off selling the rifle as-is to a collector, and using the proceeds to buy a new, better rifle.

Hot: the 6.8 Remington SPC

An easy change. You need a new bolt, barrel and magazines. However, the idea, while tempting, is not without shortcomings if you own more than one rifle. If you need to do this, be ultra-organized. Otherwise, you will find yourself one day at the range with a .223 rifle and 6.8 magazines and ammo, or vice-versa. The ammunition is not cross-compatible, nor are the magazines.

While developed as an improved military cartridge for the M-16/M4, the 6.8 is an entirely acceptable deer hunting cartridge. A deer rifle, built on an AR platform, with 5-round magazine, will certainly turn heads in the hunting camp. Or would have in an earlier era. Now, it is more common than before.

(Note: the 6.8 and the 6.5 – see below – are no more compatible with each other than either is with the 5.56. They each require different bolts, magazines and barrels. Advocates of one or the other view adherents of the opposing mid-size AR cartridge as best misguided and at worst a heretic. Arguments can and will ensue if the two are compared).

Hotter: The 6.5 Grendel

Bumping things up a notch is the 6.5 Grendel. It produces more velocity than the 6.8 does, using a larger case but one that still fits within the standard AR-size magazine. (Note: like the 6.8, you need different magazines, but they will fit a .223/5.56 lower.)

It gives you more velocity, but in the opinion of some the velocity gain comes at too great a price: recoil. As a cartridge for a precision marksman it would be a good choice. Converting a rifle would require a new bolt and barrel, and new magazines. But the cost of the conversion and the cost of the ammo are higher than that of the 6.8.

Tempting, but No-Go: 7.62X39

The lure of the AK cartridge in an AR has been strong for many years. The positives are, or have been, considerable. The ammunition, even in modern more-expensive times, is much less expensive than .223/5.56. The rifle works the same way regardless of caliber, and the controls are the same, so anyone trained on an AR-15/M-16 in 5.56 can work one in 7.62X39. And an AR in 7.62 avoids the social and PR stigma of being an AK.

Mechanically, converting is easy: new bolt and barrel, new magazines.

However, the downsides are very bad. The 7.62X39 is sharply tapered, compared to the .223/5.56. It does not work well in a "straight-then-curved" shape magazine like that of the standard AR. Most of the magazines that were made for the AK/AR Frankengun were either low-capacity, unreliable, or both. To make matters worse, much Com-bloc 7.62X39 ammunition is corrosive. Some of it is only mildly corrosive, but some is so bad it will rust the rifle next to the one you're firing. The direct-gas impingement system of the AR does not handle corrosion or corrosively-primed ammunition well. Most 7.62X39 ammunition uses steel cases, which the AR extractor does not always work well with. The cheapest surplus 7.62X39 ammunition has a well-deserved reputation for casual accuracy. Even from a good rifle, the best such ammo will do is often 3-4 inches at 100 yards. Sometimes a lot larger groups are the norm. Given the accuracy expected from the AR, going backwards to the AK is not wise.

Left to right: 7.62X45 (no-go, no ammo) the 7.62X39, a 5.56 and a 6.8.

The biggest, .30-06; the middle, a .308; and the small, a 5.56.

Can't Be Done: 7.62X51 NATO/.308 Winchester

The standard AR isn't big enough for the .308. To get that caliber you have to get a whole new rifle, one based on (or called) the AR-10. The downsides are many: the rifle is larger and recoil is much heavier. You can't get something for nothing, and to handle the power the rifle needs bigger parts. The heavier bullet generates more recoil. Everything about it is more expensive: rifles, ammunition, magazines and training.

So, converting an existing AR-15 to .308 is not feasible, and you have to buy a new (and larger) rifle to get a .308. Luckily, the existing .308 Stoner-system rifles accept AR-15 sized accessories. You can count on the existing pipeline of stocks, scopes, grips, etc to install in your new .308.

Some real exotics in the AR system are the 6X45, the .300 Whisper and various iterations of a .45 caliber straight-walled cartridge such as the .450 Bushmaster. The problem is not usually one of barrels (you can have custom barrels made) or magazines. No, often the problem is simple: ammunition. While the .450 Bushmaster is factory-loaded, many of the others are not. So, to add to the problems of a non-standard caliber is the need to reload every single round you'll ever fire. Only you can decide if that sounds like fun, or drudgery.

Some Simple Ones: 6X45 & 300 Whisper

The 6X45 is easy: it is simply the .223 case with the neck opened up to take a 6mm bullet. Olympic Arms has offered barrels from time-to-time in 6X45, and there are a number of custom barrel makers who can turn one out for you. Why? Simple: you live in a place that does not allow .22 rifles for deer hunting but want a relatively inexpensive conversion. All you need is a barrel. A .223 bolt and magazines work just fine. You will, however, have to load your own ammo, but that doesn't seem to be a problem for a lot of shooters.

The .300 Whisper comes to us from the fertile mind of J.D. Jones. It is a .221 Fireball case (same head and rim as a .223) necked up to .308" bullet size and loaded to the same overall length as a .223 cartridge. The idea? Subsonic, suppressed heavy-bullet thwacking of miscreants. In it, you can load and fire a 190 grain .308" bullet at just under sub-sonic, and if you also have a suppressor, the noisiest part of the experience is the bolt slapping back and forth. I've watched people shooting a .300 Whisper, and the sound of the brass hitting the ground was louder than the bullet hitting the backstop. If you want one, contact J.D. Les Baer offers a 6X45 rifle, ready for varmint or deer-shooting.

The S&W M&P545 is clearly marked as to caliber.

The Soviet 5.45 on the right, is close enough to the 5.56 that you can easily rebuild a rifle to accept it.

A Good Little Gun: 9mm Parabellum

The 9 is a mutt to some, and a jewel to others. While it fits the AR-15 platform as a conversion, it is best when it is its own little gun. First, it isn't easy to convert back and forth. A .223/5.56 rifle can be made into a 9mm with the right parts: bolt, barrel, magazine and adapter blocks. However, the conversion is either pricey or cludgy, and it cannot be done in the field. The 9mm is a blowback system, so there is no gas tube. The bolt is not locked. There is no "bolt-carrier assembly" as the bolt and carrier is one piece: the front of the carrier is machined as the bolt. Instead of being bored out to receive a bolt assembly, the Colt 9mm carrier is machined to have a 9mm bolt face on its front, complete with extractor and ejector slot.

Colt pins two adapter blocks into the lower receiver fill the magazine well and accept a 9mm magazine. Rock River Arms machines the lower forgings to accept only a 9mm magazine; Olympic uses modified magazines to fit the mag well. The 9mm buffer is a different design and weight than that of the 5.56. The buffer spring is a different part number.

By the time you'd gotten all the correct parts, and done the work, you probably could have bought a 9mm carbine or SMG.

Other (non-Colt) conversions use slip-in adapter blocks and replacement bolts to take the place of the .223 bolt. While they can be functional, they are not compatible with Colt parts or magazines. You will be at the mercy of the specialty manufacturer who made it.

You cannot take a 9mm and easily or cheaply make it a .223/5.56. First, the upper receiver has no hole for the gas tube. Holding the receiver in some sort of fixture and locating the hole to drill it isn't easy. Also, the 9mm upper lacks the recess cut on its left-side interior as clearance for the .223/5.56 cam pin. Since the 9mm doesn't cam, it doesn't need it, and Colt omitted it. Holding, locating and milling the upper for that recess makes drilling the gas tube hole look easy. Easier, but more costly, would be a complete .223/5.56 upper.

As a further complication, Colt uses a 9mm-specific hammer in their 9mm ARs. Other makers use standard AR hammers, or lightly-modified hammers.

Why a 9mm? After all, the .223/5.56 has much better terminal ballistics. The advantage of the 9mm is simple: training. Indoors, the .223 is obnoxiously loud. New shooters, or shooters new to a rifle who are training, can learn bad habits simply due to the noise, and without both earplugs and over-ear muffs, they may suffer some hearing

The S&W M&P545 bolt is marked, so there is no confusing it with a standard one.

loss over time. Also, many indoor ranges are rated only for handgun cartridges, not rifle. The steel backstops of many indoor ranges are not made of steel hard enough to withstand the regular pounding of high-velocity .223/5.56 bullets. With a 9mm carbine you can conduct indoor wintertime training with the 9mm. It doesn't hurt that 9mm ammunition is generally less-expensive than .223. With frangible 9mm ammunition, close-range reactive targets and shoot houses now become possible training venues. (And decrease lead exposure due to indoor firing, too.) Falling steel plates should not be engaged with .223/5.56 closer than 75 yards, for even the best steel spits fragments back. (They bounce off the plate, and then the legs, ground or other plate stands. From there they can carom back to the shooters.) With frangible ammunition in a 9mm, falling plates at ten yards are safe. And the steel lasts longer, too.

The ability to engage close-range (relatively speaking, that is; you still should not be closer than 10 yards) steel plates brings another use for the 9mm CAR: competition. There are a growing number of USPSA clubs who have at the club level "Pistol Caliber Carbine" divisions. There, you shoot a standard USPSA handgun match, but use your 9mm AR. Interestingly, in many cases an average shooter, using a 9mm AR, can keep up with a Master or GM using an Open Division handgun.

Other Handgun Calibers

There are conversions to make the AR into a .40, 10mm and/or a .45 ACP. None is Colt-compatible, all are from specialty vendors, and none offer much if any advantage over the 9mm. If the 9mm is for training, then larger and more expensive calibers offer no advantage, and in fact they present the disadvantages of increased cost and recoil to say nothing of decreased magazine capacity. The added power is not much, in the scheme of things: even a big handgun caliber is modest at best compared to a rifle caliber.

A 9mm carbine can be a useful training tool, as well as a relatively less-expensive one. You can also enter some really cool matches with them.

One thing about the 9mm: since there's no gas tube, the distance from the front sight to the muzzle is a mere legal detail, not a mechanical limitation.

CHAPTER TEN

Chapter Ten

THE UPPER RECEIVER

The upper receiver contains the bolt and carrier, secures the barrel and gas tube, contains the charging handle and provides a location for securing the handguards.

Types

Upper receivers come in a number of materials. For the most durability and utility, only forged receivers made of 7075-T6 alloy should be used. (These are also known as mil-spec.) These can be identified by the forge codes on the receiver. The forging company that hammered the hot aluminum into shape will have their code mark on the upper portion of the receiver. It may be in the "web" of the carry handle, or on the upper just below the rail of a flat-top version. Uppers machined from bar stock will lack forge codes, as will those made of polymers. Bar-stock uppers tend to be less elaborate than the forged ones. While they can provide good service, I've never really been all that happy with the look of a billet upper. But that's just me. A lot of shooters like and use them. If one catches your eye, don't let me drive you away.

Here you see the forge marks, indicating who forged this upper.

The uppers (and the lowers they fit on) come in two takedown pin sizes. Most will have front and rear takedown pin diameters of .250 inch. The quarter-inch pin is the original, and the standard for M-16s and all derivatives. These are called the "double take-down" pin upper, and they can be placed on any double take-down pin lower, manufacturing dimensions permitting. (With dozens of manufacturers, and nearly a half-century of manufacture, there are inevitable instances where one lower and one upper may not fit.) In my own rifles, I have some uppers that won't fit on lowers. Such is life.

The other takedown pin size comes from an attempt by Colt to prevent adverse legislation. The front pin on those is 5/16 inch in diameter (.312") and instead of being captured by means of a spring-loaded plunger, the pin set simply has a screw slot in the head of the pin, and in the screw that bolts into it from the other end. Colt made this change to preclude the use of M-16 upper assemblies on AR-15 (semi-automatic) lowers, and to create the impression among legislators that their product was somehow not the assault weapon being discussed in one or another ban. The rear pin is still the same .250 inch size as the double push-pin sets.

The efforts failed, the legislators did what they did, and the manufacturing and armorers headache that the uppers represent persisted in Colt products for several decades. The large-hole uppers can be fitted to small-hole lowers (and vice-versa) by means of offset pins and sleeves. However, the effort is not usually worth the time, as a matched large-hole upper and lower will take any and all other AR-15/M-16 parts. (At least all but the direct full-auto parts, in the case of the AR-15.) So, if you have an old large-hole Colt rifle that is in need of upgrading, it can have new barrels, stocks, handguards, etc., installed as would any other rifle. As long as the upper and lower aren't separated, they can continue in service for a long time. If you simply must, absolutely have to have, a large pin hole flat-top upper, then you have two choices: find a Colt (good luck with that) or go to Daniel Defense. They list a flat-top

The best makers test (and destroy in testing) their parts. This one is soon to be a sacrificial lamb to the altar of QC.

This Sun Devil billet upper has everything you want in an upper: a flat-top, a forward assist, an ejector lump – and it looks good, too.

Here is a bin of uppers in-process. They've been machined and gauged, but not anodized.

big-hole upper on their web page. At $189 it is going to cost you less than a Colt, but for all the work I have to wonder if simply selling your Colt (for the name) and buying a new rifle might not be a wiser option. (I know, a near-heretical statement in a book devoted to gunsmithing, but there it is.)

Fitting the Mis-Matched

Inevitably, someone will have uppers and lowers of the two types that they simply have to fit. The large-hole upper cannot be used on a small-hole lower (and vice-versa) without extra parts. If the two are simply assembled, the slop between the upper and lower will lead to unreliable function. To fit a large-hole upper to a small hole lower, you need a bronze bushing to sleeve the upper. Available at many hardware stores, it is simply a .250" ID and a .312" OD sleeve. It will be too long to fit, but careful cutting with a jewelers saw or trimming on a lathe will produce a bushing to fit the upper hole.

I've done the big upper-to-small lower conversion perhaps half a dozen times. They all worked for me, including the 9mm CAR so assembled. The location of the axis of the holes is slightly offset, and I've heard some complain that the offset is enough to prevent reliable function. I'd like to point out that the locations of the pivot holes of receivers manufactured decades apart, by different companies, when all involved are using different drawings, is not guaranteed. That's why you buy a three-dollar bushing, trim to fit, and give it a try. No luck? You're out three bucks and some labor. There are also offset bushing conversion pins you can try.

To fit the small-hole upper to a large-hole lower you need an offset screw, one where the outside heads of the screw are the large-hole lower diameter, and the center is the small-hole diameter. Rifles so fitted are subject to the same dimensional problems as the conversion above. If the bushing is lost, the slop returns. If the offset head screw is improperly installed, the rifle cannot be assembled.

Any fitting of a large-hole upper or lower to a small-hole counterpart is a cut-and-try, hand-fit process. It is generally a bad idea, and making it work depends on a good dose of luck, as well as skill and careful thought as to how the whole process is going.

All AR-15/M-16 uppers have a threaded portion at the front, where the barrel nut screws on. Above the barrel nut threads is the gas tube hole. 9mm uppers will lack this hole, and as mentioned earlier a 9mm upper cannot be

There is a whole lot of machining that goes into each upper, even with most external surfaces as-is from the forging.

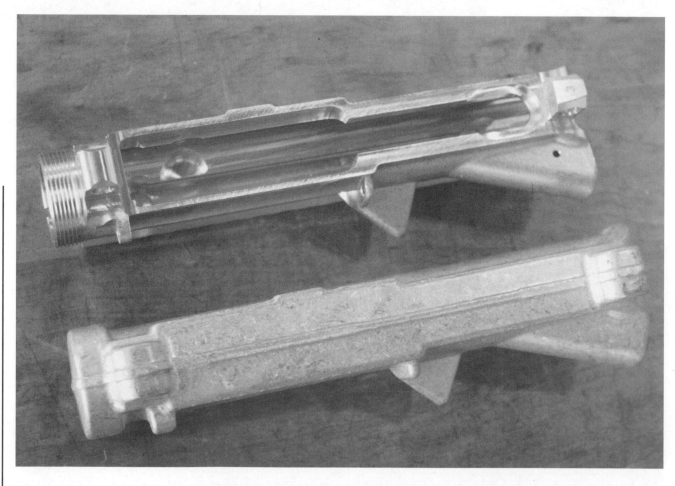

Here you can clearly see the ejector lump and forward assist housing, before the insides of the forging are machined.

This M-16A1, like all early ARs, lacks an ejector lump on the upper receiver. That can be a real hassle for left-handed shooters.

re-built as a .223/5.56 upper. All forged uppers will have an ejection port door, spring loaded to hinge out of the way when the bolt cycles. This door should be kept closed when stored, racked or in a case, to keep dirt and dust out of the mechanism. If you buy a billet upper, I would consider it a competition rifle and not a primary defensive rifle.

Early AR-15s and M-16s purchased on Air Force contracts lack a forward assist. The forward assist is used to force the bolt closed when it would otherwise not fully close. The forward assist should rarely be utilized. If a cartridge is so bent, dented, creased or otherwise damaged that it will not fully chamber with normal function, you should not force it more. You will only wedge it in place. The only use of the forward assist is in a "Chamber Check" where you have eased the bolt back to look and feel for a chambered round. When the bolt goes forward again during a Chamber Check, it will not be doing so with the normal force. Then, and only then, should you use the forward assist to fully close the bolt.

Some rifles have an ejector lump, a pyramid-shaped portion on the receiver directly behind the ejection port. Some rifles, lacking the pyramid, can eject brass to the rear in such a direction as to be uncomfortable or hazardous to left-handed shooters. The Colt 9mm SMG uppers lack a forward assist, and the ejector lump is a moulded plastic part that rides on the ejector door shaft and takes the place of part of the (cut-down) ejector door.

All modern, mass-manufactured uppers have both the forward assist and the ejector lump. Some low-volume specialty production uppers may lack one or both, to provide builders trying to assemble "retro" or early-1960s-configuration rifles with an upper to meet their needs.

I should point out that you southpaws will not be happy trying to build or use a clone SP-1 or XM-177. Since both those lack an ejector lump, the hot brass will be hurled into your shoulder, or graze your cheek, at high speed. Do yourself a favor: eschew retro, and stick with the modern uppers.

Sighting Considerations

Uppers also differ in the design of their sights. The three types are the A1, the A2, and the flat-top.

What kind should you get? That depends on what you want it for. Flat-top for a scope, or for the currently popular "M4-gery" look; A2 for an iron-sight target rifle; and A1 for the retro carbine. For a basic, working rifle, I'd lean toward the C7, an A1 rear sight with ejector lump upper. But you know the best parts? Unless you live someplace heinous, you can have them all.

Upper Receiver Visual Inspection

Why inspect? Perhaps you're buying a used rifle. Or maybe you've left it in the safe too long, and you want to re-acquaint yourself with "skippy."

There are four things to check on the upper receiver besides the finish: the ejection port cover, the sights, the forward assist, and the fit of the upper to the lower. Checking the finish is easy: look for scratches, gouges, dents, or cracks from having been dropped or otherwise abused. Look for the marks of tools that would indicate abuse. If you see extensive gouging and pry marks around the ejection port, be suspicious. Those usually come about from someone who had a malfunction and felt the need to pry at the bolt and carrier, or a partially-chambered round, to get them loose. You should immediately do a full check of the bolt and carrier, chamber and headspace. If you're buying, start bargaining down the price, hard. If it is yours, you'll want to be asking who borrowed your rifle and treated it in such a wretched manner.

The ejection port cover should swing freely, powered

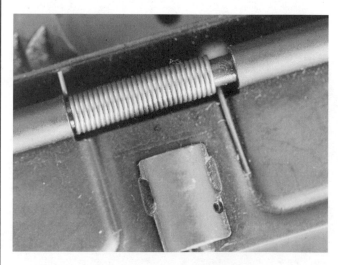

Here is a correctly-installed dust cover spring.

by the spring. It should snap closed, and open easily when the bolt is moved. The locking latch on the cover is staked in place and should be tight on the door. A loose assembly housing is cause for replacing the cover assembly. So let's do it.

Ejection Port Door Replacement

You rarely will need to replace a door. Occasionally you'll have to re-fit a spring that has slipped in its seat. The easiest way/time to replace the door is with the barrel removed. However, if you're working on an assembled rifle, instead of a bare receiver, taking the barrel off just to replace the ejection port door is simply making things more difficult for yourself. To replace the cover without removing the barrel, have on hand the new cover and a supply of the "E" clips for the cover rod as well as two pair of fine-tipped needle nose pliers. If you're particularly skilled and careful, you'll only lose/damage one e-clip for each one you install. Heavy-handed armorers, or those of you who work in cluttered spaces, will lose three or four for each one they install. Luckily they are cheaper than dirt. (They're $1 each, if you buy Colt parts at retail. They're $0.75 each bought in bulk.) And they're still easier than removing a barrel.

Look at the spring that powers the door to see if it was installed correctly to begin with, and if so, to remind yourself how it goes back on. The longer leg of the spring should be pressed against the door itself, in one of the stamped grooves of the door. The short leg should be against the upper receiver. The long leg should be closer to the muzzle than the short leg, and both of them should be coming off of the hinge pin from underneath the rod, next to the receiver.

Grasp the old "E" clip at its center with a pair of needlenose pliers, (standard size) and pull it straight away from the upper receiver. Once it comes free (if you're careful you might even be able to re-use it) push the hinge pin towards the buttstock. As the pin clears the front hinge boss on the upper receiver, the spring will lever it up. Keep the cover flat against the upper as you then pull the pin the rest of the way out.

To reassemble, insert the hinge pin through the rear pivot boss and push it into the back of the new door. (The grooved end of the rod goes in first. Make sure the latch is showing on the door.) Push the pin halfway across the dust cover opening. Slide the spring onto the pin, with the short leg of the spring pointing up and coming from underneath the pin. Once you have the spring on the pin, press the pin

Here is the wily little "E" clip that holds your dust cover on the upper.

and cover flat to the upper. Now wind the spring one turn (the long leg goes up and away from you, then back down), back to where it started. Press the spring flat into the opening of the cover and push the door pivot pin the rest of the way through the coiled spring. Once it passes through the front pivot boss on the receiver, you can let go of things for the moment.

To install the "E" clip takes delicate maneuvering and steady hands. The best way is with those two pairs of needlenose pliers. Hold the "E" clip with one set of pliers, not on the center, but closer to an end. (The end towards the handle or top rails works well.) Hold the "E" clip against the groove in the hinge pin. Then use the other pliers to press against the center of the clip, forcing it onto the hinge pin. If you try to hold and push it with just one set of pliers, in the center, when you press it, the clip (obstinate little devil that it is) will pivot away from the pin and not snap on.

Changing with the barrel off is easy: the hinge pin comes out and goes back in from the barrel end. You don't even have to remove the "E" clip from the door pivot rod. Twisting the spring using the short end is a bit more difficult, but nothing compared to the hassle of removing and installing the "E" clip.

Forward Assist

Required by the Army, and initially refused by the Air Force (that was back in the early 1960's; everyone is more-or-less happy with it now), the forward assist is something you only want to use in very limited situations. The only one, really, is after a loaded chamber-check. Any other use is likely to simply make a recalcitrant cartridge become a wedge. To check function, pull the charging handle back half an inch. Then, while holding the charging handle back, press the forward assist. You should feel the pressure

of the forward assist as you push it, working against your effort to hold the bolt slightly to the rear. Older rifles may have the "teardrop" assist; newer ones should have the "button" assist. The teardrop has an oval shape to the button, while the button is circular. (Those building an XM-177 clone, take note: teardrop.)

To change or install a forward assist, place the upper receiver on a padded bench top. Bags of lead shot can hold the rifle in place, or an assistant can keep it stable. Remove the charging handle and carrier assembly. If the BUIS or optics are in the way, remove them as well. Use a drift punch to drive the roll pin on the forward assist housing mostly but not completely out. The forward assist assembly and spring will then come out the rear. The forward assist assembly comes assembled, and there are usually no individual parts to be had. The assembly itself is not expensive (around $16, with spring and new roll pin), so trying to repair parts of the assembly is usually a waste of time.

To install, start the new roll pin into the hole in the receiver. Once it will stay there on its own, insert the new assembly, with the spring over it. (If you left the old one still sticking in the F-A lump, simply tap it back down on the next step.) As you insert it, orient the assembly so the flat spot on it is toward the carrier. Press the forward assist to the front against its spring until it stops. Then ease up slightly, and while holding the forward assist in place tap the roll pin down flush. When the pin is in, the forward assist should not fall out the rear. Press and release it to make sure the spring is working, and then install the charging handle and carrier assembly and do the forward assist function check.

Tightness Check, Continued
Sights, Barrel, Handguards

Checking the sights is simple: if the rifle has already been zeroed, then check to make sure the paint from the painting-in process hasn't been disturbed. (Zeroed rifles should have the sights painted-in, to keep them at the zeroed setting and disclose unauthorized changes. Jump to that chapter, if you need to.) If the rifle has not yet been zeroed, then the front and rear sights (of either A1 or A2) should be mechanically zeroed: the rear centered within the windage adjustment range, and the front sight should have the top edge of the post shelf level with the shelf cut in the front sight housing. The rear sight should not wobble, or flop back and forth between the unmarked and the "L" setting (A1) or between the small and large aperture (A2). Additionally, the A2 adjustments should have the elevation wheel stopped at the 3/6 or 3/8 setting markings, with the wheel two or three clicks above bottomed-out.

Barrel tightness is checked by grasping the upper receiver in one hand and the barrel at the front sight housing with the other and twisting and pulling forward and back. As with the carrier key tightness check, any movement at all is too much, and the barrel nut tightness needs to be inspected and adjusted.

Handguards might or might not move, if plastic, without movement being a problem. The standard handguards can move some, and it isn't anything except perhaps annoying. Railed handguards that clamp on the barrel nut, or replace it, that move are not installed correctly and must be inspected for cause. The solution will probably be to remove them, tighten the barrel nut, and re-install the handguards properly.

Fit to Lower Check

While the fit between the lower and upper is not critical, excessive movement can be objectionable. The test is to grasp the upper and lower, one in each hand, and wiggle them. This is not like wrestling alligators, you aren't trying to wrench the parts away from each other, just check their fit. Wriggle them a bit, and that is enough. You will find the fit of uppers to lowers on rifles fall into four broad camps:

Head-Scratching Tight: What the Heck?

The upper and lower don't move when you wiggle them. The fit is so tight you need a hammer to drive the takedown pins in and out. While not good for reasons of ham-handed disassembly (the pounding of assembly and dis-assembly can lead to marred receivers and busted detents), it doesn't hurt anything otherwise. The tight fit will also loosen over time, as the rifle is repeatedly taken apart and assembled for cleaning and inspection. It may, however, take quite some time to loosen. Do not attempt to loosen it by filing, stoning, lapping or otherwise removing metal or altering surfaces. The anodizing of the aluminum is only a few thousandths thick, and once worn through the softer substrate will wear quickly. If a rifle is so tightly fitted that disassembly is a problem, swap uppers and lowers between rifles until you have a proper fit in all the rifles. (Just keep in mind the prohibitions against swapping short barrels onto non-SBR lowers.)

Mmmmm, Good: Goldilocks

"Just right." The upper and lower have little or no movement when closed, but the pins can be pushed with fingertips or the aid of a small tool like the ChamberSafe or tip of a cartridge. Properly cared-for, the "just right" fit will last a long time.

"Say, Sarge": All Right, I Guess

The upper and lower move, but the movement isn't so great it feels wobbly, or is so great the user objects.

Wait a Minute: I'm Not Signing for That

The upper and lower are so loose that they can be seen to visibly wobble when assembled. While the movement does not change accuracy, it can be disconcerting to see the upper wobbling on the lower. Target shooters dislike it, some because they think such rifles are not accurate, others, because a wobbly fit interferes with their shooting position and sling tension: if the upper moves, you have to adjust to get your eye lined up behind the sights.

Does It Matter?

Fit of upper and lower has no bearing whatsoever on accuracy or function. While the USAMTU goes to great effort to fit uppers and lowers (even using layers of epoxy and steel shims as a filler to close the gap) the loose fit does not change accuracy. If, however, the fit is loose enough to be objectionable, the wobble can be removed by means of a small polymer fitting called an Accu-wedge. It fits under the rear takedown pin and acts as a crush-fit washer between the interior of the lower and the rear takedown lug of the upper. Accu-wedges are apparently quite common overseas. The extreme wear on rifles and carbines, and the in-theater unit rebuilding of serviceable rifles and cabines, mean that many of the upper and lower fit of weapons is quite loose. Adding an Accu-wedge keeps things tight and increases user confidence in the weapon.

J-P Enterprises also makes an upper-lower fit tightener. Called the Accu-cam, it is a steel pin with two angled surfaces on it and a tightening screw. To use it, close the upper and lower, insert the Accu-cam, and then tighten it with a screwdriver. The angled faces will wedge against each other and press outward. It allows for a variable fit, tightening the fit only as much as you need it to. It has the drawback of requiring a screwdriver to loosen and tighten. Lacking a properly-fitting screwdriver, you can't disassemble the rifle for cleaning or service. The JP part is useful in a competition rifle, but not for a duty weapon.

Also for use as a competition rifle are custom lowers made with an adjustment screw in them. Sun Devil and Iron Ridge Arms make lowers (AR-10 in the case of IRA) that have a vertical screw in the lower, at the location of the rear takedown pin. The screw (hidden by the pistol grip) acts as an adjustable internal shelf. To fit, you install the upper and then gently adjust the screw until the upper has little or no wobble but does not bind or need to be forced to fit. If you tighten too much, you have to force the parts to close, and that isn't good.

Use blue Loctite (so you can still take it apart or readjust if you need to on a new upper) and you're done.

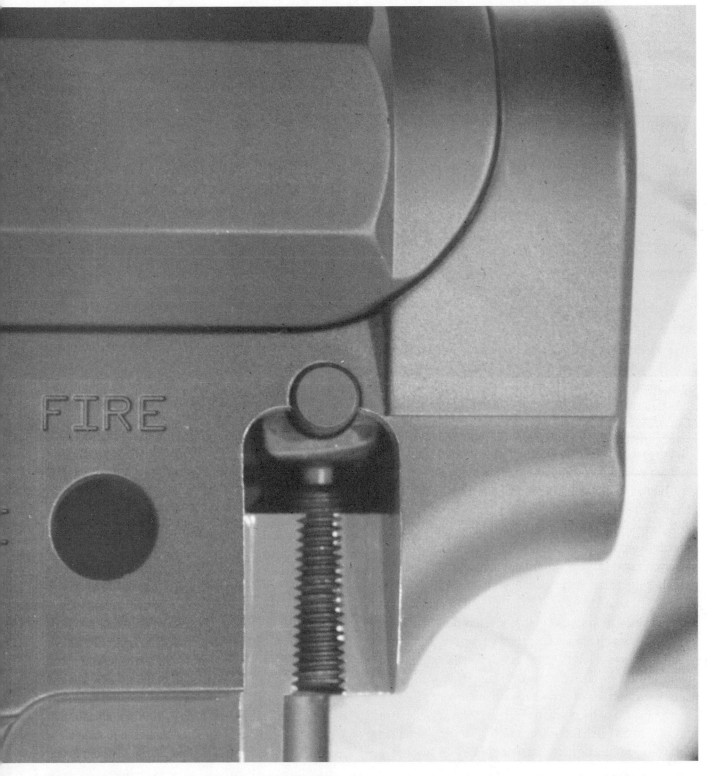

The Sun Devil lower, sectioned to show the fit adjustment screw. Tighten this just enough to take out the wobble, but not enough to make the rifle difficult to assemble or disassemble.

Chapter Eleven

THE CHARGING HANDLE

The charging handle is a "T" shaped bar used to draw back the bolt and carrier. On the left side of it is a small spring-loaded latch that catches in a slot milled on the upper receiver. This catch keeps the charging handle from rattling around loose.

Keep the charging handle latched to the upper receiver all the time. If you lock the bolt back, push the charging handle forward until it latches. Why? Imagine leaving the charging handle back after you lock the bolt open: If you then insert a loaded magazine, and press the bolt catch to send the bolt home and chamber a round, it has to collect the charging handle as it goes forward. The bolt has plenty

of energy to do so unless the handle catches on your sleeve, seatbelt, wall, etc. Then the loose charging handle will prevent the rifle from fully closing. You may not notice until you need to fire the rifle. At that moment in time, life will suck. And leaving it loose looks sloppy.

Replacing the Charging Handle

The charging handle is rather small. To increase the leverage and make the handle easier to grasp, you can replace the latch with a larger one. Sometimes this is not

This charging handle has been NP3 plated, along with the bolt/carrier assembly. Overkill? Perhaps, but it sure is easy to clean.

possible. Some handles have been seen with the roll pin holding the latch in so securely staked, Loctited and served with restraining orders that it will not budge. (I once broke a drift pin trying to loosen a roll pin. I ended up simply swapping charging handles with the officer.) Changing latches is easy, more or less. I recently discovered a field expedient for the task: the Brownells barrel pin block. OK, "field expedient" in that when I go to the rifle classes, I have a toolbox filled with all the tools needed to assemble a rifle. (Ned and I once assembled a box of parts into a rifle, at the range in half an hour. We did it for the US Army 1st Lieutenant who was supervising the range we were at. Favor? Sure. Show-offs? Not if you can do it.) The easy way is to save and re-use the roll pin. The hard way is to drive the pin out, lose it, hope the one included with the new latch fits, and then get three hands to tap it in.

Place the charging handle on the barrel block, with a clearance hole under the pin.

Tap the roll pin partially out. The latch is driven by a spring. Check that the new latch fits properly. If it moves freely, press it in place to line up with the roll pin and press the assembled handle and latch into a corner of the Brownells block until the latch is held in place. Then tap the roll pin back into the handle. When it comes to

Here is a PRI Big Latch, low profile. I much prefer this to the big ones with the loop as a lever.

securing the pin, I'm a belt-and-suspenders man: I stake the aluminum of the charging handle over the roll pin, to keep it in place. I then apply a dab of dark-colored paint, or a drop of Loctite, to secure it and disclose attempts at tampering. If the new latch will not freely move when you check it for fit, file or stone the surface of the new latch until it does.

It is possible to get a latch that is too large; they can

Use the Brownells barrel pin block as a means of holding the charging handle while you work on the latch.

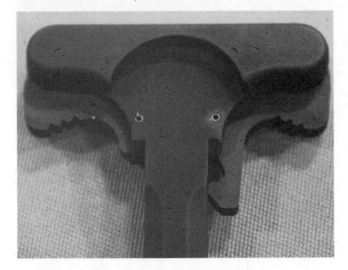

Badger Ordnance now makes an ambi charging handle. Grab it on either side and it unlatches and works. Lefties rejoice.

catch on clothing and gear, or offer too much leverage, leading to a bent or broken charging handle. However, many users are quite happy with the biggest latches available. On this part of the rifle, personal preference does matter. Me, I'd save the biggest latches for competition guns.

Why go to the trouble of painting and even Loctite and painting in the pin? Because if it comes loose it will make a mess of things. The charging handle is a close fit to the upper and lower receivers. If the pin drifts out, it will begin banging against either the upper or lower, marring the aluminum and making a mess of things. Save yourself the hassle, and make sure the pin is in to stay.

PRI Gas-Buster

The bottom edge of the charging handle is also the juncture between the upper and lower receivers.

Sometimes a puff of gas will jet out of there with each shot. The amount of gas escaping will vary from rifle to rifle, and swapping uppers on lowers can alter the amount. (Of course, if you don't have a dozen rifles that you can swap uppers and lowers for fit, that option isn't open to you.) While barely noticeable to some, it can be a major annoyance to others, especially shooters wearing contact lenses. Some police departments, with savvy armorers, allow uppers and lowers to be swapped to solve the problem, they just issue the officer who is complaining a new rifle, one that doesn't spit gas. The rest of us? Too bad.

The parts solution is a charging handle known as the "Gas Buster." Available from PRI, it has a small shelf protruding underneath the "T" that blocks the gas flow and eliminates the problem. You must, however, make sure that any new charging handle installed on your rifle does not impact on the leading edge of the stock on a tele-stock assembly. (See the stock section for further details.)

The PRI Gas Buster has a lip on the bottom, to block gas puffs that might jet back into your face.

The standard charging handle has a gap between it and the upper/lower receiver joint.

You can clearly see the joint between the parts on this welded charging handle. Junk it and get a good one.

Here is the welded charging handle, as seen in the rifle.

In the early years of AR-15 manufacture, many non-Colt and non-DoD approved manufacturers made parts any way they could. People wanted rifles but Colt was at times prissy about making or selling, so manufacturers stepped in. One of the cheaper (and shoddier) approaches was to make charging handles out of two pieces. Instead of a single forging, machined to shape, they would make the bar one piece and the T-handle another. Then they would weld the two together. The welding is obvious. If you encounter such a charging handle either in a rifle you've bought, or a parts kit, replace it with a new one. If the parts kit came from a reputable source, call and complain.

Steel vs. Aluminum

The military has no problem with aluminum, but apparently the police are much harder on gear. I have seen enough bent aluminum charging handles recently that the use of steel charging handles can be strongly recommended. It would be better if shooters properly treated their rifles and didn't bend the charging handles.

But steel prevents bending. Bent charging handles create inoperative rifles.

Now, in all fairness, there is a change happening in firearms training and tactics. The much heavier emphasis on tactical, as opposed to competition use, has called for a lot harder use of rifles. I know respected trainers who have bent or broken charging handle after charging handle until they went with steel. And their rifles are viewed as tools, to be used for the attitude correction of miscreants and other felons. The weight is not a big deal; you're adding only a few ounces to the rifle. But the cost can matter. An aluminum charging handle (the one that came with the rifle) costs maybe $12. A replacement steel one can run $50-60.

You may never bend one, or need one. But when you do, you're out of action until you get a new charging handle in there. All those of you who carry a spare one in your rucksack, raise your right hand. (Put your hands down – most of you are fibbing.)

A bent charging handle isn't the only outcome of hard use. You can bend or break the front tab, doing the malfunction drills. Inspect and replace when needed.

You don't have a problem until you do. A bent charging handle means an inoperative rifle.

BOLTS AND CARRIERS

The bolt is the smaller portion of the assembly that protrudes from the front of the carrier. It has seven lugs on it, spaced evenly for eight lugs, but the extractor takes the place of the eighth lug. (It takes the place of it, but does not take any of the load from firing. That would be far too much to ask of it.) Before inspecting the bolt you must remove and disassemble the bolt and carrier. To do so remove the carrier assembly from the rifle. Set the rifle aside.

Disassembly

On the left side of the carrier is the head of a cotter pin. Pull the pin out. The cotter pin holds in the firing pin, which now can drop free. If the firing pin is heavily caked with powder residue, it may have to be pulled out. Removing the firing pin frees the cam pin, on top of the carrier, nestled underneath the gas key. Turn the cam pin in either direction, one-quarter turn. The head is

rectangular, and the long side will now be parallel to the gas key. Pull the cam pin up out of the carrier. The bolt can now be drawn forward out of the carrier.

The direct-gas impingement system of Stoner rifles (all AR-15s, M-16s & AR-10s) directs a jet of gas out of the gas tube and into the receiver. If the rifle has been fired at all, there will be gas deposits on all the parts you just handled, sometimes enough to require that you use some muscle to separate the parts. Scrub the parts clean. At the very least, use paper towels or hand towels to wipe the parts as clean as possible. In training or during practice it may not be possible to scrub properly, that is, using brushes, a tank of solvent and compressed air to clean a rifle. However, even when firing hundreds of rounds a day (or more) your rifle can be kept functioning reliably with an occasional wipedown and re-lube.

One thing to keep in mind: the system was designed with reliability in all conditions as the imperative. The gas system as a result is generally viewed as "over-gassing" the

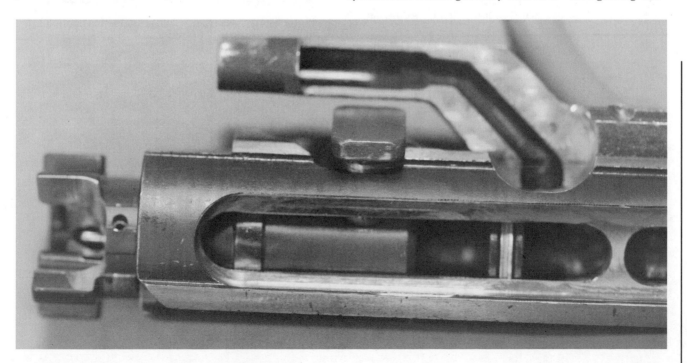

Here you see the far side of a bolt, sectioned and open.

rifle. There are several approaches competition shooters take to reduce the over-gassing or the over-driving of the carrier and bolt. Those modifications can be a good thing in that they increase scores in matches. However, they bring with them increased maintenance, cleaning and inspection demands, and if they fail on the target range or in training it is only a day's score on the range, or training time, that suffers. Since a duty or defensive rifle must be counted on to function reliably in all conditions, changes from the mil-spec standard to competition standards should be strenuously resisted. Do not give in to the temptation to make your home defense M4-gery as "soft" in recoil as your Open Division competition rifle.

Carrier Scraping

While the outside is relatively easy to clean, the inside of the carrier can be difficult to clean. Outside, scrub with brushes and solvent, wipe and you're pretty much done. If you've neglected it for a while (as in many hundreds of rounds) you may have to use a brass brush to scrub it clean. The interior, where the bolt rides, has powder residue caked on at high heat and pressure. To remove the carbon you need one of the tools designed for cleaning the interior: the Mark Brown tool (Brownells), the CAT M4, or the MOACKS from Michigun. The first time you scrape an otherwise unscraped rifle, you'll be surprised at how much carbon falls out of the previously "cleaned" rifle.

Can you overclean the interior? Perhaps. However, the interior is chrome-plated, and it will be difficult to seriously wear the carrier. The carrier is made of alloy steel, surface-hardened to be harder than sin. It is a literal lifetime part. You could use the same carrier for the rest of your life,

through a dozen barrels and several replacement uppers, and it is likely to be as good at the end of 100,000 rounds as it was to start with.

Inspection & Repair: Carrier

Once the carrier is clean, look first at the gas key. It is secured to the carrier by means of two bolts or screws. Those bolt/screws should have been staked. That is, the metal surrounding the head should have been struck with a sharp instrument of some kind with the result of "dinging" the key in order to peen steel against the bolt/screw head, trapping it in place. (The key in the first photo shows no signs of staking at all.) Thus they are prevented from working loose. While older rifles are often staked properly, many modern-assembly rifles are given a modest or insufficient staking. Some receive none. The test is simple: grasp the carrier in one hand and the key in another. Attempt to move the key by wiggling or twisting it. If it shows any movement at all, the bolts are loose. To re-secure the gas key you must first remove it. Use an appropriate allen wrench (the bolts come in one of two sizes, 5/32" and 9/64") and unscrew the bolts. Remove the key from the carrier and the bolts from the key. Scrub all parts clean and use an aerosol de-greaser to remove any residual oil. Scrape off any caked-on powder residue or remaining thread-locking compound.

Discard the old screws. The proper torque limit of the screws according to Colt is 35-40 inch-pounds. Other manufacturers indicate they use a higher figure, up to 55 in-lbs. The screws themselves are rated for not much more than that last figure. If the old screws have been

The CAT M4 tool, shown here scraping a bolt tail and the carrier tunnel.

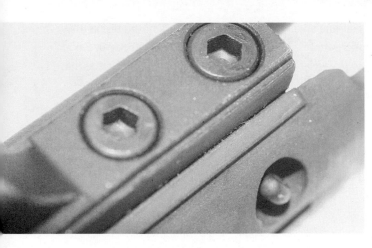

Here we have a carrier key, just as it came from the factory. Note the complete lack of staking, a serious oversight.

Once you're sure the screws are tight, slide the MOACKS onto the carrier, and line it up with the cap screws.

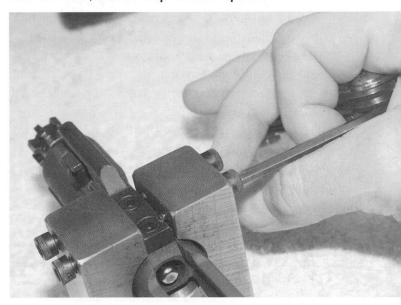

Tighten the staking screws until the screw head bottoms out. That's it, you're done.

over-torqued, they may break off when you try to tighten them again, or after a short period of firing. The screws are inexpensive enough that starting with new ones is an inconsequential expense, as well as good quality assurance. Apply red Loctite (at least red, the stronger Loctite the better; do not settle for blue) to the degreased screw threads. Apply a thin bead to the base of the key, either on the key itself or in the key seat on the carrier. Tighten the new bolt/screws between 35 and 50 in-lb, using the setting of a torque wrench or firmly by hand. If you use a regular-length allen wrench and tighten it as much as you can with your bare hands (no vise, no breaker bar), you will be in the correct torque range.

Wipe the inside of the bolt recess in the front of the carrier with a cleaning patch, to remove any Loctite that may have worked its way there, and the outside edges of the key, where the Loctite oozed out. (A good Loctite application allows the 35 in-lb minimum to be your default setting, and will stay securely fastened until you go to remove it later. Lacking Loctite, go to 50 in-lbs.) Last, stake the screws. The old method is to use a chisel-headed or pointed staking tool and a large ball-peen hammer. Either adjust your vise jaws to nestle the carrier firmly in the opening, with padding (leather or shop cloths) underneath, or place the carrier on a solid wooden (not metal-topped) bench and keep it in place with a 25-pound bag of lead shot. Lacking those, then enlist a trusting assistant who can keep the carrier pinned in place on the bench top with his/her hands to keep it secure while you strike the punch with your hammer. Then place the staking tool adjacent to the screw head, on the key, and strike it firmly to upset the metal. As an "insurance" measure, counter-stake. To counter-stake, take a spring-loaded marking punch and apply it to the screw head. The smaller markers will only leave a mark, so you'll need more than just a pencil-sized marker. Place the marker against the screw head,

just "later" on the clock than the stake that was done to the key. That is, if the key was staked at 3 o' clock, then counter-stake at 3:30. Screws loosen by rotating counter-clockwise, so you want a peen on the head to lock against the peen on the key.

The preferred method of staking is to use the MOACKS (Mother Of All Carrier Key Staking tools). The MOACKS uses hardened screws and a holding fixture. Place the carrier with key in place and tightened down, in the MOACKS. Line up the key screws with the MOACKS screws. Tighten the MOACKS screws until they stop. Loosen the MOACKS screws and remove the carrier. Then counter-stake with the spring-loaded punch. Michiguns also offers the MOACKS II and the Pocket MOACKS. As much as I love Ned, for a one-time use the tool is a bit pricey. However, if you have more than one rifle to do, it is

Here you see properly-staked screws on the carrier key.

worth every penny. And worth more, if it keeps your key tight on a defensive rifle.

Properly staked, the gas key is not easily removed from the carrier. As gas keys have a long service life, removing it 20-50,000 rounds later is not a common job. If a properly-staked key must be removed, then simply use a bench grinder or milling machine to cut away the staked portion of the key, and then unscrew the bolts. If the Loctite is still secure, then a careful application of heat with a heat gun or propane torch will break down the Loctite. (The 50,000-round figure is only an illustration and estimate. If you do replace the key then, that rifle will probably have already gone through four or five barrels and as many bolts. The cost of replacing the old key with a new one is miniscule. At current prices, the rifle in question will have consumed $12,500 in ammunition, the barrels will have cost $1,250 to $1,600, and the bolts $250. A new carrier and key assembly can be had for $100, and a new key with screws is $10.)

The only reason to replace a key is that your testing has shown it to be too worn to provide an adequate gas seal even with a new gas tube. Given the low cost of gas keys and the near-indestructability of carriers, it may be prudent to simply treat the gas key as part of the new barrel. When you replace the worn barrel with a new one, also replace the bolt assembly, gas tube, gas tube pin, gas key and test once everything is assembled.

The added cost of parts (key, screws, gas tube and gas tube roll pin) is less than $40, it adds a few minutes to the time spent in replacing a barrel, and it ensures that everything is fresh, new and in-spec.

Carrier Designs

The original carrier is the M-16 design, where the lightening cuts on the top and bottom are the same lengths. If you hold the carrier up and look at it from the side, the area where metal has been removed on the top and bottom end at the same location near the rear. On an M-16 carrier, the bottom lip of that cut is the surface that strikes the auto-sear and allows for full-auto or burst fire on the M-16. Lacking the auto-sear, the surface serves no function on an AR-15. No function that is, other than to create a great deal of unnecessary controversy. The BATFE is very careful in describing what a Machine Gun is, when it comes to Federal interest or prosecution:

The National Firearms Act (NFA), 26 U.S.C. Chapter 53, defines the term "firearm" to include a machinegun. Section 5845(b) of the NFA defines "machinegun" as "any weapon which shoots, is designed to shoot, or can be readily restored to shoot, automatically more than one shot, without manual reloading, by a single function of the trigger. The term shall also include the frame or receiver of any such weapon, any part designed and intended solely and exclusively, or combination of parts designed and intended, for use in converting a weapon into a machinegun, and any combination of parts from which a machinegun can be assembled if such parts are in the possession or under the control of a person."

(Quote from ATFE web page, and relevant NFA paragraph)

The important parts here are "which shoots" and "combination of parts" sections of the definition. If you have a complete bag of M-16 parts, and an AR-15, you could be construed as possessing a machine gun. You have all the parts and the rifle they could fit into even if the receiver

Here we have the carrier variants, back end, seen from the bottom. Right to left: M16, original Colt AR, later Colt AR.

has not been modified. However, any single part in and of itself is highly unlikely to be a problem. As the carrier is the least important full-auto part, and it does have some use in semi-auto rifles, the BATFE has been unconcerned about M-16 carriers. However, "unconcerned" and "approving use" are different things.

All letters with questions concerning the use of M-16 carriers in AR-15 rifles sent to them have been addressed by the BATFE by first repeating the definition of a machinegun (as seen above) and then mentioning that the crux of the definition is performance: if it does not fire more than one shot, it is unlikely to be defined as a machine gun, as long as the rifle in question does not have all the M-16 parts.

The conclusion we can draw (attention: this is not legal advice, only experience and engineering observation) that a rifle that has an M-16 carrier, and that is the only M-16 part present, is highly unlikely to even be noticed, let alone draw official attention. Nevertheless, the subject is evergreen on discussion boards, with the question coming up at regular intervals. Each time it comes up, you can count on a pretty standard response: the old-timers will groan "this again"; the newbies who think they know things will earnestly post their "information"; and the thread will lurch along for a few days until it is all hashed out all over again.

Why would you want an M-16 carrier? The extra weight of the M-16 carrier has, on occasion, been needed to provide reliable function in otherwise marginally-reliable rifles. Some NRA High Power shooters use M-16 carriers for their extra weight, as some of their handloads exceed regular chamber pressures, and the mass is useful in preventing parts battering. However, it is easier (and legally less-gray) to increase the mass of the buffer weight. AR-15 and M-16 carriers differ by 0.9 ounces. The Colt carbine buffer weights increase by at least that much in each step

The two firing pin variants: on the left the original M-16 and AR-15, and also now the modified AR-15. On the right the Colt "exposed firing pin" variant carrier.

from "H" to "H2" to "H3" and buffer weights are of no concern to the BATFE.

However, any unreliable rifle, whose reliability problem is occasional doubling, which has any unaltered M-16 part in it, is bound to draw attention. So, it is incumbent on you to make sure the rifles in your safe are: A) 100% reliable and do not double (covered in the trigger work section), and B) If they have any M-16 parts in them, you know of it and ensure they are either modified to AR-15 configuration or function correctly. The best solution is probably to exchange any M-16 parts for properly-fitted AR-15 parts. Proper fitting is important, as a rifle that has an entire set of M-16 parts, (except for the auto sear) but which doubles, and is not corrected, meets the definition of a machine gun, and could be (and has been) cause for legal difficulties.

The question of M-16 carriers and how they can be used to let experimenters make a semi-automatic rifle function as a machine gun, caused Colt to modify their carriers. They went through two variants before settling on the latest configuration.

Variant 1: Here, Colt milled back the lower shelf so it could not make contact with the auto-sear. Also, they milled the relief shelf of the firing pin so the head on the firing pin was exposed. They also milled a notch into the top corner of the hammer. If the rifle were modified so it (unlawfully) functioned as a "follow-fire" full auto, where the hammer is not caught by the disconnector and follows the carrier forward, the hammer notch on the Colt rifles would catch on the firing pin head and thus stop the rifle.

Variant 2: Colt mills the bottom-rear of the carrier completely off.

Variant 3: Colt mills the bottom rear of the carrier completely off, but does not mill the firing pin slot.

Why the last one, leaving the firing pin shelf alone? Simply for ease of production for Colt. All carriers are machined as M-16 carriers during the manufacturing process until their last step or steps in the CNC machine. Then, if the carriers are to be for a production batch of M-16 or M4 rifles, they are removed from the machine for heat-treating, phosphate finishing, gauging and assembly. If they are for AR-15s, then the machine makes one last cut to relieve the carrier of its lower shelf and produce Variant 3 carriers. The carrier production machines can produce machinings quickly and in advance of need, and the production staff can then leave them stored in oil. If the carriers have been machined to create the firing pin slot, they are AR-only. However, by making the V-3 type carriers in the production process, Colt can grab a bin full of unhardened M-16 carriers, apply one last machine cut to them, heat-treat and parkerize them and then assemble them into AR-15 rifles. Colt thus has to store, and keep track of fewer parts. And the parts they do keep on hand can be used for either of their product lines.

The only "spec" then is the accounting spec, of less to keep on hand, and keep track of.

Unless a carrier has been mis-machined (in which case it will prove unreliable in any rifle it is installed in) a carrier is a lifetime part. Short of damage, neglect or abuse, it will not wear out. It is a hardened steel part that is not subject to large forces or excessive heat. Older carriers were chromed to ease cleaning. While a chromed carrier can be useful, it isn't necessary. The military switched to parkerized carriers for overseas duty simply as a means of reducing shine. The shiny surface of a clean carrier, showing through an open ejection port, may give away the position of a soldier or Marine. Thus, all rifles and carbines approved for overseas deployment will have parkerized carriers.

Properly done, a hard-chromed carrier is as durable as a parkerized one. However, there is no reason to search out, and pay more for, a chromed carrier than a parkerized one unless you like the look, want the ease of cleaning, or need a retro part.

Altering Carriers

In the event you have M-16 carriers on hand or in rifles, and do not wish to have even a potential for legal difficulties, what to do? The simplest is to exchange them for one or another AR-15 carrier. You'll easily be able to find someone to trade with. However, simple can be expensive. What if the carrier you traded for is mis-machined? Too bad. Selling and buying means your rifle(s) are down until you get the new parts. A simple and inexpensive route is to use a bench grinder to grind off some of the lower shoulder where the auto sear engages. It need not be pretty, nor extensive, simply enough to preclude engaging an auto sear. 1/8" of steel removed should be enough.

Competition Carriers

There are custom-made carriers that are offered to make the AR rifle "better" in one regard or another. They should be avoided for defensive or duty rifles. Some may have some use in Precision Marksman rifles. The two choices, basically, are: heavier and lighter.

Heavier carriers are used by long-range target shooters. They usually use reloaded ammunition, and their reloads can often brush against the upper limits of chamber pressure of the .223/5.56 cartridge. As an example, standard 5.56 ammunition pushes a 55 grain bullet, in the XM-193 load, to 3150 to 3200 fps. Moving up in weight,

The competition carrier is fine for matches but not for defense.

a 69 grain bullet may be going only 2800 fps, both out of 20-inch barrels. Long-range competitors may be using 75, 77 or 80 grain bullets and pushing them fully as fast (or faster) than the 69 grain bullets. They do so by changing the powder from those suitable to 55 or 69 grain bullets to loading slower-burning powders. They need more mass in the carrier to keep the bolt closed as long as possible. They also use an adjustable gas tube, to close down gas flow and throttle the amount of gas from the slower-burning powder fed to the rifle to a manageable level. However, a rifle so-tuned may not function at all, let alone reliably, when fed standard 55 grain FMJ or factory tactical ammo.

Lighter carriers come from the USPSA/IPSC 3-Gun shooters. They want a rifle that cycles as quickly as possible, with the least amount of disruption from felt recoil that they can manage. They too take advantage of the "over-gassed" AR system and install an adjustable gas tube or gas block. They then install a lighter than usual carrier (either a stainless steel one that has had additional milling cuts done to it, or one made of aluminum) and adjust the gas flow until the rifle cycles 100% reliably but does not bottom out at the rear of the buffer tube. The carrier and spring do not strike the rear of the buffer tube, and thus do not add vibration to the recoil. The lighter mass cycles as fast as, or faster than, a standard carrier, even with reduced gas flow.

The downsides to both options are greater than can be allowed in a defensive or duty rifle. They also add cost, in some instances a lot. A standard, parkerized, mil-spec carrier, with key and screws, costs about (as of mid-2009) $85. A Match, heavy long-range carrier can easily run as much as $200, bare. On the other extreme, the lightweight carrier must be used with an adjustable gas block, or the carrier velocity will be too high, and the mechanical dwell time of the bolt opening will be too short. Without a properly tuned adjustable gas block, the rifle will recoil violently and often leave fired cases in the chamber. Even if it does extract, the violent cycling can jar the magazine and create failures to feed. So, the long-range match carrier adds $125, while the lightweight one (plus gas block, and tuning) can add double that to your rifle cost.

How much difference can a carrier make? JP Enterprises (a very good competition carrier maker) offers a lightweight stainless steel carrier that weighs, with bolt, key and internals, ready to go, a mere 8.7 ounces. As a standard AR-15 carrier similarly equipped weighs 11.3 (and the M-16 is 1.5 heavier still at 12.8 ounces) we're talking about a difference of 23%. JP makes it lighter by cutting the diameter smaller where it isn't needed as bearing surface and making scalloped cuts on the sides around the bolt. Their aluminum carriers are lighter still, weighing in at a wispy six ounces ready to go. JP is very up-front about their carriers, telling you that they are not intended for, and must never be installed in, a duty weapon. They are competition-only parts, and JP tells you so many times.

Now, if you're building a competition rifle, go for it. But be aware that your rifle will be very touchy. If you drive to a match and find that you left your match ammo behind, the ammo you buy at the big-box sporting goods store may not function reliably. On that day, life will suck. For a rifle built or meant for defensive use, leave the competition gear for competition use, and use only mil-spec parts in defensive/duty rifles.

Bolt and Firing Pin

You have to remove the bolt from the carrier to clean it properly. (No, I'm not kidding; I've seen rifles where the bolt was "cleaned" but never removed from the carrier.) Bolt cleaning is relatively simple: wipe the powder residue off the exterior. Where cleaning can become difficult is on the area known as the tail: the curved area the firing pin fits through. That surface is exposed to the hot gases of combustion and will build up a layer of caked and baked-on carbon. If you scrub the carbon off with a brush, you risk also brushing off one or more of the gas rings. The loss of those will cause decreased carrier gas pressure and a malfunctioning rifle. To clean off the carbon you need to carefully scrape it with a brass plate (such as a modified .50 BMG case) or use a special tool such as is built into the MOACKS, or the "fork" of the CAT M4.

The bolt on the AR-15/M-16 is a high-stress part that has to be heat-treated to a high level of hardness in order to do its job at all. To do it well, the bolt has to be machined to a nearly-finished set of dimensions, then heat-treated and finish-machined to final dimensions after hardening. The machining must be precise at both stages, and the tooling

This is a Colt, magnetic-particle inspected bolt. It is a good one, but not necessarily the best one.

on the second stage must be exotic carbide or ceramic cutters. The steel alloy used in AR bolts is very precisely defined, and very difficult to work with.

As an aside, it is also not very modern. The alloy is known as Carpenter 154. The Carpenter Steel Foundry began making steel in 1889. They made the steel that the Wright Brothers used in their engine. Carpenter developed some of the first stainless alloys here in the United States. The specifications for this alloy were high-tech in the 1950s, when the Armalite company was developing the AR-10 and AR-15. However, there have been some amazing advances in steel technology since the Chevy Bel Aire was a new car.

Once heat-treated and finish-machined, the bolts are shot-peened to relieve stresses, parkerized, then subject to a Proof Load. They are (the good ones, anyway) installed in a test fixture, and a cartridge loaded to 130% of the maximum pressure of the .223/5.56 cartridge is fired. Each bolt is then inspected with a Magnetic Particle machine, also known as a Magnaflux machine. If the bolt shows no cracks, it is marked ("MPC" is one such marking, used by Colt) and sent to assembly. If a bolt shows a crack, it is scrapped. A good manufacturer, if faced with a production batch where more than a few bolts fail, will scrap the whole lot. All of that work, and all the potential for scrappage, raises the cost of true, mil-spec bolts. (They'll also investigate the cause of the failed bolts. It may be the alloy, in which case the steel mill will pay for a new lot of steel. It may be the heat-treat, and someone could be fined or lose their job.)

"Mil-spec" bolts can be any number of things. A truly mil-spec bolt has gone through all of the above, in the production line of a true military supplier. There are not many such manufacturers. A lot of other, second-tier manufacturers will make bolts that meet all the dimensional and material specifications. However, only one, or a few, of the bolts in each production lot from those manufacturers will be proof-tested and magnetic particle inspected by them. The rest will be measured to make sure they meet the drawing specs, but will not be M-P tested. Then the whole lot will be sold as "mil-spec bolts."

Some clever and unscrupulous "manufacturers" or "surplus dealers" will bid on the scrap steel from rejected bolt lots, and then sell the bolts as "mil-spec." This does not happen often, as the real mil-spec manufacturer will often crush, chop or otherwise damage such rejected lots, to prevent exactly such a situation.

Bolt Cleaning

Use a brush to clean the locking lugs, bolt face and body. Avoid using a brush on the gas rings, as we'll discuss later. The rear tail of the bolt is exposed to hot gases on every shot. It will become crusted with carbon. Use a CAT M4 tool to scrape the tail clean. If you try to use a knife, you'll likely cut yourself. If you use a plastic brush it will have no effect. A bronze or stainless steel brush risks removing gas rings, to be lost in corners or the shag rug. Once clean, wipe with an oiled cloth.

If you're going to inspect your bolt lugs for cracks, this is the place to start. These two both take the most load, and have the least support.

You, however, won't have such leverage. So, if you want to be sure, buy from suppliers who tell you the specs: is it marked? Is it M-P inspected and proof-fired? If it is not, decide if the cost savings are worth the (admittedly minor) risks of a bad bolt failing on you. Me, I'll use any for training and match guns. For a defensive gun I'll only use a bolt that is fully proofed and marked. If it doesn't have an "MPC" or "MPB" or such marked on it, it isn't in the ready rack.

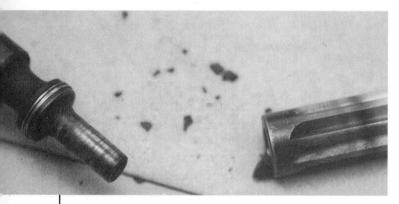

The MOACKS bolt-cleaning attachment, with the carbon it scraped off one bolt.

Bolt Inspection

A departmental armorer may be inspecting and replacing bolts in a large number of rifles. You will be looking for a bolt or a few bolts to build your personal rifles. The only answer to the question of "who makes mil-spec bolts?" is to go to a reputable supplier. The departmental armorer can have a clear understanding and agreement that "X" number of bolts that fail in an unusually early timeframe will cause all bolts to be returned. A supplier who deals only with real-deal mil-spec manufacturers will not have a problem with such an arrangement, as their bolts won't fail.

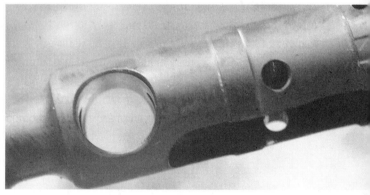

You can see how thin the bolt is, where it is machined for the cam pin.

The bolt has a number of areas that need regular inspection. Once you've cleaned the bolt, inspect closely the cam pin hole. The cam pin hole is the large one that goes transversely through the bolt body. The side walls of the hole are thin, and if a bolt has been over-hardened the walls may crack. As with the staked gas key we never saw this fault in the old days. However, the radically-increased production of AR-15 rifles and M-16s for government use has lead to some few marginal parts slipping through. Any crack at all here is cause for the bolt to be declared scrap, and it must be replaced. If the bolt or rifle are relatively new, then the manufacturer should be informed, and a warranty repair or replacement requested.

Another location to check for cracks is each on locking

Here's another bolt, from a different maker, with the same break. Yes, I'd be seriously put out by this.

Seen from underneath, with the upper off the lower, you can clearly see that the bolt is still locked into the barrel extension.

Until you get a new bolt, this rifle is out of service.

lug, at the rear, where they join the bolt body. The locking lugs are the highest-stress portion of the bolt, and a bolt that has seen too many rounds can fail there. Finding cracks, and retiring the bolt before a lug breaks off, can prevent damage to other parts. Failing to find a crack can lead to a broken barrel extension (and thus a new barrel) or a rifle that fails when needed most, leading to a loss greater than a mere bolt and barrel.

Firing pins can chip, wear, get bent or be dropped. One measurement to check annually is firing pin protrusion. The firing pin must protrude from the face of the bolt far enough to set off the primer. Too little protrusion, and the rifle will not fire. Too much, and the rifle may pierce primers, which is bad for the bolt. (It greatly decreases the service life of the bolt and firing pin.) To check, you need the bolt out of the carrier, the firing pin, and a firing pin protrusion gauge. With the bolt and firing pin clean, insert the firing pin into the bolt. The rear tail of the bolt will stop the firing pin, on the flange. The easiest way to set this up is to insert the firing pin into the bolt, and stand the bolt and firing pin on the firing pin tail, on the table or bench.

Now select the "MIN" end of the gauge, and press it to the bolt face to the side of the firing pin, then wipe the gauge across the firing pin. The firing pin should NOT pass over the exposed firing pin tip. If it does, the firing pin is not protruding enough, and there is something wrong. Replace it with a new firing pin, and then check that one for protrusion. The firing pin may be bent. To check, take it out of the bolt and roll the pin across a smooth tabletop. If there is any visible wobble, replace the pin. There is no point in trying to straighten a bent pin. Replace it. I've had people proudly show me the firing pin they tapped and whacked and re-bent until they got it straight. However, each time they hit it, they added stresses to the pin, and who knows how long a "straightened" pin will last? A firing pin is not expensive, so if it is worn, shipped, bent or otherwise shows wear, replace it.

Select the "MAX" and repeat the process. The MAX end of the gauge MUST pass over the firing pin tip. If it does not, there is too much protrusion and the rifle may pierce primers. Again, replace it. Replaced firing pins should be discarded. Ideally, they should be broken or visibly bent before being discarded, to prevent their re-use. Leaving them around simply makes it possible for them to be installed in another rifle, leading to problems. If it fails, mangle and toss it.

Firing pins should not be used as disassembly tools. You'd think "It's a hardened piece of steel, and it's hard-chromed to boot." Yes, but there are only a few thousandths of steel difference between "long enough" and "not long enough." It only takes a bit of change in the length of the tip to drop it from "Acceptable" to "Too Short."

Other Materials?

The hot property for a while in the AR field was titanium firing pins. The idea was that by lowering the mass, we'd speed the firing pin velocity and thus decrease lock time. The problems were not many, but serious. First, titanium is a lot less able to shrug off impact wear than steel. So once they reached the end of their service life (which was quicker than steel) they'd just quit. Also, if you ran into a batch of ammo with hard primers, you might experience a few misfires. So, Ti firing pins are competition-only items.

Bolt Costs, Service Life and Spares

Why such fussing over bolts? Here's why: a bad bolt can make a rifle inaccurate. A bad bolt can break, leaving the rifle inoperative. Bolts should not be mixed or exchanged between rifles, even if all are mil-spec, and even if all rifles are from the same manufacturer.

Now, the government manuals warn soldiers, airmen, sailors and Marines that exchanging bolts between rifles can be dangerous, and people might be injured or killed. With all due respect to a bunch of (now, anyway) hardened combat vets: stop being whiny worrywarts. True mil-spec bolts and barrels will be readily interchangeable, from the earliest M-16 (not A1) to the newest M4. My resistance to changing things is that not all bolts are true mil-spec, and even if they do fit, you can be changing accuracy and/or reliability. Once you have a rifle that works, why risk screwing that up, showing off to your buddies that you can swap bolts?

An inexpensive bolt from an internet supplier picked at random, bought in volume, can run as little as $40. A real Colt bolt, mil-spec, MPC inspected and so-marked, can run over $150. How many bolts do you need on hand for spares? Does price matter? Does MPC inspection matter? Consider a department with 1,000 rifles. If they're all Colt, then maybe one bolt will break in the course of the service life of a barrel. Probably not; more like one in 10,000.

The military deems the service life of a barrel and bolt to be 7,500 rounds. But that is an average, taking into account a large volume of full-auto fire in some units. The service life of a barrel and bolt in non-military and/or law enforcement use is certainly going to average higher than that. If a particular rifle is one you take over and over to high-volume rifle classes, it may have reached the 10,000

round figure in 5 years. If a department only uses it in quarterly qualifications, it may take 20+ years to reach 10,000 rounds. In either case it may or may not be worn out and in need of replacing. Only testing and inspection can tell for sure.

The inexpensive bolts may break in two or three instances in a thousand barrels, in shooting 10,000 rounds each. They may not. Does the difference matter? (One might argue that a department that gets the 2-3 breaking bolts through simple random chance instead of a department that gets none of the future-break bolts, might have a different opinion.) One way to consider it is this: the price differential between the cheapest bolt and the most expensive is at the moment $120. That is less than the cost of half a case of training or duty ammunition. Depending on the ammunition used, the price difference between best and "good enough" bolts may not even buy enough ammunition to function-test, zero and duty-qualify a single rifle. A serious USPSA/IPSC competitor could shoot up the $120 bolt-price difference in a weekend of practice.

In the service life of the rifle, a cheap bolt and 10,000 rounds of ammunition costs the same as the expensive bolt and 9,500 rounds of ammunition.

Cheap is not good, in this context.

Really Cheap Bolts

The cam pin hole through the bolt is precisely machined. It is also staked on the bottom, so the cam pin can be inserted from only one direction. Lacking this staking, the bolt could be assembled with the extractor on the wrong side, the left side. When fired, the bolt will attempt to eject the empty to the left, where there is the significant lack of an ejection port. We have only seen this once in over 20 years of AR-1/M-16 gunsmithing, but once was enough. If your rifle is a type known as a "Frankengun" or one made

Cheap bolts don't usually do this unless there is a bad round of ammo. But they can cause all kinds of other problems. Avoid cheap bolts.

of randomly-acquired assembled parts kits, look specifically for this feature. If you find the bolt lacks this staking, replace it immediately.

It would be prudent for a departmental armorer, faced with a rack of confiscated weapons to be used by officers, to suggest replacing all bolts that are not "MPC" or "MPB" marked with new bolts from a known source.

You, the individual, can decide for yourself what kind of bolt you want.

Hard Chrome

Hard chromed bolts are rare, and now seen on either rifles made very early in the life cycle of the AR-15 (early 1960s) or on custom rifles made today. The problem back then was a byproduct of the process called "hydrogen embrittlement." Hydrogen, driven into the steel by the plating process, would cause the parts to become even harder, hard enough to break sooner than expected. The solution was to heat-soak the parts after plating, to allow the hydrogen to escape. However, that added cost. The government determined that plating offered no advantages (the idea that a dark bolt could be cleaned as easily as a chromed bolt comes easily to someone who doesn't have to do it daily) and the risk of embrittlement was not worth it. Custom makers can charge enough to cover the cost, and some owners desire the plating regardless of the cost. There is no good technical reason for someone to seek out hard chromed bolts, and pay extra for them. If you like it, get it. Otherwise, don't worry about it.

Firing Pin

Inspect the firing pin tip. It should be hemispherical, smooth and clean. If it is chipped, dented, bent or otherwise marred, replace it. Do not replace it with a Titanium firing pin. Ti firing pins are competition-only items, and even competition shooters view them with a certain amount of wariness. Ti is light and tough, but it fails without much warning. The chrome-plated steel of the standard firing pin is heavier (not by much), tougher, and fails mostly through abuse.

Inspect the collar or flange of the firing pin. The collars come in two sizes: the standard, and (you probably have guessed by now) the Colt-modified. In a change done to try and preclude full-auto modifications, and prospective legislation, Colt modified the carrier as mentioned previously. The bottom of the forward part of the carrier, leading to the firing pin tunnel was given an access slot. The plan was simple: The hook on the top of the modified AR-15 hammer would ride up into that slot if the

(unlawfully so) modified disconnector didn't catch the hammer. The notch on the hammer was thus meant to catch on the enlarged collar of the Colt-modified firing pin, bringing things to a halt.

As an inadvertent aspect of the design, the larger collar of the modified firing pin tends to get bumped by the hammer every time you fire, and the edges of it (the collar) can become peened. If you feel a sharp, raised edge, the collar has been peened. The edge can easily be removed with a lathe or drill press and a careful application of a fine-cut file. (Please, use a file handle when filing on power equipment!) Or it can be hand-filed or stoned. Finally, you can simply exchange the peened firing pin for a new one.

On every inspection, scrub the carbon off the firing pin.

Again, when reassembling the carrier, be certain that the firing pin flange is in front of the cotter pin. In the above illustration, the top box is correct and the bottom box is incorrect. Perform the palm-slap test to be sure, as a firing pin installed incorrectly will fall out.

The retaining pin, or cotter pin, can become worn from use, dry-firing and repeated disassembly. As with many other parts, they don't cost much, and replacing them when they become worn is inexpensive insurance for proper function.

Extractor and Ejector removal

One weak point of the AR system is the extractor. Unless the rifle in question has the latest and full set of extractor springs and buffers, it is likely "under-extractored." To remove the extractor, hold the bolt in one hand, and using a thumb or fingertip, press the extractor into the bolt (toward the firing pin tunnel). Then use a punch to press the extractor pin out of the bolt. In the field, the cotter pin tip can be used to press the extractor pin completely out. (Some suggest using the firing pin to start, but I have to express some reluctance to using it. It is much too important as the primer igniter to risk wearing it out by using it to take the bolt apart.)

Once it's out, you'll find the interior will be caked with powder residue despite your best efforts at cleaning the bolt. Scrub or wipe the extractor clean. Inspect the lip. It should be complete, not chipped or cracked. One way to gauge the wear on an extractor is to draw the extraction end of it across the tip of your pinky finger. The corners will feel like "kitten teeth": sharp and grabby. If they do not, the extractor is probably worn and should be closely watched or replaced. Inspect the extractor spring. Inside of it should be a small polymer cylinder. That is the extractor tension booster, which Colt calls the "harmonic dampening buffer." The insert increases the tension of the extractor, reducing the likelihood of it slipping off a case that is resisting the extraction process. The earliest rifles lacked this buffer. Later ones (but still early in the evolution of the AR-15/M-16) had cream, olive or red buffers, in that order. Those are increasing in strength as they increase in darkness of color. The newer ones are blue, the newest black. Blue is good, black is better. If your extractor either has a light-color booster, or none at all, replace the spring and install a new blue or black buffer with it.

The newest springs for the extractor are gold in color. A black buffer with an older-style spring will work, but the best combination is a black buffer with gold spring. The "black and gold" combination was developed for the M4 carbine and works just fine in the full-sized rifles as well. The US Army feels that the blue booster is good enough for rifles and only mandates the black ones for M4 carbines. On this point, I have to disagree with the Army: when it comes to the extractor, more is better.

Many companies make an extra booster, one that wraps around the extractor spring. The one I and the instructors in our classes use the most, and have complete confidence in, is the MGI D-Fender. It is "D" shaped and fits around the extractor spring with the curve matching the curve of the extractor tail. It boosts the extractor tension by up to four times as much as the non-D-Fender extractor tension. Yes, it is possible to match up all the boosters: black insert, gold spring, D-Fender. The rifle will function

normally except for one special instance: if you insert a round directly into the chamber, and then ease the bolt slowly forward (in an attempt to be as quiet as possible) the bolt may not fully close. Many rifles will close. Some won't. You will have to use the forward assist to finish chambering the round and closing the bolt. A short period of experimentation (ON THE RANGE, and SAFELY!) will quickly determine which camp your particular rifle falls into.

When will you ever need to know this? When you plan on loading your rifle as quietly as possible. Since that is an esoteric need, I doubt "over-extractoring" is a problem you are going to encounter.

There are many other extractor boosters out there. If they were made for the AR in particular, then they probably work well also. One approach to vigorously avoid is the "hardware store" approach. Sooner or later someone notices that the boosters look very much like a small rubber "O" ring. And that someone will probably suggest that they can get a box of a hundred of those rings at the hardware store or auto parts store for a mere five or ten bucks. However, the environment of the AR is very harsh. The abrasive gases are very hot. The pressures and cycling rates severe. And the solvents and lubricants may be harsher than those found in other applications. The AR-specific rings have been formulated or tested (more likely both) to withstand any known solvent, including

The D-Fender boosts extractor strength. This is a must-have, and ignore all advice to the contrary.

New Jersey tap water. A good booster such as the D-Fender is a lifetime part that can be transferred from rifle to rifle. There is no need to practice false economy, so decline the kind offer of hardware-store parts.

Cheap Extractors

Extractors are not that expensive and there is no need to economize on them. They are also highly-stressed in normal function. Any extractor that shows signs of having been made from a casting (mould marks, etc.) should be replaced with a mil-spec part from a known supplier. Any that show signs of wear; rounded edges, chipping, etc. should be replaced. Any that fail the "kitten teeth" test should be replaced. In the scheme of things, extractors are inexpensive. Buy good a good one or good ones.

By now, you've read my suggestion not to skimp on

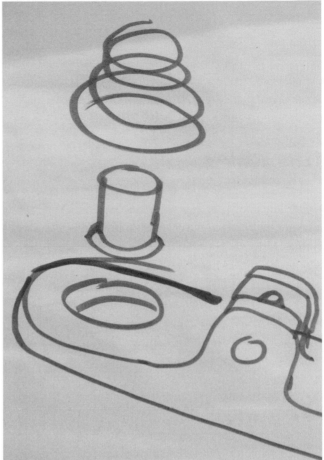

The extractor spring goes in after the little buffer, rim down. The larger coil of the spring goes in, and you'll hear or feel a snap when it seats.

Cheap extractors soon fail. Avoid them.

parts. If you've been keeping track, the "five dollars here and ten dollars there" approach has probably cost you an extra hundred bucks. Trust me, it is money well-spent.

Extractor Spring and Buffer Installation

The spring is flared: one end has the last coil wound to a slightly larger diameter. The internal buffer also has a head on it like a nail. Insert the buffer into the spring from the wider end of the spring, with the head of the buffer matching the flare of the spring. You cannot simply cram the spring into the seat in the extractor. To install it, you must treat it the same way you'd put a tire on a wheel, or the gas rings into the bolt: catch one edge first. Tip the spring slightly and insert the end of the flared coil into the seat in the extractor. (Use the tip of a centerpunch, or

a small screwdriver blade to press the coil down.) Then work around the edge of the spring, pushing the leading edge into the extractor seat using your fingers or a small screwdriver. Once you get all the way around, you aren't done.

Hold the extractor between your thumb and forefinger, pressing directly down on the spring, Press firmly. You'll hear a click as the spring finishes seating. If you do not hear a click, the spring may have already been seated.

Check the installation by trying gently to pull the spring out. It should resist. If it comes out, you didn't press hard enough. Repeat the seating process and then press more firmly. If it won't click into place, then either the spring or the extractor is incorrectly formed. Try again with another spring. If that one also will not click into place, switch to another extractor. Continue until you have a correctly-assembled spring and extractor.

Which Spring and Buffer Again?

The Army decided that the new gold spring and black buffer was needed only for the M4 carbines, and not the rifles. The Army being the Army, there are probably a lot of rifles that have the carbine extractor spring in them, and still a few M4 carbines with the older spring and buffer in them.

The rule of thumb is simple: you want as much extractor tension as you can get, in all rifles and carbines. If you have the gold Colt/Army springs, use them. Wolff springs of the same strength are green. Use the stiffest spring you have or can get, and a blue or black buffer.

Gas Rings

The gas rings in the bolt of the AR are important to proper function. They ensure a gas seal between the gas tube and the vents in the carrier until the carrier begins cycling, If the gas seal is insufficient, the bolt and carrier will not be impelled backwards by gas sufficient to ensure complete cycling, and the result will be the dreaded "short-stroke." Gas rings are very cheap, you should keep a large supply ready. To inspect, remove one with the tip of a pin or sharp punch. A very sharp knife will do. The ends of the rings will have the appearance of two snakes facing each other. Rings wear as the bolt cycles back and forth inside the carrier. Compare the worn rings to a new one. A good rule of thumb is: if the "neck" of the snake heads is half of its original thickness or less, replace the rings. All of them. The bolt-stand test is better. Gas rings are installed just like a tire on a rim; hook one end in the groove, and then work the ring around the perimeter of the bolt, sliding the ring into place as you go. If you try to snap it into the groove all at once you will bend it and reduce it to scrap.

The bolt takes three rings. It is entirely possible for a rifle to work properly with only two, and I have seen some working properly with just one, but three is what it takes. Do not bother to mis-align, or stagger in spacing, the gaps in the rings. Extensive testing has proven it makes no difference in function. The idea of installing the rings crossed on each other had never occurred to me. After a

Never say "I've seen everything" until you actually have. This was a first, after 20+ years of working on ARs. Yes, the gas rings are overlapped, and the rifle does not like it.

recent class, however, I have to note it and advise against it. If you do not notice the crossed rings right away, they will become apparent when the bolt resists all attempts to re-insert it into the carrier. Closely inspecting the rings before inserting the bolt into the carrier takes only a moment, but can save hassle and embarrassment.

There is a near-cult around the one-piece gas ring. Those who favor it extol its virtues and assure all who listen that it will cure short-stroking, baldness, a bad complexion and high interest rates. My experience has been that the standard rings are all that you need. Provided you do not lose one or more in cleaning, they will last thousands of rounds. If you replace the rings every 5,000 rounds (barrels are good for 10,000 to 15,000) you will probably still be prematurely throwing away rings, ones that are still in good shape. What the one-piece rings can do is cause problems. If the rings are too tight, they will create sufficient friction when the rifle is hot, dirty and dry that the rifle may begin malfunctioning.

If your rifles work with standard gas rings, use them. If they don't, find the problem instead of masking it with one-piece rings. (Sorry, one-piece ring fans.)

When you scrub the bolt, do not use a brush around the gas rings. You can easily flick a ring out of its seat and toss it across the room, never to be found. To scrape the carbon off the bolt tail, use a tool designed for the job like the MOACKS, CAT M4 or a modified .50 BMG case.

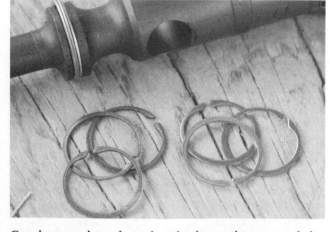

Gas rings are cheap, buy a bunch, change them as needed and don't waste a moment on regretting tossing old ones.

Ejector Removal

The ejector is a spring-loaded plunger that can prove quite difficult to remove. It requires the smallest of the punches in an armorers kit, the 1/16" punch. Mis-handled, you can break the punch and still fail to remove the ejector.

To test the ejector for proper function, press down on it with a larger punch than the 1/16" punch. The ejector should require a strong push to move it, and it should move back to full height with no hesitation when you remove the pressure. If it binds, or is excessively easy or difficult to move, it needs to be serviced.

One situation where the ejector will need service is if a combination of factors stack up against the rifle: If the chamber is a .223 instead of a 5.56; if the weather is hot; and if the rifle has been fired enough to heat it noticeably. And if the cartridge case has a head hardness at the lower end of the allowable range for the case brass. In such a combination, the brass can protrude into the ejector hole (i.e., as the .223 chamber and heat increase pressure, the soft brass flows more than hard brass) and when the bolt turns to unlock, some of the extruded brass can be shorn off. The slivers of brass can build up inside the ejector hole until they bind the ejector and it stops ejecting. The usual symptom is the distance that brass is thrown from the rifle when fired decreases until the brass finally fails to eject.

The other extreme in ejector movement is caused by a broken or altered ejector spring that is not pushing the

The combination of a sharp-edged ejector and soft brass leads to shavings rudely shoved down into the ejector tunnel. Your rifle will not like this, and you'll have to get the ejector out before you can deburr the leading edge of the ejector.

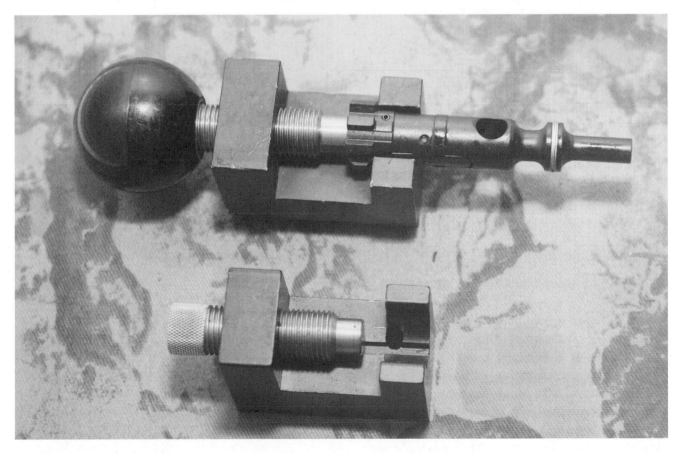

To remove the ejector without hassle, you really need one of these fixtures. Without them, removing and replacing the ejector is a struggle.

ejector forcefully enough. Both problems show up with the same symptom: failure to eject (which is often "diagnosed" as the gas system not delivering enough gas, and which leads to the unknowing "gunsmith" sometimes drilling the gas port larger. Obviously not the correct solution.)

The best way to remove the ejector is with the aid of a tool, either the Brownells ejector tool (080-792-002) or the Young Manufacturing Tool, (939-000-003), both available from Brownells. The big advantage to the Young tool is that it is self-contained. The Brownells tool still requires a small vise to hold the bolt while you remove the ejector retaining pin.

Place the bolt in either tool and turn the screw to compress the ejector. On the Young tool, first align the bolt so the ejector retaining pin is in line with the clearance hole for it, drilled in the tool. Once compressed, gently clamp the Brownells tool in a vise, or place the Young tool on the bench. Now with your 1/16" drift punch and hammer, tap the retaining pin (#4) partially or fully out of the bolt. Loosen the knob on the fixture, and the ejector (#5) will rise out of the hole. Remove the ejector and its spring. Clean the hole out. A large straightened paperclip or section of pipe cleaner is useful to scour the bottom of the hole clean. You can also bend the very tip of the paperclip to retrieve any broken bits of spring that might still be in the hole.

If, in the case of brass shards, the ejector does not rise out of the hole, you must apply hydraulics. With the bolt clamped vertically in a vise, apply a few drops of oil to the ejector. Now place a punch loosely against the ejector and begin tapping with your hammer. You aren't trying to drive the ejector down, you simply want to cycle it against the spring and oil, and flush the brass out. After a short while of ejector pumping, the ejector should start rising as you tap it. Once it is free you can grasp it with a pair of needlenose plies, or remove the bolt from the vise and tap the bolt face against the bench to remove the ejector.

To install the ejector, reverse the process. Oil the spring before inserting it. When inserting the ejector be sure to line the retaining slot cut in it with the hole for the retaining pin.

Ejectors and A1 Rifles for Southpaws

In some instances the M-16A1 or the Colt SP1 rifle, lacking a ejector lump, will throw brass at the left-handed shooter's face. Now, if you are a left-handed shooter and you are depending on this rifle for defense, my suggestion is to buy a new rifle or buy a new upper (remember: large

hole for the Colt) and get something with an ejector lump on it. For use in practice, training, or competition you can alter the ejector to minimize the problem. Remove the ejector and its spring from the bolt. Clip a couple of coils off the spring and reassemble. Test-fire to determine the new ejection pattern. You can even simply exchange all the parts from an M-16A1 or Colt SP1 upper into an A2 or C7 upper. Simply swapping the parts from one upper to another solves the problem, albeit at the cost of a bit more work than clipping ejector springs.

Reassembly of the Bolt and Carrier

Reassembly is easy. Insert the reassembled bolt into the carrier. Make sure the extractor is on the right side, the one with the gas vent holes. Push the cam pin down into the cam slot and into the hole in the bolt. It will only fit with the long leg of the rectangular "box" on top running parallel to the bore. Rotate the cam pin 90 degrees. Insert the firing pin from the rear and press it forward. Once the firing pin is fully forward, insert the cotter pin from the left side.

This is your assembled test: clean and lubed, stand the extended bolt on its head. If the weight of the carrier drops it down, you need new gas rings. Replace all three.

Re-Assembled Carrier Checks

Having inspected the carrier and its parts and assembling them, you need to check your work. The check on an assembled carrier is simple:

Tap the rear of the carrier into the palm of your other hand. If the firing pin comes loose and falls free, you did not have it forward enough when inserting the cotter pin. If the flange is in front of the cotter pin, life is good. If the flange of the firing pin is behind the cotter, pin, you have a non-firing rifle and life is bad.

Now pull the bolt forward to full extension. Stand the bolt/carrier assembly on the bolt face. If the weight of the carrier causes the carrier to slide down the bolt toward the table, your gas rings are worn and need replacing. If it stands without collapsing, there is enough friction.

Chamber and Headspace

Before we move on, someone will ask why headspace here, and not in the barrel section? Simple: headspace is a function of the fit of bolt to barrel, not just the barrel itself.

Headspace has two definitions: the general one is the amount of space in the chamber, from front to back and from side to side. The technical definition is the measurement of the chamber from the face of the bolt when closed, to a "datum line," which is a circle of a specific diameter, on the shoulder of the chamber. A chamber could be tighter (as in "narrower") than is proper, while still having correct front-to-back dimension, or headspace.

Headspace in the real world is an allowable range of values. Both cartridge cases and chambers are manufactured within a range of sizes, limited by manufacturing tolerances and industry agreements such as that the largest cartridge case made to spec must still be smaller than the smallest chamber reamed. The typical value that a chamber is allowed to "wander" in manufacturing is .006". A too-small chamber will cause a cartridge at the largest dimension to wedge into the chamber and be difficult to remove. (This can be a problem when replacing barrels, and the symptoms can be subtle and misleading.)

A too-large chamber provides too much room for case expansion. When a cartridge is fired, the case expands to the size of the chamber. If the amount of expansion is more than the elastic limits of the brass of the case, the case may split or break. A too-wide chamber, or one that has been ovaled from polishing, may split cases on their side walls. A chamber that is too long will create stretching lengthwise, and the cases will break around their circumferences, resulting in the bolt extracting the broken-off base but leaving the forward part of the case in

The barrel is screwed into the barrel extension. The gap between the bolt face and the chamber shoulder is the headspace.

With a clear view of the chamber, you can see how the cartridge fits, or doesn't. Headspace is the chamber fit, but bad ammo choices can mean headspace problems.

the chamber. The next round fed into the chamber will not have sufficient room and will wedge tightly in place. With luck the corrective action taken to remove the wedged round will also extract the front half of the previous case. However, the excessive headspace condition still exists, and case separation will happen again and again until the barrel is replaced.

Cases that have been reloaded too many times can also break. The brass can become work-hardened. If the case shoulder has been set back too much in the resizing station of a reloading process, the rifle with that ammunition will have excessive headspace. (In this situation, excessive headspace is the fault of the reloaded ammunition, not the rifle.) Unless any potential source of reloaded ammunition has been commercially processed, or reloaded by an experienced and careful reloader, police departments avoid it, even for training. It is false economy for them to save a few taxpayer dollars on ammunition, only to risk the repair or replacement of an expensive rifle.

You, however, have only one taxpayer to lean back on: yourself. So, you may find that you are using mostly reloaded ammunition, in which case you had best read up everything on reloading and make sure your ammo is loaded correctly. Also, avoid the use of a small-base sizer. A generation ago it was viewed as necessary. Now, we know its usual function is to prematurely wear out brass.

Chamber Descriptions

As we saw earlier, the chamber is the rear of the barrel from the bolt face, up through the leade, until the rifling is fully established. The chamber proper is the area from bolt face to the shoulder. The shoulder tapers the case body to the neck. Forward of the case neck is the leade, which is a cylindrical section where the bullet rests, and the forcing cone, which is the taper of the lands as they rise up from the leade to their height.

The bullet, when leaving the case upon firing, must move forward from the case neck, along the leade, or cylindrical portion of the chamber, until it strikes the forcing cone. The shorter the distance it moves, the less likely it is for the bullet to tip (microscopically, I might add) and the greater the theoretical accuracy. However, the longer the bullet moves forward before it strikes the forcing cone (all other things being equal, which they often are not), the lower the peak chamber pressure. Accuracy and pressure are also affected by other variables. For instance, if we make the cylindrical section (the leade) narrower, the bullet cannot angle as far when tipping. Or, if we use longer bullets, there will be less tipping. A gentler taper in the forcing cone will decrease pressure. But it cannot control bullet tipping as well, and thus it potentially decreases accuracy.

There are two chambers commonly found on the AR, with a new custom one that is well-defined and gaining some acceptance for those who want both accuracy and reliability, as well as a whole host of "custom" "close enough" and other chambers of dubious design.

The two common chambering dimension sets are the .223 Remington and the 5.56X45 NATO chambers. Relatively speaking, the .223 chamber has a narrower, shorter leade, and a sharper angle to the forcing cone, all done to increase accuracy. The 5.56, relative to the .223, has a larger and longer leade and a gentler taper to the forcing cone. The 5.56 dimensions are selected to reduce peak pressure and to allow the use of tracer rounds, which are extremely long for their diameter and can be very sensitive to the .223 chamber. The leade dimensions can be a separate issue from the chamber and shoulder dimensions. While the 5.56 generally has a larger chamber than that of the .223, that is more a matter of tolerances in manufacturing. A large chamber is more forgiving of powder residue and environmental crud than a tight one. Thus, military rifles' chambers tend to have larger dimensions than non-military chambers.

The problem arises when a rifle that has a .223 Remington chamber fires a cartridge loaded to 5.56X45 specifications. The 5.56 has been loaded to be used in a chamber that will handle higher pressure and different bullet construction. If fired in a chamber that is not designed to deal with the 5.56 by decreasing the potential peak pressure, the pressure may be greater than desired. Not past safety limits, but problems may arise. The case may be over-expanded and fail to contract enough for reliable or clean extraction. The ejector may shave off extruded bits of brass. While the AR is designed to get dirty when fired, it is not designed to shave off bits of brass. If in firing a particular rifle the powder residue has noticeable amounts of copper or brass shavings, sparkling particles or small pieces of brass in the action, there is something wrong.

That wrong thing might be a .223 leade instead of a 5.56 leade.

The custom chamber that is gaining some use is the Wylde chamber. It combines some of the .223 and some of the 5.56, with an eye toward accuracy with reliability. However, to get a barrel chambered in .223 Wylde, you'll probably have to go to a custom gunsmith or barrel maker, which is expensive.

A .223 chamber that is fed 5.56 ammunition can also "blow" primers. There, the primer is loosened from the pressure so much that it falls free of the case during the extraction and ejection cycle. If allowed to rattle around inside the receiver, it can create mischief.

Checking Headspace

The measuring tools for determining headspace are called (not surprisingly) headspace gauges. They come in three sizes: GO, NO/GO and FIELD. A correctly-headspaced rifle will, when tested with gauges, accept a GO gauge, not accept a NO/GO gauge, and never take a FIELD gauge.

Also not surprisingly, the civilian .223/5.56 gauges and the military 5.56 gauges have slightly different dimensions. However, the overlap between them is so great that civilian gauges can be used. Of what use is a FIELD gauge, if the rifle should not accept a NO/GO gauge? The NO/GO guage is just barely beyond the largest size a rifle chamber should be and still work properly, reliably and without risk of brass separations. A rifle that will just barely close on a NO/GO gauge will be hard on the brass (it won't last as many firings when reloaded as a smaller chamber would) but it is, in the military context, still safe to fire. The military, after all, is not the least bit concerned about the useful reloading life of brass. As long as it does not break when fired, they don't care if the once-fired case is stretched, mangled, or otherwise abused.

The FIELD gauge is the outer limit of safe function and reliable brass life, as a one-time-use product. A rifle that will accept a NO/GO gauge but not accept a FIELD gauge is considered still useable in the military. In a peacetime environment it would probably be sent back for a new bolt, barrel or both. In a wartime setting, in a combat theatre it would be handed to the next soldier who needed it. A unit armorer overhauling rifles in Iraq, or piecing together the undamaged bits of otherwise scrapped rifles, will issue any rifle or carbine that fails to accept a FIELD gauge. Non-military AR shooters and police departments are not under the pressure to retain otherwise-functional rifles that our theoretical NCO in Iraq faces. For the rest of us, and law enforcement, a rifle that accepts a NO-GO gauge must be pulled from use and serviced.

Any rifle that will accept a FIELD gauge is unsafe to fire in even a military situation, and must have the bolt, barrel or both replaced. For the rest of us, any rifle that accepts a

You need headspace gauges to measure headspace. Get your pair from the same maker, and don't mix brands.

NO/GO gauge should be inspected to determine if the bolt, barrel or both need to be replaced. It should not be used until the situation has been corrected.

Headspace gauges are delicate measuring instruments and should not be dropped or mis-used in measuring. To measure headspace, you need to remove the bolt from the carrier, remove the extractor and ejector, and scrub it clean. (I know of people who will check headspace by simply dropping the gauge into the chamber and attempting to close the bolt on it. So I have higher standards, and a clearer knowledge of what is what in the chamber I just measured.) You must also scrub the chamber and locking lug recesses clean. Any powder residue or brass shavings left in those areas could produce a false reading. If the barrel is out of the rifle, then reaching the chamber is easy. If the barrel is installed in an upper receiver, do not remove it. Acquire a 10-inch section of small-diameter PVC pipe that just fits over the end of the bolt tail, and press the bolt end into it. You can also use surgical rubber hose, although the turning part becomes less-certain in feel. Then use the PVC pipe as a handle to reach down into the receiver, to insert the bolt into the barrel extension.

First, place the GO gauge in the chamber. Orient the bolt as it would be as it is closing, with the extractor to the ejection port. Press it forward and then turn it. The bolt lugs should rotate freely underneath the lugs in the barrel extension. Remove the bolt and the GO gauge. Insert the NO/GO gauge and repeat the process. The bolt lugs should not pass under the barrel recess lugs.

A brand-new bolt and a brand-new barrel will both have high spots on their locking lugs. When they are fired, the high spots will quickly iron out, adding a part of a thousandth of an inch to the headspace. Since the acceptable range is six thousandths, that "part" is not a

Excess headspace (or bad reloading practices) can lead to this: a case separation, and a need to do a field malfunction clearance.

problem. A heavily-used rifle that was already close to needing a bolt or barrel replacement might nearly allow the NO/GO gauge to be accepted. Again, not a problem. Once the high spots have been ironed down, the headspace is not going to increase short of a near-catastrophic event.

(Note: Colt chambers are almost always on the large side of the headspace range. It is not unusual to find a brand-new Colt rifle that almost accepts a NO/GO gauge. On some, it has been possible to "catch" the lead-in taper of the lugs against each other and start to cam the bolt closed on the gauge. This is normal.)

As with almost all things firearms related, headspace gauges can be purchased from Brownells. When buying gauges, buy all two or three of a set from the same manufacturer. Don't mix brands.

A Peculiar Headspace Problem

While excessive headspace can lead to short case life and broken cases, headspace that is under minimum, but not so short as to prevent the bolt closing on a cartridge, can be a more subtle problem to diagnose and correct. The bolt, driven by the buffer spring, has quite a bit of power and leverage to close over the chambered cartridge. It is entirely possible that the headspace can be slightly under minimum, and yet the bolt will close so vigorously that the cartridge is squeezed/crushed into the chamber with the bolt fully rotated behind it. Now if the headspace is far enough under minimum, the bolt won't close at all. There just isn't enough room for the cartridge. Or if it does somehow close, it is so hard to open afterwards that it is obvious to even the casual observer that there is something wrong.

But a chamber can be enough under minimum to cause other problems, but not so under that it is obviously difficult to open. The problem with figuring it out is that the symptoms it demonstrates will be the same symptoms of other problems: the rifle will short-stroke.

If you have a rifle that consistently short-strokes, and you've tested for the following conditions:

Gas key is tight;
Gas rings are present, and pass the friction test;
Gas tube is not worn on receiver end;
Gas tube is tight on front sight end;
Front sight housing is vertical, gas port not blocked;
Ammunition works fine in other rifle

think of headspace. (Do not immediately proceed to drilling the gas port!)

How does under-minimum headspace cause short-stroking? When the bolt crashes home and compresses the cartridge, the bolt ends up tensioned back against the locking lugs, pressed back by the squished case. When the cartridge is fired, it then does two things: 1) it expands, driven by the combustion pressure, putting even more stress on the bolt; and 2) the slightly compressed cartridge will have a slightly higher chamber pressure due to the slightly smaller space it is in.

Coefficient of friction depends on many things, but one variable is that the greater the pressure between two surfaces, the higher will be the coefficient of friction. (That's why you put weight in the back of a car or truck in the wintertime: the increased coefficient of friction due to the extra weight keeps the tires from slipping.)

The increased frictional load on the locking lugs can require so much more effort to unlock than normal that there is significantly less left over to power the carrier back once it is open. Add a little more powder residue and some brass dust, let the rifle heat up and dry out, and it will start short-stroking in a few rounds or a magazine or two. As mentioned before, to many experimenters/gunsmiths/ armorers, short-stroking is an open invitation to drill out the gas port. In this particular situation, it would be the wrong thing to do.

The right thing to do is scrub, measure headspace, and then if it is found to be under minimum, adjust it.

Fitting New Barrel/Bolt

There are two ways to fit a new bolt/barrel combination, besides simply purchasing them as a set from the supplier (which is an approach that is highly recommended, as it saves you a great deal of work). One method is the military armorer method: a box of bolts. Each barrel, upon arrival, has its headspace checked using bolts from the "box of bolts," until one matches correctly. Then the bolt is taped or otherwise secured to that particular barrel, and the two are used as a matched pair when it comes time to re-barrel a rifle. (That, by the way, is what the supplier did to provide you with the headspaced bolt and barrel combination you had ordered in order to re-barrel your rifle.) The downside is the cost of maintaining a box of bolts for no other reason than headspacing. Maintaining the "box of bolts" is easy for the supplier, they'll have hundreds or thousands of each on hand all the time anyway. For the military armorer, it's all just taxpayer's money, anyway. For you, keeping a box of bolts at $150 each on hand just to check headspace adds up faster than anyone wants to endure.

Bolts are fitted to barrels this way when the barrel is chrome-lined. Chromed chambers cannot be reamed to adjust headspace without both ruining the reamer and removing the chrome from the chamber.

Adjusting Headspace

One of the requirements of mil-spec production is that all bolts and barrels have their chamber/locking lug dimensions held to such strict tolerances that any combination of any barrel from any maker, at any point in time, with a bolt similarly selected, will still result in a properly-headspaced bolt/barrel combination. So a bolt made by Colt in 1967, matched to a barrel made by Colt in 2007, should have correct headspace. And they usually do. If you plan to replace barrels, and use chrome-lined ones, purchase a matched bolt to that barrel, from the manufacturer. Colt, Stag, Lewis Machine & Tool and FN all make bolts and barrels for the military. Bushmaster and Armalite do not, but their bolts and barrels are held to very high standards, and a matched bolt/barrel combo from either of them will be entirely suitable.

Where you may encounter headaches is if you mix brands. Yes, the military expects a Colt bolt to work with an FN barrel and any other mil-spec combination. But mixed combinations increase the odds that a slight dimensional mis-match will leave you with an inoperative rifle.

When you buy barrels to replace worn ones, unless you have an imperative for accuracy or hand-fitting, buy a bolt and barrel, pre-headspaced, from the same maker. Barrels made of stainless or carbon steel, on the other hand, can be reamed. That is the second method of adjusting headspace.

The new non chrome-lined barrel is first measured for headspace. If it matches the bolt and headspaces correctly, then there is no need to adjust headspace. If the headspace is excessive, it cannot be adjusted. Check with another, preferably brand-new bolt. (You should have one or two on hand if for no other reason than as a standard to measure against.) If your standard bolt is a Colt, Stag, Lewis Machine & Tool or FN (in other words, a real mil-spec manufacturer) and the headspace on the new barrel

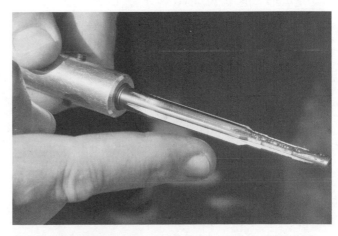

To adjust headspace, you need a finish reamer and a non chrome-plated chamber.

is still excessive, then the barrel is faulty: return it with an explanation why. Find a new barrel provider.

More likely, the headspace will be under minimum, and the bolt will not close on the GO gauge. To proceed you will need a chamber reamer. For this, you need a Finish reamer, in 5.56. (Using a 5.56 Finish reamer will save working on the leade later.) Reamers come in two size/uses: Rough and Finish. The Rough is what gunsmiths and factories making barrels from barrel blanks use. It is undersized by a large amount, and the cutting flutes are designed for fast removal of large amounts of steel. In a production line or custom gunsmith shop, the barrel blank would be reamed with the rough short of the final dimension, and then the Finish reamer would be used at the end of the fitting process. The Finish reamer is a full-diameter and length chamber size cutting tool, meant to cut small amounts and leave a smooth surface behind.

You'll also need cutting oil. Cutting oil differs from lubricants by being a thicker consistency and is meant to reduce the friction of cutting and to carry the chips of cutting away from the tool. In a pinch you can use a standard lubricant; it will just mean the reamer will have to re-sharpened after a being used in couple of dozen chambers, instead of the normal 50-or 60.

Chamber reaming requires the Finish reamer, cutting oil, a large tap handle, headspace gauges and a cleaning rod and brushes.

Firmly clamp the barrel vertically, with the chamber end up. While it is possible to ream a chamber with the barrel still installed in the upper receiver, it is awkward. If you have the right tools to make a five-minute job of barrel removal, you should do so. Otherwise you'll need extension bars for the tap handle and reamer, and the bolt, to check headspace.

Place a tin can or plastic bucket under the muzzle of the barrel. The bore will drip oil, and without the cup the mess will be difficult to clean up.

Scrub the chamber again. Measure headspace, and note the fit of the bolt in the barrel recess with the GO gauge in place. Remove the gauge. Clamp the finish reamer in the tap handle, and either brush cutting oil on the reamer or dip the reamer into the oil. Ease the reamer down into the chamber. Do not drop it in. The sharp edges of the reamer, if dropped, will dig into the chamber and can cause cuts too deep to be reamed or polished out when you are finished. Once the reamer stops, start turning it clockwise, applying moderate (a few pounds worth) of pressure downwards. You will feel the reamer edges bite into the steel and begin cutting. Turn the tap handle one complete revolution once you feel the edges bite and begin to cut. Lift the reamer out while still turning. Once it is

out, note exactly where the edges of the reamer have small curls of steel on them. Most likely they will be on the front edges of the shoulder flutes. However, it is not unusual to find some steel on the body section of the reamer, directly behind the shoulder flutes.

Reamers wear with use. As they dull in production-line use, the edges are re-sharpened. Sharpening can decrease the overall size of the reamer. The reamer starts as the largest dimension allowed by the chamber drawing specs, and as it sharpened each time it gets smaller, so sooner or later it reaches the minimum chamber size. Then it should have been discarded. However, the barrel maker may have used it longer than that. That is why you are adjusting the headspace, as they happen to have shipped a barrel that was under the minimum. Or they shipped a barrel that was right at the minimum and the bolt you're fitting is right at the maximum. Your brand-new reamer is in the larger range of the allowable dimensions and will bring your chamber to the size you need.

Brush the chips off the reamer, scrub the chamber clean, and measure headspace again. It is not likely that the headspace is correct, however, you must "sneak up" on correct headspace. If you ream too much, and create excessive headspace, you cannot fix it. Unlike other rifle designs, there is no way to correct excessive headspace by altering or adjusting other parts.

Repeat the above steps as needed, until you get results.

Once the chamber will accept the GO gauge and you can close the bolt, you are not necessarily done. A custom gunsmith will stop as soon as the chamber accepts the GO gauge, clean up and reassemble the rifle, and then proceed to test-fire it. What the custom gunsmith is looking for is how many rounds the rifle will fire before the minimum-size chamber becomes too dirty and the rifle then malfunctions. The smaller the chamber, the longer the brass life for his client, and the greater (all other things being equal) the accuracy will be. If the client is shooting reloads that run right at the absolute maximum the rifle accepts, and shooting at 600 yards or more, every tiny detail matters. And the client may be willing to scrub the chamber every hundred rounds to keep the rifle "clean enough."

For defensive use, that isn't a desirable situation. The chamber on a defensive-use AR should be reamed larger than the minimum, without exceeding the maximum. As the gap between those is only .006" that doesn't leave much margin for error. The solution is tape. Take a dial calipers and measure the length of your GO gauge, from the base to the tip. A typical length (measured from a GO gauge in the tool kit) is 1.648". (Note: This is not the measurement of the chamber headspace; it's simply the arbitrary length of the gauge from nose to base.) Masking tape, depending on the brand, is just about .003" thick.

So, as soon as the reamed chamber will accept (barely) a GO gauge, you apply a single layer of masking tape to the base of the gauge. Check the length it adds by measuring the gauge without, and then with, the tape.

Your new "ream-to" length is for the reamed chamber to smoothly accept the GO gauge with the tape on the bottom, without extra movement or wobble of the bolt. You will reach that new goal in a very few turns of the reamer.

(Once you have measured a few, you can become quite sensitive to gauge fit in a chamber. Will the bolt just barely turn on the gauges? Does it turn smoothly and easily? Can you tilt the bolt from side to side when the lugs are locked on the gauge? Each of these conditions may only be a thousandth of an inch different, but you can feel them with practice.)

Once the chamber has been properly reamed for headspace, scrub the chamber and locking lug recesses of the barrel extension clean. Repeatedly push clean patches down the bore until there is no oil left. Reassemble the rifle and proceed to zero and test-fire on the range.

Installing and Fitting Gas Tube

A new barrel, along with a new bolt, should also involve installing a new gas tube. Gas tubes can be long-term items, capable of serving through several barrels, but they are inexpensive enough that a new one is a wise investment with a new barrel. Also, if the gas tube is worn on the receiver end, from the carrier key rubbing against it, the new barrel may begin short-stroking from loss of gas, and the problem may not be easy to track down.

The new tube, once the barrel has been torqued in place, will have to be aligned with the carrier key as outlined earlier. The best method is to start with the tube untouched by the barrel nut flanges, so it rides straight

The gas tube has to project straight into the upper receiver, and not bind on the gas key. If it binds, you must either re-set the barrel nut, or bend the tube so it smoothly enters the gas key.

through into the receiver. Then, it is a simple matter to use the carrier without the bolt as a gauge, and judge the tube alignment with the carrier key. The trick to getting proper alignment of the gas tube to the carrier key is one that I've had some customers view with alarm: I simply use a large screwdriver to gently bend the tube a small amount to allow the carrier key to ride closed over the tube without rubbing.

If the barrel nut is properly torqued, and the gas tube appears greatly out of alignment with the carrier key, remove the tube and inspect it. It may have become bent in installation, or during storage. Compare it to a new, fresh-out-of-the-wrapper-or-storage tube gas tube.

(Gas tubes are commonly packaged and shipped in a plastic bag. It is prudent for you to store them in clear plastic tubes, or cardboard tubes, to give them some protection when stashed in a box or drawer with other parts.)

Bending a gas tube to make it conform to the expected shape is OK as long as you do not bend a kink in it or crease the tube. Kinks will restrict gas flow. Creases will be prone to cracking and will leak gas.

Carefully bent with the screwdriver, gas tubes are quite forgiving. In the old days, when a lot of the parts that people's ARs were built with were somewhere between dodgy and crappy, I found a lot of tubes needed aligning. Even after having to yank the tube all over the place to make it line up and smoothly slide into the carrier key, the tubes lasted as long as the barrel, and often longer.

Gas Tube Maintenance

A lot of pre-assembled cleaning and maintenance kits for the AR will have pipe cleaners in them. Or even a tiny little bottle brush. These are meant to clean the gas tube. Here's a tip: you don't need them. The gas tube is a self-cleaning system and does not need you to scrub it. My brother worked for a long time as a production engineer in an engine plant. When I asked him about using fuel injector cleaners, he almost snorted coffee out his nose. At the pressure a fuel injector works at, nothing can stick. And so it is with AR gas tubes. They are not going to get clogged with crud. At the pressures they operate at, any crud that tries to hang around will get shot out. And if there is some residue, the tube pressure will increase to adjust (a simple matter of Boyle's Law) and motor on or blow the crud out. Now, if you find yourself in the clutches of a superior who insists on clean gas tubes, don't argue. And don't tell him or her, "Sweeney says I don't need to." Training Sergeants do not take kindly to citations of outside authority.

Simply clean the damned tube until you graduate, and then don't give gas tube cleaning another thought.

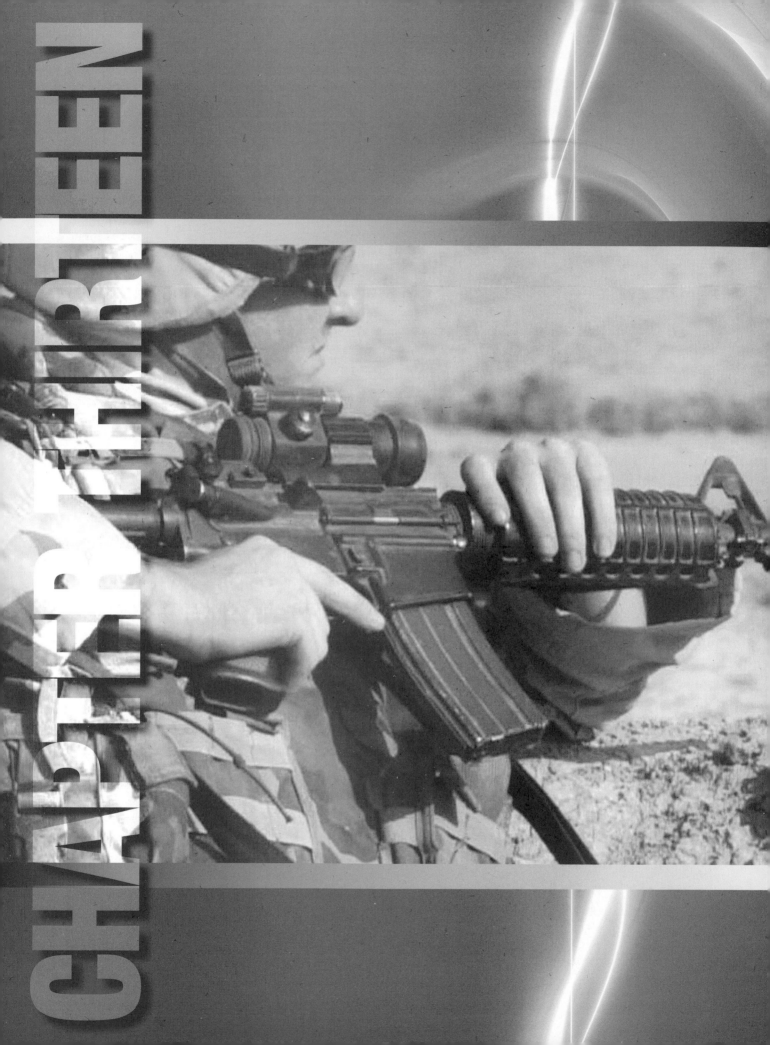

Chapter Thirteen

BUFFERS AND RECOIL SPRINGS

The AR-15/M-16 rifle, as do all self-loading rifles, needs a recoil spring to cycle the action. Due to the lightweight design of the AR, the spring also requires a buffer, or extra weight. The earliest buffers were simply plastic tubes that rode inside the tube and in front of the buffer spring and gave the spring a bearing surface against which to work on the carrier and bolt. The carrier and bolt, blown off of the gas tube by the gases, cycle back

The buffer retainer is in the bottom of the lower, drilled down through the threads of the tube loop.

The buffer and spring must be contained by the retainer, or every time you go to disassemble your rifle, the buffer will try to smack you in the face.

into the buffer tube inside the stock, compressing the buffer spring. Once the energy of that action has been absorbed by the springs' compression, the spring then uses the stored energy to push the buffer, carrier and bolt back forward. Experience early in the production evolution of the AR demonstrated that a simple plastic and aluminum buffer lacked the mass to reliably handle the cycling of the carrier and bolt. Specifically, the low mass did not provide enough mechanical dwell time, allowing the bolt to unlock too early, and with too much velocity. Also, the mass was insufficient to keep the reciprocating parts from bottoming out in the buffer tube. In addition to increasing the harshness of the recoil

impulse, the vibration disturbed magazine feeding and the impact shortened the cyclic time, bringing the bolt forward too soon in the cyclic sequence, leading to the feeding problems.

The rifle was not so adversely affected, and making the buffer heavier solved the problem. The carbines, however, required several mass increases.

Tubes

The buffer and spring ride inside a tube screwed to the rear of the lower receiver. The rifle tube can be recognized by its greater length and the lack of a rib. The carbine is much shorter (except for the "Post-ban" stocks)

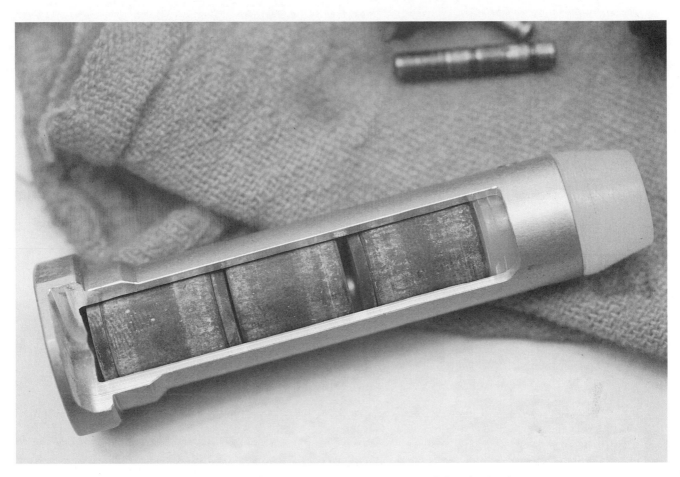

A cutaway carbine buffer weight, showing the internal weights, their spacers and the plastic plug.

Cheap buffers are nothing but problems. This no-name unit caused problems even before the plastic cap began to shred.

And to add insult to injury, the crappy buffer weight also lacked the separate internal weights.

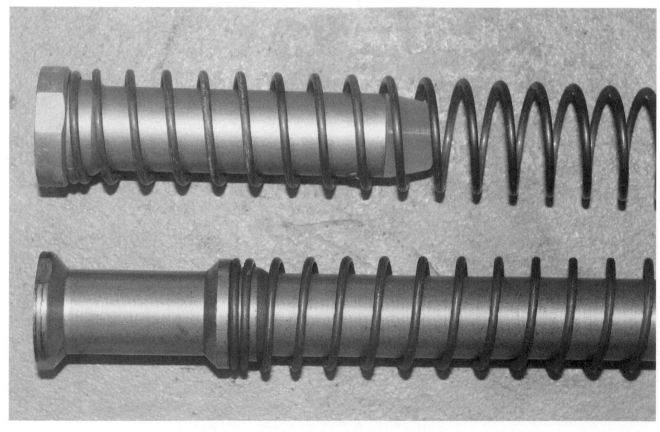

The difference between a carbine buffer (top) and a rifle buffer (bottom) are easy to see.

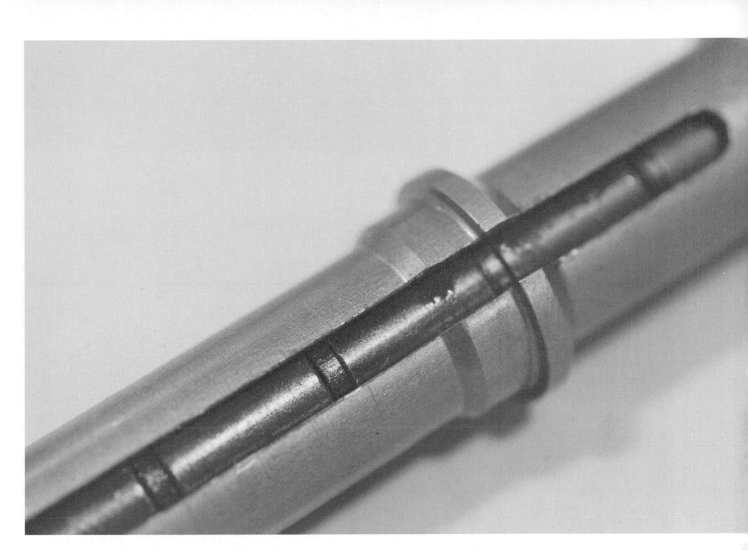

This is a correct rifle buffer, showing the internal weights to create the dead-blow hammer effect.

and has a rib on it to guide the sliding stock. Handgun-specific tubes lack both the "spine" for the telescoping stock slider, and the threaded hole in the rear of the tube for the fixed stock. A handgun AR with a buffer tube that has either of those is a firearm asking for official interest and censure. Translation: the BATFE is likely to determine it is actually an SBR, complete with the headaches that come from such a pronouncement.

To remove the buffer and spring, push the rear takedown pin across and hinge-open the action. At the rear inside of the lower is a small plunger at the face of the buffer. Depress the plunger and the buffer spring will push the buffer out of the tube. Once the head of the buffer clears the plunger, grab the buffer and pull it and the spring out of the tube. It may take some wiggling to get it past the hammer (which should be cocked) but it does come out.

The buffer is designed to sound like there are loose parts inside. The buffer acts as a dead-blow hammer. As the bolt closes, the carrier strikes the barrel extension. In mechanical terms, a steel-on-steel collision is very elastic and bounces more than any other collision. The carrier bounces away from the barrel, then is pushed forward again by the buffer spring. The problem with this is a matter of timing, and one that arose in the early days of the AR, in testing for military use. If, in full-auto fire, the hammer happens to fall as the carrier is moving away from the barrel on a bounce, or has moved away, then the hammer cannot fully strike the firing pin. The result is a live round in the chamber, with the hammer forward: a failure to fire malfunction. The internal weights move back and forth inside the buffer. As the buffer spring launches the buffer forward from the compression of cycling, the weights inside slide to the rear of the buffer. As the carrier strikes the barrel extension, and the buffer stops, the weights inside move forward. They strike the inside front of the buffer just about the time the carrier would be bouncing away from the barrel extension. Thus, no bounce. Bolt bounce is not a problem limited just to the AR-15/M-16. The later model of the AK-47, the AKM, also has a set of parts in it to control bolt bounce.

Semi-auto rifles do not need anti-bounce parts. The bouncing is an extremely short-duration event, and

before even the fastest shooter could fire a second shot the carrier is long finished bouncing from the first shot. In the AR there is no good reason to have two different buffer weights, one full-auto and one semi-auto. So we have the same parts in both. However, in the AK the parts needed are extra, so there is no point in installing extra parts in a semi-auto AK, which is why the anti-bounce AK parts are rarely seen.

Rifle vs. Carbine

The springs for the rifle and the carbine are the same diameter, and made of the same steel alloy. The rifle springs have 41 to 43 coils, and the carbine springs have 37 to 39 coils. The brand-new length of the springs is approximately 12.75" for the rifle and 10.5" for the carbine springs. If you've bought a used rifle or carbine, and find that a spring has been shortened by cutting off coils, it should be replaced. (Any rifle that has a shortened spring in it also needs a complete inspection, as the spring was probably not cut without "reason." You'll need to find what the problem was that led a previous owner/armorer/gunsmith/hack to cut the spring.) Springs shorten with use. When a spring has gotten much shorter than the starting length, replace it. As long as a rifle spring is more than 12 inches long, and a carbine spring more than 10 inches long, they are still serviceable. When they have shortened to those lengths or shorter, replace them.

Rifle and carbine springs cannot be interchanged. While the lengths and number of coils would seem close enough that in an emergency you could get by, resist the temptation. "Emergencies" tend to linger on, as the equipment is "obviously" doing fine. It is hard on the rifle or carbine to be "getting by" with the wrong spring.

The longest spring I've ever observed was 50 coils long, The rifle it was in was regularly short-stroking and failing to eject. (Big surprise there, eh?) Count the coils!

Unless you are going to be regularly using maximum loads (say, for long-range target shooting) you do not need an extra power buffer spring. Avoid them.

Buffer Weights

Selecting the rifle buffer is simple: there is only one. Except for the very earliest buffers, there is just the one rifle buffer: six inches in length. For the carbines, there are a host of buffers, and one in particular is to be avoided. The shorter carbine buffer lacks the second

Some love the reduced felt recoil of the plunger-buffers. Me, I'd rather stick with something that is less-likely to break when Mr. Murphy turns his attention to me.

spring shoulder found on the rifle buffer. Some of the carbine buffers can be found made of a plastic moulding instead of machined aluminum. These will be filled with lead shot. While they weight much the same as the proper aluminum carbine buffer, they are a cause of unreliable function. A carbine containing this buffer should have the wretched plastic abomination exchanged for a proper buffer. (Wrong spring, wrong buffer – where did you buy this rifle, anyway?) The proper ones are made of turned aluminum, 3-1/4 inches long, with a nail-like head and a plastic tip. If you shake the buffer you can hear and feel the steel weights inside clacking back and forth. Those are the dead-blow weights. If a carbine works properly with a regular buffer, then leave it alone. If, however, you experience occasional malfunctions of unknown origins such as failure to extract, especially if you find the extractor has bent or broken the rim of the cartridge, replace the buffer with one of the heavier ones Colt developed.

The first-heavier one has an "H" stamped on the top of the head, in the center. In the H buffer, one of the steel weights has been replaced with a tungsten-carbide weight. As an extra measure, Colt developed the H2 buffer, with two weights replaced with T-C. (If your wallet can take the strain, the buffers on all your carbines should be replaced with H or H2 buffers. Even otherwise reliable carbines have a slight decrease in felt recoil when a regular buffer is replaced with an H or H2 buffer.) In extreme cases, a carbine may need the H3 buffer. This is not the latest Hummer truck, but a buffer where all three of the steel weights have been replaced with T-C weights. If a carbine really needs an H3 to work well, it would be best to perform some tests, and if need-be surgery and find out why.

Do not, under any circumstances, exchange buffers between rifles and carbines. The rifle buffer is too long, and firing a carbine with a rifle buffer in it will cause the buffer tail to strike the end of the tube at higher than designed velocities. The carbine may well not cycle far enough to even work "after a fashion." Even if it does, it will certainly be very hard on the carbine, and noticeably harsher in recoil than a carbine with a proper buffer in it. The carbine buffer, being too short, allows the carrier of the rifle to cycle too far, and the result is the carrier key striking the portion of the lower receiver into which the buffer tube is screwed. If you are lucky, the result will be that the carrier key screws shear off.

If the screws do not shear off in time, the lower receiver will crack at the buffer tube threads. The only repair for that particular mistake is a new receiver. Remember: the lower has the serial number, and it is the firearm.

Buying a new lower means buying a new firearm, with all the paperwork that entails in your jurisdiction. Install the proper buffer, and avoid the hassles of a new lower to correct the mistake.

Buffer Weight Variations

Buffer weights, like carrier weights, can differ. As with the carriers, 3-gun competitors adjust the cycling mass, and the gas flow, to reduce the felt impact and thus increase shooting speed. How much difference can it all make? If you consider the cycling mass of a standard rifle (bolt/carrier group and buffer weight) you're shuttling 16.45 ounces, just over a full pound, every time you pull the trigger. If you were to build a competition rifle (and NOT a duty or defensive rifle) using a lightweight stainless JP carrier, and a low-mass JP buffer, you'd be cycling 11.7 ounces, a weight that is only 71% of the standard. Combined with the "just enough" gas flow that an adjustable gas block/tube offers, the felt recoil becomes much lighter. Combine all that with an effective compensator, and recoil becomes negligible. However, reliably is now on the razor's edge, and maintenance is a daily schedule item. Again: rifles built to such specifications should be considered competition-only rifles, and not duty or defensive tools.

The weights of the buffers are:

Original, plastic (looks like a WWII german grenade) .... 1.9 ounces

Current, for all rifles .... 5.15 ounces

Carbine, standard .... 2.9 ounces

Carbine, "H" .... 3.8 ounces

Carbine, "H2" .... 4.7 ounces

Carbine, "H3" .... 5.6 ounces

9mm Carbine .... 5.5 ounces

JP Enterprises low-mass competition rifle buffer .... 3.0 ounces

Special Buffers

There are buffers available with extra functions added. Some have a spring-loaded plunger sticking out of the back end. Others are hydraulically-loaded. They serve the same purpose: to reduce the impact of the buffer as it strikes the rear of the buffer tube. They are mostly a competition device. The recoil of the .223/5.56 is not so great that we need to reduce it for defensive uses. However, in the competition world, where the scores between winning and losing may differ by very small margins, anything that improves scores is sought, tuned, adjusted and fussed over. One might argue that a real-life shootout is scored, and that anything that improves one's chances should be adopted. But the downside of most competition equipment is that when it fails, it prevents the rifle from functioning. A standard buffer is nearly indestructible. You can literally use it after it has been run over by a wheeled vehicle. The custom buffers? What happens if the spring breaks, or the hydraulic fluid leaks, or the plunger gets bent?

Leave the competition equipment for competitions.

Now, if you want a competition rifle, then by all means, go for it. However, be aware that Newtonian physics do not cut you any slack just because you're shooting in a match. The softer felt recoil of the hydraulic buffers comes at a price. That price could be a rifle that is less forgiving of the powder your ammo is loaded with. Or it could mean more cleaning, as the rifle is more sensitive to crud. Install, test, and be certain of the results before you enter a match.

Putting It All Together: Timing

So, how can you tell that your system is proper? Simple: does it work? There is a lot of acceptable variance in ejection angle and distance, and we can only go by approximates, but here goes:

In all instances, you want the brass to go perhaps six to eight feet from you. (We'll assume for the purposes of demonstration that you're shooting standing.) Less,

and you have something slowing the system. More, and things are being run too vigorously. This obviously varies depending on the load. If you are using a relatively soft load, like Federal American Eagle, the distances will be more like six feet. Something like XM-193, or Mk 262 Mod 0 or 1, eight feet or more.

Angle? That depends on barrel length and ejector lump. Non-lump rifles and carbines will throw the brass back, that is, if you are firing at 12 o'clock, the empties will be at 4 or 4:30 o'clock. That'll be tough on lefties. Over-driven guns will throw them even further behind, slower guns, more to the side.

Ejector-lump rifles and carbines will be throwing empties at about 2 or 2:30. If they are being launched forward, your carrier velocity is too high. (They are ricocheting off the ejector lump.) Thrown to 3 o'clock or behind, slow bolt velocity. However, the bigger clue on ejector-lump guns is the distance. A slow-bolt gun will sort of dribble the empties out, instead of snappily tossing them out.

However, the angles and distances, unless extreme, are not that much to be concerned about. As I said, if the rifle runs reliably, and the brass isn't mangled, you're close enough. Leave it alone.

Chapter Fourteen

THE LOWER RECEIVER

By law, the lower receiver is the firearm. It is the part with the serial number on it, and is the part that must be accounted for by law. The rest of the parts are simply random "stuff," much like chairs, desks and paper clips, items that have to be accounted for according to the terms of your insurance policy, or not. But the lower receiver must also be accounted for according to state and federal law.

(Left) This M-16, or one like it, is likely to cost you $12,000, if it is a transferable. If it isn't a transferable, you can't have it regardless of how much money you have.

Lower Markings

The only markings required by federal law are a serial number and the name and city of the manufacturer. Model designations, caliber designations and other markings are not needed, but a lower lacking any markings but a serial number and makers name isn't as common as it used to be. In the old days it was common for new manufacturers in the AR field to start production with as few costs as possible, markings included. So a rifle with few markings is likely to be an old one from the early days of AR manufacturing.

Some lowers will be marked "pistol" as a means of

These markings mean something. Basically, they mean if you're caught with it, you will spend time in a Federal penitentiary. The generic ones mean nothing at all.

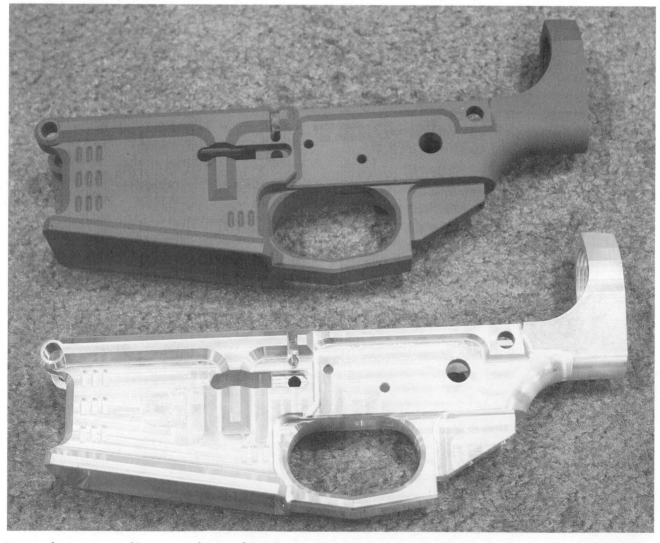

If someone tries to sell you this lower, run. Either it is for a submachine gun, or it is a faux-marked one, using the Colt trademark in violation. Either way, you don't want it, unless it comes to you on a Form 4.

You can have many markings put on lowers, depending on whom they come from. Or you can get a custom one, like these Iron Ridge Arms .308 lowers.

ensuring that the owner doesn't get into trouble. The idea is simple: since an AR can be a pistol, if you mark it so, the owner is less likely to get in trouble from an unknowing officer. Which is fine, except that an AR that was made as a pistol can be re-made as a legal rifle. Then, what do you do with the "pistol" marking? (Sometimes this all gets so confusing.)

One aspect of marking that has started to become known (not exactly common) is to mark a semi-auto-only rifle with "SAFE-SEMI-FULL" or "SAFE-SEMI-BURST" markings around the safety. The markings in and of themselves do nothing to either make the rifle an actual machine gun or change its legal status. A quick look into the rear of the lower, to determine that there is indeed the lack of an auto-sear or hole for it, will determine that a rifle is still a semi-auto only rifle. As my friend Jeff Chudwin has said more than once: "Just because you can, doesn't mean you must." Can you have a rifle so marked? Sure. Must you? No. Will it cause legal problems? Only if you're very unlucky.

With CNC pantograph software now common, it would be possible for someone to legally take a semi-automatic rifle and re-mark it with "M-16A2" "US Government Property" and "SAFE-SEMI-FULL" or other martial markings. Not smart, but not against the law, either.

It would however, curiously enough, be against the law for such an owner to mark their rifle with "Colt" "Harrington & Richardson" or "Hydramatic," as they would be violating copyright or trademark law. As long as it is still just a semi-auto rifle, the BATFE would probably not show any interest. The BATFE is concerned with function, not markings. The receiver seen in the photo above would be of interest to them because of the hole above the selector pivot, not because of the markings on it.

Post-Ban Rifles

During the Assault Weapons Ban of 1994-2004, rifles meant for law enforcement use had to be clearly marked as such. The common location was on the right side of the magazine well. There are a great many rifles in circulation that are not now controlled rifles: they are not SBRs, they are not machine guns, but during the ban they were marked as LEO-only.

They now are not. When the ban ended, the various AR manufacturers had small or large numbers of LEO-marked rifles in inventory, and with the law expired, no restriction on sales. In fact, some AR owners sought out rifles so-marked, both to express defiance of an unfair (and now expired) law, and to remind themselves to not let such legislation pass again.

Law Enforcement Only (LEO) Marked Rifles

Unlike the full-auto parts conundrum, the LEO-marked rifles are easy: the markings now don't mean anything. The BATFE has posted a letter on their web site explaining it all:

As of September 13, 2004, the provisions of Public Law 103-322, the Violent Crime Control and Law Enforcement Act of 1994, covering semiautomatic assault weapons and large capacity ammunition feeding devices are no longer in effect. The regulations implementing these provisions also are no longer in effect.

Law enforcement officers and police departments who obtained semiautomatic assault weapons are no longer required to use such firearms only for official use.

Law enforcement officers and police departments may now sell or transfer semiautomatic assault weapons to persons who are not prohibited from receiving firearms.

Law enforcement officers and police departments may now sell or transfer large capacity ammunition feeding devices to anybody.

SAWs and LCAFDs are no longer prohibited. Therefore firearms with the restrictive markings are legal to transfer to civilians in the United States and it will be legal for non-prohibited civilians to possess them. All civilians may possess LCAFDs.

A "SAW" was an semi-automatic assault weapon. An "LCAFD" was a large-capacity ammunition feeding device.

(From www.atf.gov/firearms/saw-factsheet.htm)

The opinion of the BATFE does not change state law, however, so relevant state laws or local statutes that restrict such rifles, or the AR in general, will still apply. (Some states wrote their own Assault Weapon Ban legislation by simply linking state statutes to federal law. When the federal law went away, so did the AWB of those states. States that enacted their own separate laws [like Illinois or California] did not have those laws disappear when the federal AWB/94 expired.)

So, a quick summary: as long as you do not have M-16 parts in your rifle, or the hole to accept the auto-sear drilled, you can mark up a lower pretty much any way you want to. Just don't go and infringe on trademarked names or logos.

What About the Future?

Some worry about a future ban. Will the old markings come back and bite the owners of LEO-Only marked rifles? How can you ensure your personal rifles are grandfathered then? The answers are: No; and there is no way to be sure. If there is a new ban, the BATFE will have to approve new markings that don't cause confusion with the old markings and the new law. (If such a law ever happens, that is. The best solution is to make sure new laws don't happen.) And there is no way to guarantee old rifles are grandfathered under a new law, as the new law (if such a thing happens again) will have all new language.

The AWB/94, having sunset, cannot be resurrected by Congress simply voting "bring the old law back." Well, theoretically they could. But the process is far too cumbersome to permit that. Any new law, even if it was worded as an attempt to resurrect the old law, would be amended, have the language re-written, some or many changes made, etc. There is no way to guarantee anything, except by making sure a new law doesn't get passed.

Other Markings

It used to be that when equipment was past its service life, it was sold or scrapped. There are a great many handguns and shotguns in collector's safes that have police department markings. Would that the old days were still here!

Markings indicating the rifle is property of a department or city can be another matter. Rifles that are plain and simple semi-automatic rifles with barrels longer than 16 inches are (as far as the BATFE is concerned) just another firearm, and can be disposed of according to State law. As long as the departmental records clearly show when and to whom (usually a dealer) the rifles went, the BATFE is satisfied. Rifles that are SBRs, owned by the city or department, must be disposed of in a manner that fully complies with and follows BATFE regulations. The easiest way to do so with an SBR would be to replace the too-short barrel with one 16 inches or longer. Write to the NFA Registry of the BATFE and request that that particular rifle be removed from the NFA Registry. Once it has been removed (and not a moment before), it is simply another rifle which can be disposed of according to local and State law. (It might, however, bring more money to the department if left as a registered SBR.) Without removing it from the registry, it can be transferred only with approval from the NFA Registry of the BATFE, on a Form 4, Form 5, or Form 10. Such transfers are a specialized area, and you will have to do so with the assistance of an NFA dealer.

If the department wishes to dispose of rifle marked as being departmental or city property, the markings can be a source of friction. Dealers and collectors will pay more for departmentally-marked firearms. However, the city attorneys may not wish them sold while still marked.

And self-serving politicians will trample any grandmothers standing between them and the TV cameras to appear on the side of Right. Basically, don't count on ever having a chance to buy a police-marked AR as surplus. And, don't ask someone who does custom markings to so mark your AR, unless of course you are a member of that department.

Short-Barreled Rifles

Barrels shorter than 16 inches fall into the category known as short-barreled rifles, or SBRs. They are covered by, and treated the same as, machineguns, but they are not machineguns. The short-barreled rifle status transfers with the serial-numbered lower. When making an SBR, the SBR maker has to mark the lower with their name and the city in which they are licensed. If you go through the paperwork and do it yourself, you have to have the lower marked with your name and city.

Machine Guns

Machine guns fall into two groups: Transferables and non-Transferables. All machine guns manufactured after May 1986 fall into the second group. That was when the NFA Registry was frozen, and no new machine guns could be sold other than to government and law enforcement agencies. The existing, registered machine guns could still be sold, traded, modified, and exchanged. However, not all machine guns purchased by police departments before May 1986 are transferable. It depends on exactly how the department acquired them. The only way to be sure is to inquire to the NFA Registry and find if the rifle in question was listed. If it is on the NFA Registry, it can be transferred (that is, sold to a non-departmental owner). If it is not on the Registry, it can only be transferred to another department. If the department still has the paperwork of the original purchase, the paperwork will indicate the rifle's status. If the original paperwork indicates that it was purchased as a transferable rifle, then the NFA Registry need only be contacted for approval of the sale. So, that "bargain" machinegun you've been talking to the local PD about may not be lawfully transferred to you. Do the research, and avoid the legal hassles.

There is a third, smaller group: Rifles transferred from the government to a department. These are un-transferable. They are either transferred on a Form 10, or are loaned to the department, and still considered government property. While the department may use, service and even alter (to a certain extent) such loaned property, it is not the department's property to sell or trade. At such time as the government requests their return, or requires an audit of firearms, they must be produced or otherwise accounted for. These are the "LESSO" guns, or the 1033 guns. They are M-16A1s a police department has bought from the government for the princely sum of $39. No, that isn't a typo: $39 each.

Why tell you about rifles you can't have? Because on a fairly regular basis, I hear from shooters who have figured out a "loophole" or "exception" or "great deal that is legal" to buy a machinegun. They are all either mistaken or kidding themselves. The law was changed in 1986. Since then the BATFE has had plenty of opportunities to plug and loopholes, exceptions or any other linguistics dodge you might have just thought up. The simple truth is: if you want an M-16, be prepared to pay $12,000 for it.

Takedown Pins

The AR design allows the upper and lower to be separated, for replacement, repair or exchange. The dual push-pins are both the strength and weakness of the AR system. They allow uppers to be switched between lowers. If that works for you and the rifles you have, great, but try as much as possible to keep "like on like." That is, keep the Colts on Colts, the Bushmasters on Bushmasters, etc. It is possible, if you have rifles from a variety of manufacturers over a large period of time that not all uppers will fit all lowers in inventory. It also raises the specter (as mentioned earlier) of the upper on a properly-acquired SBR to fit on a non-SBR lower. (As mentioned before, the non-SBR with the SBR upper on it is an unlawful weapon. Even for a police officer or police agency. Having a badge is not a free pass as far as the BATFE is concerned)

If at all possible, keep the uppers and lowers mated as they came from the factory. If you've built your own rifle, and the upper and lower fit properly, leave them as a matched set.

Pins, Springs and Detents

The dual push pin system of the M-16, and the AR-15s that fit them, use pins that have a nominal quarter-inch diameter. 0.250 inch in diameter on the shanks, they are machined with heads on them. The thick head with one flat side is the front pin, and the thin domed head is the rear pin. They also have grooves machined into the side, where the detent pin rides. That groove has two small depressions machined into it, at each end of the groove. The depressions keep the pin in place when the pin is fully opened or fully closed. The groove is closed on each end, so the pins do not leave the lower when they are pressed out to allow the upper to be removed.

Colt Screw Head

In a futile attempt to forestall future legislation, Colt manufactured AR-15 rifles for the non-military market with the "large pin" front pin. (These were manufactured from the early 1970's to the early 2000's.) This pin is 5/16 inch in diameter, a nominal .312 inch and the center of the pin hole is offset from where the center of the smaller pin would be located. The large pin does not use a spring and plunger, but instead the large pin is drilled and tapped on the end that is on the left side of the receiver. Colt fitted a screw-threaded bolt there, and the head of the large pin and the screw-thread bolt are slotted for screwdrivers. To disassemble the Colt large-pin upper you need a pair of large-blade screwdrivers. The small-diameter front pin of a

The Colt screw-head front takedown pin. You need two screwdrivers, and you can't match this upper or lower with a double push-pin set, without offset pins or adapters of some kind.

You can't mix these uppers and lowers without a lot of work. If you have one type, get the proper upper or lower for it, don't mix them.

regular rifle cannot be fit to the large-pin upper/lower (for the lower has a larger front hole, too). Large pin uppers and small-pin lowers (and vice-versa) can be fitted to each other by the use of special offset pins. However, it is usually best to leave a large-head upper and lower assembled as a set. As Colt rifles, a large-pin upper and lower have some value, often more than a non-Colt pair would have. However, by the time you get down to the stripped upper and lower set, the additional value is pretty much gone.

If, however, you want a multi-upper rifle, and have a Colt rifle to build on, you may be in luck: you could probably sell or trade the all-Colt rifle for enough to get you most of the way to your new set: push-pin uppers and a lower rifle.

Transition: a New Colt

The newest Colt use double push pin uppers and lowers. They are, however, shipped with the same sort of two-headed screwdriver pins as the old one. Just in the correct diameter. So, if you have a new Colt, with the correct diameter front pin, you simply remove the Colt two-headed abomination, and install a correct pin as described below. However, not all is sweetness and light.

You see (I kid you not, and I cannot make this stuff up) Colt made a bunch of rifles with the old/new correct .250 inch pin diameter and shipped them with the two-headed screwdriver pins. But they didn't drill the hole for the plunger and spring. So unless you're prepared to drill a long, small diameter hole into your frame, you can't install the correct pin. You're stuck with the screwdriver pin.

Front Takedown Pin Installation

Installing or removing the front takedown pin on a double push-pin lower takes a bit of fussing. Starting from a bare receiver, you'll need the spring and detent, the front takedown pin (the front one is the one with a flat on the side of the pin head) a 1/8" or 3/32" drift punch and the assembly tool.

Insert the assembly tool into the receiver takedown holes, from the left side. The end of the tool you want in the lower receiver pin holes is the one with the hole drilled through it. Push the spring through the hole in the tool, into the receiver. Then push the detent. Now use the punch to compress the detent and spring. When they have been compressed enough that the installation tool will turn, rotate it a quarter-turn. The detent and spring are now trapped in the receiver. Remove the punch, leaving the tool in place.

Now if the receiver lacks a buttstock, stand the receiver on the rear flat. If it has a buttstock on it, you may have to stand, or place the buttstock on the seat of your chair, between your legs. Make an inverted "V" with your thumb

and forefinger of your left hand. Place the V over the tool at the location of the detent. With your right hand holding the front takedown pin, use that pin to press the assembly tool out of the receiver, while using the "V" of your fingers to keep everything compressed.

You want to prevent the detent and spring from launching themselves, while replacing the assembly tool in the receiver holes with the takedown pin. Once down, the detent will snap into the groove (unless you pressed the takedown pin in groove-side towards the detent, in which case it is already captured) and the assembly is done.

To remove the pin, you need to get an angled edge inside the groove, to lever the detent back. A 1/8" allen wrench, with the inside edge of the short leg filed on an angle, is the preferred tool. A small screwdriver like those used on eyeglasses will also serve the purpose. The trick is to lever the detent back so it no longer captures the front takedown pin. Once the detent is compressed, rotate the takedown pin. Cover the area with your free hand when you pull the detent out of the lower. The usual result of not covering the area is the detent and spring launched across the table, onto the floor, and get lost in the proto-dustbunnies.

Why take the pin off? If you want to get your lower refinished, it cannot be re-anodized with any steel still attached to it. You may also want the pin off to paint the lower.

Internals, Pin Diameter

The trigger mechanism of the AR system is very simple. However, that simplicity can be deceptive if something goes wrong. One thing to keep track of: hammer and trigger pin diameters. Colt (I know this sounds repetitive, but they actually did all the things I mention for what seemed to them as good reasons) changed the pin diameters. The original AR-15/M-16 hammer and trigger pin diameters are a nominal .155". The M-16, in all its variations, since the beginning, use this pin diameter. All other manufacturers use this diameter. The early Colt AR-15s use this diameter.

Colt, attempting to prevent legislation, changed the pin diameter for a number of years. Known as the "big pin" (not to be confused with the big pin front takedown pin lowers) lowers use pins that are .170" in diameter, and can be obtained only from Colt. Obviously, hammers and triggers made for one diameter cannot be used on pins (or in lowers) of the other diameter.

If the department has a mixture of rifles in inventory, and some are large pin while others are small, it would be prudent to either mark them in some way or restrict the large-pin rifles (which will probably be fewer in number) for use on the range as training rifles.

This is the correct spring arrangement on the hammer. Anything else is wrong.

Disassembly and Inspection

If you are thinking of buying an AR, or you want to check your work, you have to know how to take the lower apart, and how to check the parts for function.

Trigger Assembly Visual Check

Open the action and remove the upper receiver, if it is not already off. Look inside the lower receiver. Push the safety, if it is not already there, to "SAFE." The hammer spring legs should be on either side of the trigger, above the trigger pivot pin and against the receiver sidewalls. (That is, outside the loops of the trigger spring legs.) The hammer should move when pressed down, but not much, and return to the trigger when released.

With the safety on, the trigger should not move, or move only a very small amount when pulled. You will see the hammer flex as you pull and release the trigger with the safety ON. The hammer and trigger must return to their original positions when you release the trigger. If they do, and the springs are in the correct positions, then the lower (at least this part of it) has been correctly assembled. Let's take it apart.

Move the safety lever/selector to "FIRE" or "SEMI." Place your thumb in front of the hammer to control its movement and only then pull the trigger. Use your thumb to ease the hammer fully forward. You can spare your thumb by using a dry-fire block, which you can get from Brownells or CrossTac.

Disassembly

Take your 1/8" punch and press the hammer pivot pin out of the lower. While a brand-new rifle may (again, MAY) require a hammer to tap the pin out, as a general rule, if you have to use a hammer on the takedown pins or pivot pins, you're doing something wrong. Typically, when I'm part of a class teaching the use or maintenance of the AR, we'll hear the "tap-tap-tap" of someone hammering at this point in the class. All of us hurry over. The person with the hammer is usually doing something wrong.

The hammer and trigger pins are identical, interchangeable, and can be inserted/removed in either direction.

The hammer is retained by a spring inside it called the "J" spring. That spring bears on a groove machined into the pivot pin. If the "J" spring is broken, it cannot be replaced or repaired. You'll need a new hammer.

When the pivot pin comes free, the hammer spring will try to relax, like a mousetrap, and the hammer may jump on you. Keep it under control with your thumb.

Place hammer on the table, impact surface down, and with the spring legs touching the tabletop away from the hammer head. Notice the spring assembly. The mousetrap closed end of the spring bears against the hammer, under the disconnector hook. The legs of the spring are on the table surface side of the hammer pivot barrel. This is correct. Any other assembly is wrong. (There are three other ways as well, which can be used as brain exercise for those adept at three-dimensional mental imagery.)

Press the trigger pin out. As the pin gets past the

I've always had good luck "pinching" the hammer into the lower on installation.

halfway point, the disconnector will jump free. Lift the disconnector out, and continue pushing the pin until it falls out. Attempt to lift the trigger out, moving it slightly forward. If it won't budge, it is trapped by the safety. For triggers trapped by the safety, you'll have to unscrew the pistol grip screw or bolt and remove the pistol grip. (Don't lose the safety spring and plunger!) Which rifles will allow the trigger to be weaseled out, and which won't? It is entirely a matter of dimensional stacking. If the trigger slot, trigger bar thickness, safety shelf location, etc., all work out, you can work the trigger out. If any of them are not co-operative, you'll have to remove the pistol grip, spring and plunger, and then the safety.

On full-auto guns, you'll need a smaller punch to remove the auto-sear, and a special tool it put it back in again. The auto-sear has its own retention spring, wrapped around the auto-sear pivot tube.

More Colt Trickery

In yet another engineering attempt at forestalling legislative restrictions and home-gunsmithing buffoonery, Colt pinned a block into the rear of some of the semi-auto rifles and carbines. They have done this for nearly two decades. (I have to point out at this juncture that there are actually two Colts: Colt Defense and Colt's Manufacturing. Rifles made for law enforcement will lack this block, but those made for the great unwashed will have the block.) The block is an attempt to do two things: preclude the use of an M-16 carrier (the upper flange of the block stops the lower lip of the M-16 carrier) and the pin hole for the block is in the location of the receiver where the auto-sear would go. Remove the block and there's no receiver wall for the auto-sear pivot pin hole.

The block makes disassembly and reassembly a bit trickier but does not otherwise change the function of the parts. (It does change the configuration of some, however.) The block is made of surface-hardened steel, and while some owners/gunsmiths have removed them without harming the receiver, there isn't any point to it. Leave it alone and learn to live with it, or trade/sell the rifle for one that lacks the block. Despite rumor to the contrary, it is not against the law to remove the block. Colt may grumble and refuse to perform warranty work on any rifle so modified, but the Colt warranty service is so spotty that losing them as an option is hardly a crushing blow. Removing the block is not viewed as a precursor to converting the rifle to full-auto, as long as the block and only the block has been removed. Other changes to the receiver might be viewed askance by the BATFE.

Again, leave it alone.

Reassembly

If your rifle permitted removing the trigger without taking out the safety, then weasel the trigger back under the safety. If you had to remove the safety, then insert the trigger into the lower. Then install the safety, plunger, spring and pistol grip. (As long as the tail of the trigger remains under the safety as you reinstall the safety and associated parts, you need not insert the trigger pin yet.)

Hold the trigger with one hand (balancing the lower receiver on that hand) and line the trigger pivot up with the receiver hole. Press the trigger pivot pin into the receiver, and one side of the trigger. Be careful here: the trigger pivot has sharp edges on its bosses. If you try to force the pin, you'll mar its leading edge against the sharp edges, and the resulting burrs will make assembly more difficult. With the trigger caught on one side, leave clearance for the disconnector in the trigger center channel. Press the disconnector in, and move it around (as you press gently on the trigger pivot pin) until it catches.

Note: You can also do that by turning the receiver sideways, pressing the pin against the tabletop, looking down into the trigger pivot hole from the other side, and watching the disconnector as you move it.

With the disconnector caught, now use the trigger as a lever to line up the trigger pivot with the last receiver hole, and press the pin flush.

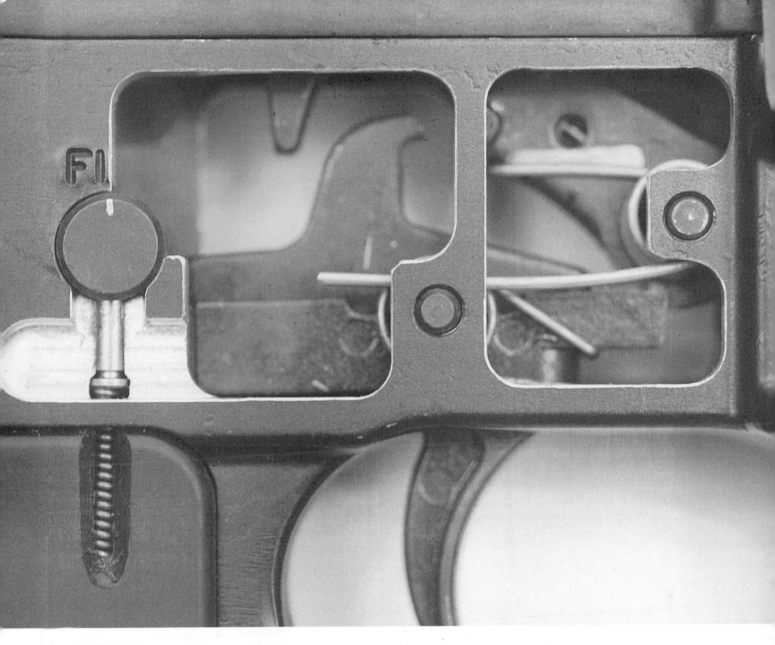

The hammer spring legs must go over the trigger pin, and on the outside.

Installing the hammer requires a bit of dexterity. First, press the safety to FIRE or SEMI. You'll need the extra trigger pivot room. Place the hammer spring legs on top of the trigger pin. Put your thumb against the disconnector hook on the hammer. Stick your first, or first two, fingers into the magazine well and pinch the hammer down into the receiver. Once there, you can (if your hand strength is up to it) hold the hammer in place while you line up the holes and press the hammer pivot pin in place.

Once started, whack the pin with a blunt object. Turn the receiver over, and using the hammer as a lever, line up the receiver and hammer pivot holes and finish pressing the pin flush.

Once together, do the basic systems checks, without letting the hammer crash free into the front lower receiver wall.

Check once again to make sure that the hammer springs lie on either side of the trigger spring coils. The trigger and hammer pivot pins do not have a capture slot on both sides, and if you let the hammer spring legs ride up on the coils, you have a 50/50 chance that the trigger pin will not be locked in place by the hammer spring leg.

All the instructors in all of our classes mention this point time and again. We go over and over it, and yet at least once in each class we encounter a rifle where the hammer spring legs are installed incorrectly. What happens to a rifle misassembled this way? Generally it works fine for a while. But the trigger pin will eventually walk out of the receiver. As it moves, it will allow the trigger to wander from its assigned path. The first malfunction that happens is usually a short burst or pair of shots, then the rifle won't fire at all.

Obviously, a burst will gain attention, and you do not want the police looking into the mystery of your rifle, when you could have avoided it by assembling it correctly.

The disconnector cannot be allowed to release the hammer until after the trigger nose has lifted high enough to catch the hammer sear.

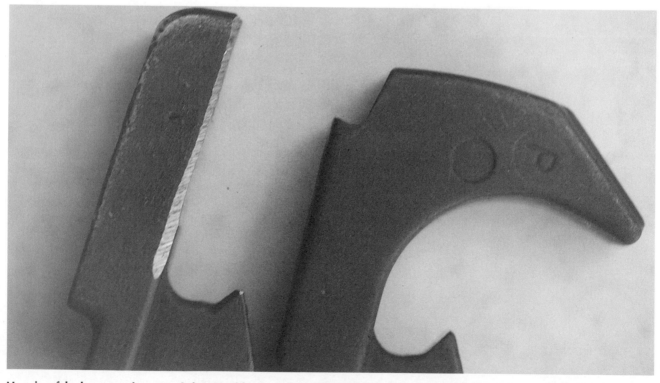

Here is a fake low-mass hammer, left (cut with a cutoff wheel), next to a Colt-modified hammer for comparison.

Semi-Auto Function

Since your rifle is back together, let's do the function check to make sure the fire control system timing is correct. First, a quick overview:

At full cock, the hammer rests with the lower notch resting against the front nose of the trigger. To fire, pulling the trigger pulls the trigger nose down out of contact with the hammer: a simple lever. The hammer pivots forward, strikes the firing pin and initiates the firing cycle. When the carrier cycles it pushes the hammer back against its spring. The trigger is still down, pressed from the trigger pull that fired the rifle and held there by your finger. When the hammer pivots down to the trigger, the disconnector is in its path. The small hook underneath the bird's-beak of the hammer is the disconnector hook. The hammer hook pushes the disconnector nose back, and then the nose of the disconnector, driven by its spring, snaps over the hammer hook.

The hammer, captured by the disconnector, stays disengaged from the trigger nose. As you gradually release the trigger, the hammer hook slides off the disconnector.

The disconnector releases the hammer, which pivots until the hammer notch strikes and stops on the trigger nose. Once the disconnector releases the hammer the trigger is said to be "reset" and the trigger can be pulled again for another shot.

Trigger Mechanism Surface Hardness

The internal parts of the AR are surface-hardened. Unless you install an adjustable trigger, trigger pulls must be adjusted (if they need to be) by exchanging parts until the "correct" pull is acquired. If you try to polish the engagement surfaces of the trigger and hammer, you may cut or polish through the hardened surface, to softer metal underneath. (Called the "substrate" in engineering-speak.) As a simple lever, the trigger and hammer engagement surfaces receive a great deal of force and high frictional force loadings. If the surfaces are soft because you filed or stoned them, they will wear, and quickly, and as they wear the trigger pull will change. Eventually the wear will be great enough to render the trigger engagement unsafe.

What Rides on the Pins: Controversy

How many M-16 parts can you have in your rifle? First, we have to make sure you can identify parts, and sort the AR-15 from the M-16 parts.

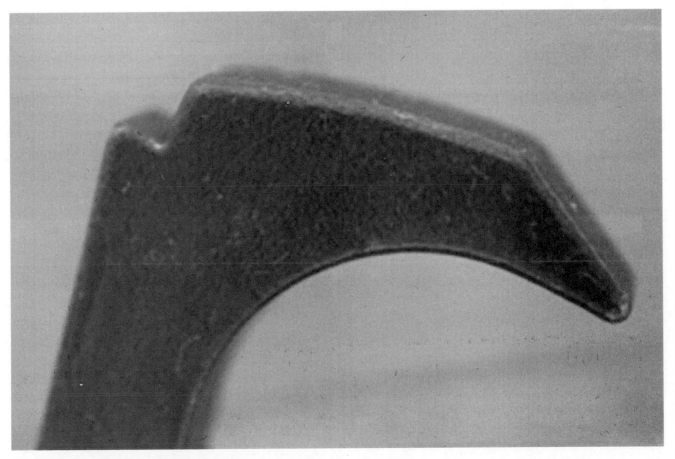

Here is a Colt AR hammer, with the firing pin notch up top.

Here is the Colt-modified trigger, to fit the Colt lowers with the internal blocks.

This is not an old Colt dual-spring seat trigger for an AR. It is a Burst trigger, meant for a select-fire lower.

This is cool to see and study, but bad to have in your parts box. This is a Burst trigger and both of its disconnectors.

Hammers

The AR-15/M-16 has been given a number of hammers though the decades. The original M-16 hammer is the "hook and lump" shape, where the mass of the hammer comes from the trailing hook of the head, and the squarish lump on the top of the hook is the hammer sear for full-auto fire. (Seen on right.) Second is the "non-lump" smooth hammer, or the now general AR-15 hammer. Here, the lump is simply ground or machined off at the factory (or afterwards) to remove the possibility of full-auto fire. If you wish to utilize military-surplus parts and do not want to have M-16 hammers in your rifles, all you need do is grind off the squarish lump on top of the hammer hook. The lump is the surface engaging any auto-sear, and without it the rifle cannot fire more than one shot except if or when it has been mis-timed. Grinding off the autosear engagement surface is all you need do to change the hammer from an M-16 to an AR-15 one. However, the hammer can be further modified. By cutting off the tail of the hammer, you turn it into the Colt low-mass match hammer, or a close copy of it. However, the engagement surfaces of the old

hammer will be the same, and there is no point in doing this to a standard trigger unless you happen to have a hammer-trigger set that produces a really nice trigger pull already. If box-stock, the mil-spec six-pound trigger pull will not be changed much if at all by reducing hammer weight. And the improvement in accuracy is one that only a long-range target shooter might notice.

The third hammer shape comes from the continued attempts at Colt to preclude legislation, and to also make unauthorized (and thus unlawful) full-auto fire. The top corner of the hammer was notched, so that if someone attempted certain types of full-auto alterations the hammer would catch on the firing pin flange protruding into the firing pin clearance slot of the AR-variant carrier and stop the rifle. If you are modifying M-16 hammers for use, you need not attempt to grind this notch into the hammer. Removing the auto-sear engagement square is enough.

The fourth hammer is the factory "Low-mass" hammer where Colt cut off both the hook and the lump, added the anti-auto notch, and used it in their Match or Precision rifles. A hammer with less mass falls faster (shorter lock time) and increases the certainty of primer ignition at light trigger pulls.

Here we have for your enlightenment an M-16 trigger. Note the open back end, to accommodate the M-16 disconnector. Swap it for a semi-only trigger, or weld up the rear of the box, just to be safe.

Not to sound paranoid, but if you have a disconnector that looks like this, ditch or alter it. That tail must come off, for this is an M-16 disconnector.

Triggers

The AR-15 trigger will have a "closed box" design. The slot in which the disconnector rides is closed at the rear, so as to preclude the installation of an M-16 disconnector. The M-16 disconnector, with its full-auto tail, is too long for the AR-15 trigger box. The trigger will also have the disconnector spring seat drilled in the slot. That is where the disconnector spring rides, and it stays secured by means of its bottom coil being wound larger, creating a wedge fit.

Other than the rear of the slot being opened or closed, there is no difference between most AR-15 and M-16 triggers. Burst-select triggers, as they use a pair of disconnectors, are different, and few of the burst-select parts can be used in a semi- or full-select rifle. However, the changes that Colt made, which we have been listing again and again, included the trigger. To further reduce the chances of someone altering a Colt so they could turn it into a (again, unlawful) select-fire or full-auto weapon, Colt chopped off one leg of the trigger. The trigger works as expected and operates normally. Why the change? To provide clearance for the trigger under the pinned-in block mentioned earlier, that also prevents the installation of an autosear or M-16 carrier. If you have a Colt with a pinned-in block and wish to install a different trigger (say, to improve trigger pull) you will have to either remove the receiver block or alter the new trigger so it clears the block.

Mil Spec vs. Target – Two Stage

A moment to dwell on triggers, as they are of vital importance for accurate shooting.

Two-stage triggers are all the rage for target shooting. If you want to see what a two-stage trigger looks like pull the trigger assembly out of an M1 Garand, M1A/M14 or Mini-14. Take off the top cover and peer into an AK-47 and you'll see another two-stage trigger. (Yes, Mikhail "borrowed" it from John Garand, but Garand "borrowed" it from John Moses Browning.) The big advantage to a two-stage trigger is a light, clean pull.

If a lighter-than-received trigger pull is desired in a defensive or duty AR, it should be acquired by either exchanging mil-spec parts, or replacing the parts with new, commercially-manufactured for better trigger pull mil-spec design parts. The experience of the instructors and students in nearly 15 years of classes has shown several things: that a 5.5-pound or greater weight pull is not an impediment to shooting a perfect score on either the NEMRT qual course or a hindrance to shooting a clean score on the NG popups at Marsailles. And the "Match" or target trigger

pulls of some designs, with pulls of 3.5 pounds, can lead to accidental discharges (and have lead to ADs) on the range while doing drills in class. It is our opinion that mil-spec parts and trigger pulls are proper for street use, and that Match two-stage triggers, if they are used at all, should be reserved for use in the police community by precision marksmen and their spotters/support shooters. Target and competition shooters, you're limited by safety and what the match rules allow.

Two-stage triggers differ from the AR mil-spec trigger in that the hammer itself has two hooks; one is for the disconnector and the other is the hammer sear notch. The hooks are arranged such that the disconnector, once it has let go of the hammer, then acts as a trigger stop for the hammer sear notch. The design allows for a very light, crisp, clean trigger pull very suitable for target work. And not for duty work. We have, on more than one occasion, had officers discharge their rifle into the ground in front of them, as they raised the muzzle to engage the target.

Now, there are two arenas for trigger consideration: police and defensive, and competition. The two-stage trigger is not, in and of itself, unsafe. The problem arises from an officer who uses a sidearm (with which he/she has probably spent more time firing) with a typical pistol trigger pull: the lightest Glock (as one example) runs 5 pounds, and has a noticeable distance it must be pulled to fire. Other pistols (or heavier Glock trigger parts) are heavier, have a longer distance to pull, or both. When an officer transitions from that trigger to the rifle with a two-stage trigger, then problems can occur. (And the problems are not the fault of the officer or the rifle.) The officer has learned through repetition, just what force, over what distance, it takes to pull the trigger of his/her sidearm. The rifle with a two-stage trigger takes less of both. An example might be in order: If the departmental squad cars have gas pedals that have very heavy springs installed, so that to go fast required a forceful push, what would be the result of an officer changing to a vehicle with a much lighter set of springs under the gas pedal? Every officer who drove the second vehicle would risk "burning rubber" when they first left the parking lot. What if the two were mingled in departmental inventory?

So it is with triggers. Unless the department issues/approves sidearms with very short, light, crisp trigger pulls, the rifles used by officers other than the precision marksman should not have such triggers either.

If you, the non-sworn citizen are using a handgun with a light, crisp trigger pull (1911s come to mind) then a light, crisp trigger pull on a rifle is not a transition problem. But if you depend on a DAO pistol with a much heavier trigger pull, then you do not want a light, crisp rifle trigger.

The use of AR-15 type rifles by Precision Marksmen is another matter entirely. The .308 bolt-action rifle used as their main weapon will no-doubt have exactly the trigger described above: short, light, clean, crisp. It makes sense that the AR-15 rifle issued as a backup or support weapon (if it is so issued) should have a similar trigger pull.

There is some worry about the durability of two-stage triggers. While the Garand, M-14 and AK all have enviable reputations for durability, the two-stage trigger parts had to be scaled-down to fit inside the AR receiver. Some have broken in a short time, just being used in classes.

There are also drop-in trigger assemblies that provide bolt-gun like trigger pulls. More on those in a bit.

Sear Engagement

Unlike many other rifle designs, there is no sear engagement adjustment on the mil-spec AR-15 sear trigger or hammer to lighten the trigger pull. Custom gunsmiths can do such things, but they do so for competition rifles. There are special pistol grips that have an adjustment screw in them, which bears against the bottom rear of the trigger. They are there to pre-load the trigger, and tip the trigger body down so the sear engagement is reduced. They should not be used on issue rifles for the police, nor defensive use. The reduced trigger pull is not needed there. Also, the reduced movement of the trigger invites grit, sand, or other foreign objects to further interfere with the trigger movement and make the rifle inoperative. One of the advantages of the two-stage trigger for competition shooters is the ability to adjust both weight of pull and sear engagement. (Yet another reason to avoid their use in a Patrol Rifle.)

The way to increase sear engagement by increasing the overlap between the hammer and the trigger is (counter-intuitively) on the hammer. The hammer sear is machined by using a "woodruff cutter," that is, one that cuts a groove. The groove cut across the hammer creates the notch, and the edge of the notch nearer the trigger pivot pin controls sear depth. You can increase sear engagement, and trigger pull weight, by stoning that edge of the sear closer to the hammer pivot pin. The stoning allows the trigger to pivot up slightly, increasing sear engagement. However, you must be careful:

Stoning the hammer notch on the rear to create more engagement lets the trigger bar ride lower from the safety at the other end. ANY CHANGE IN THE HAMMER SEAR NOTCH CONDITION MUST BE IMMEDIATELY FOLLOWED UP BY RE-FITTING THE SAFETY (AND EVEN FITTING A NEW SAFETY) TO TAKE UP THE SLACK.

Failure to do so may result in an unsafe rifle, where the safety does not fully block the trigger movement.

Disconnectors

The original AR-15 disconnector was simply an M-16 disconnector with the full-auto tail removed. However, to prevent the installation of full-auto parts in their rifles, Colt modified the disconnector so it lacked a tail entirely, and moved the location of the disconnector spring seat in the trigger. The new location made it impossible to install an M-16 disconnector in those Colts, as the slot in the M-16 disconnector for the spring, and the seat in the AR-15 trigger didn't line up. However, use in the field showed the flaws of the design: With the disconnector spring so close to the pivot hole of the disconnector, the spring sometimes lacked the force to fully pivot the disconnector forward. The result was a disconnector that timed Early, and the rifle could double. (Oh, the irony: the "correction" creates the very problem it was intended to forestall.) Colt moved the spring location on the disconnector back (and had to do so on the triggers for those rifles as well) to increase the leverage the spring had.

However, the expense and manufacturing hassle of having two incompatible designs finally forced them to the solution that all other AR manufacturers had gone to: the latest Colt design is the same as others: an M-16 disconnector with the tail cut off. And Colt triggers have two disconnector spring seats.

If the rifle you are working on has one of the earlier Colt disconnectors and you find you need a replacement, you will have to either replace it with an identical Colt part, or replace the disconnector and trigger with a new-style set. The new disconnectors will not fit one of the two earlier Colt triggers. The trigger has a recess drilled in it for the disconnector spring. Some Colt triggers were made with both disconnector spring seats drilled. If your rifle has a trigger of that type, you'll have the option of two different disconnectors to use. The correct, rare, Colt disconnector, may cost as much as a new paired set of disconnector and trigger from a mil-spec supplier who is not Colt.

Disconnector Timing

The dance that the hammer, trigger and disconnecter do has to be correctly timed. If not, bad things happen.

The disconnector must not release the hammer from the disconnector nose until the trigger nose has risen enough to be in the path of the hammer sear notch. If the disconnector releases the hammer before the trigger has risen enough, it is said to be "Early" and can lead to a very specific two-shot AR rifle: one shot when the trigger is pulled, and another when the trigger is released. If the disconnector is "Late" it may not release the hammer hook at all, once the trigger has risen to its fully-up position.

Timing Check

To check timing, make sure the rifle is unloaded. Cycle the bolt. Press the trigger and hold it back. Cycle the bolt again. Now gradually release the trigger until you hear the disconnector release the hammer. Stop your trigger finger at that moment. The mechanism has reset, and the hammer now rests against the nose of the trigger. Then continue to release the trigger, noting trigger movement, post-reset. It should move little if at all once the hammer has reset.

What is the correct timing? You want the disconnector to release as late as possible, while still letting go of the hammer without fail. If the trigger moves a noticeable amount after rest, the disconnector is Early. As long as the rifle does not double, Early is not a problem. But it should be inspected regularly. Obviously, if when you ease the trigger forward like that the hammer releases so early that the trigger cannot stay in the hammer notch, and the hammer falls to the firing pin, it is too early and must be corrected. A Late disconnector is one that fails to let go of the hammer. When you are firing, and you lift your finger off the trigger, the trigger spring can push past a late disconnector. However, if the disconnector timing is right on the edge (literally) easing the trigger forward slowly can cause the sharp edges of the disconnector and hammer hook to bind and catch. The trigger mechanism must re-set every time you work it, regardless of how slowly your finger moves.

You can also do the timing check visually, with a Brownells hammer stop installed in the lower, and the upper receiver removed. You can then both see and feel the movements as you check the mechanism. To re-cock the hammer, simply press it back with your thumb.

DO NOT dry-fire the mechanism with the upper off without the Brownells buffer. You can damage both the lower receiver and/or (counter-intuitively) the hammer.

It is possible to observe the workings of the trigger and hammer by using the pins to "install" the hammer and trigger on the outside of the receiver. While getting the springs to work is difficult (if anything gets out of balance, parts get launched across the room) without the springs you can see how things work simply by moving them with your fingers.

Altering the disconnector to adjust timing is a delicate affair. It is better, if you have the parts, to use the military armorer method: swapping disconnectors until one fits with proper timing.

Early

An early disconnector releases before the trigger is high enough to catch the hammer hook. The disconnector must be tilted forward enough to delay release until the trigger can catch the hammer. The surface for adjustment is the underside of the disconnector nose. The nose rests on the trigger as its stopping point. You'll need a vise and large file. File the surface flat and parallel to its original angle for a couple of strokes, re-install and test the timing again. As you remove steel you'll see the disconnector releasing the hammer later and later. Stop when the trigger barely moves after the disconnector releases the hammer, and you ease up on the trigger. De-burr the edges, cold blue, and oil when you re-install.

Late

Unlike the nose, and adjusting the Early disconnector, you cannot file the underside of the disconnector hook. The hook is subject to a great deal friction and force, and is cycled each time the mechanism is fired or hand-cycled. If the surface hardness of the disconnector hook is removed by filing, the wear may change the angle of the hook and lead to a disconnector that has turned into an early-release one.

The first thing to do is to take a fine stone and simply remove the tool marks that may be on the disconnector hook and hammer hook, where they bear against each other. Disconnectors are stamped via a process known as "fine-blanking." Hammers are cast or forged. Both processes may have left tool marks or rough areas. Often, simply removing the opposing tool marks that are hooking onto each other can bring a Late disconnector back into proper timing. If that fails, you use your large file to remove a small amount of steel from the tip of the disconnector hook, not its underside. The surface exposed by filing the tip is not subject to wear, and thus cannot change timing through wear. By removing a small bit of steel and shortening the hook, you make the hook release happen earlier in the timing of the mechanism. The amount needed is very small.

In either case, Early or Late, removing too much steel makes the disconnector inoperative. However, the cost of a disconnector is small, and it may well be worth some experimentation. Go out to the gun show and buy a disconnector. Mark it with paint or something so you won't get it confused with other disconnectors you might have. Take your replacement disconnector, and set aside the perfectly-working one in your rifle, and then experiment the new disconnector to scrap. As you file you'll see the timing change, and can adjust in each direction, Early and Late. Once you have learned all you're going to learn from the sacrificial disconnector, ditch it, re-install the untouched original and your rifle is back to normal.

Safety Fitting

The safety rides over the rear of the trigger, and when rotated to the "SAFE" position, traps the rear of the trigger and prevents it from moving out of engagement with the hammer sear notch. The side walls of the disconnector slot of the trigger rise, and are stopped by, the safety when the selector is set to SAFE. When you press the selector to FIRE (or SEMI) the milled shelf in the safety has been rotated around, and the trigger now has clearance to lift in the rear, and release the hammer. To install or remove the safety, you often must remove the pistol grip, which contains the safety spring and plunger. Once the pistol grip is off, the safety should simply lift out of the left side of the receiver. However, "should" and "always" are not the same when it comes to triggers. The dimensions of the safety, trigger, receiver and the pivot points of those parts sometimes "stack." That is, the manufacturing tolerances sometimes add up such that the safety can't be installed or removed unless you also remove the trigger pivot pin, which allows it to rest lower in the receiver, and thus clear the safety pivot.

Each rifle will be an individual case, and you'll have to learn on each one of yours what it will allow.

The safety must stop the trigger from moving enough to release the hammer and fire the rifle. If, when you check the safety function (i.e., press the lever to "SAFE" on an unloaded rifle and press the trigger; if the hammer falls, the safety doesn't work) the trigger moves some, but the hammer does not fall, you need to check the safety performance. Remove the upper (if it isn't already off) and with the safety on, do the check again. Watch the trigger and the hammer. If, after pressing the trigger, the trigger moves back to its original position, and the hammer also moves back (the trigger cams the hammer as the sear moves) then the safety is working properly. If the trigger stays in the pulled position, then it is not working properly, even though the hammer doesn't fall.

There are no adjustment surfaces on the safety and trigger. You can only "adjust" the fit by swapping parts. As the trigger, and its fit to the hammer are what determine trigger pull, weight and crispness, swapping out triggers should be a last-resort option. Instead, install another safety/selector and try again. Continue until you either find a safety that works properly, or you run out of safeties to try. If you run out of safeties, then pull the trigger out of the receiver, set it aside, and install another trigger, Start over again, checking safety fit.

If, after all this you cannot find a combination of the triggers and safeties on hand that works, you have a problem. Most likely, the problem is in the receiver itself and cannot be fixed by filing, cutting or adjusting. You will have to either find a custom gunsmith who can weld and fit a trigger to the safety (the trigger needs higher rear walls on the disconnector channel) or you need to replace the lower receiver.

Safeties
Standard

The standard safety should click on and off with authority. If it flops around or is so stiff it takes two hands to move, you'll have to take a look and see what is going on in there. The spring and plunger in the pistol grip are the usual culprits but sometimes a defective safety lever passes QC, and the detents are not deep enough. While it is possible to adjust them by using a drill press, it is usually easier to just install a new safety and send the old one back.

The AR safety is solid in the middle, it does not have many slots and ridges.

Ambidextrous

Ambidextrous safeties are quite popular, but they are not without drawbacks. Some designs can be bulky enough, or have the lever proportioned such that the right-hand paddle interferes with the trigger finger of a right-handed shooter. The question is: are ambidextrous safeties considered a part that must be installed on every rifle, or only on rifles used by left-handed shooters? It is not difficult to learn to use a single-sided safety from the other side, and if at all possible left-handed shooters should be taught to do so. After all, there is Murphy's Law to contend with: If anything can go wrong, it will. You know, you just know, that if you are wedded to an ambi safety, that the day you have to pick up an AR and use it for defense it will be the only one you own lacking an ambi safety, or a battlefield

The safety/selector out of this M-16A1 is not something you want in your AR-15.

pickup lacking one. Right-handed shooters should also learn to do so, when firing from the left shoulder, as they would be doing when firing after being wounded on the right, or shooting around right-hand corners.

AR-15 vs. M-16

As we've discussed earlier, most AR-15 internal parts, considered as objects in a manufacturing stream, are M-16 parts until one last machine cut or grinding operation is made. Much of the surplus parts stream is composed of M-16 parts of one kind or another.

How Many Full-Auto Parts Can I Have in a Rifle?

The question comes up in every class, and the only really safe answer is "none." If all the parts in the lower are either semi-only parts, or full-auto parts that have been modified to be semi parts, you are safe. A rifle with those parts, and those parts only installed, that fires more than one round would then obviously be defective, right? That is the hope, and the legal defense, which usually works.

The BATFE position is pretty clear, in that they view any full-auto parts with suspicion.

In a recent court case, David Olofson, a Drill Instructor in the Wisconsin National Guard, loaned an AR-15 to a friend. The rifle malfunctioned at the range, drawing the attention of a law enforcement officer. The rifle was confiscated, tested and deemed not a machine gun. It was then tested again and by altering the test procedure (done by the BATFE testers), the rifle was then deemed a machine gun. Mr. Olofson is now serving a prison sentence for unlawfully transferring a machine gun. While the courts' decision may be overturned on appeal (there were more than just a couple of questionable matters in the rifle and the legal process), that would hardly get Mr. Olofson his time, money and reputation back. If you must be cheap and use surplus full-auto parts in a semi-auto rifle, alter them so they are clearly unable to work in a full-auto rifle.

ENGINEERING WARNING!

Let us suppose you assemble a rifle with all auto parts: carrier, hammer, trigger, disconnector, safety. (Leave out the auto sear.) Correctly done, the rifle should not fire in any other manner than in semi-automatic mode. However, if your work is not perfect, if the parts are the least bit out-of-spec, you could end up with a rifle that doubles now and then. Bingo! You just made a machinegun, and earned a trip to Ft. Leavenworth. The fact that you didn't correctly adjust the timing of the disconnector is no defense. You have the M-16 parts in there; the rifle fires more than one round. It is a prosecutorial slam-dunk: the rifle meets the definition of a machinegun exactly as written, and you did the work.

As you remove parts one at a time and replace them with semi parts, the likelihood of full-auto (defective) fire diminishes. But one full auto part and a bad trigger job that doubles are a suspicious condition. More parts, more suspicion.

Engineering does not trump Law. And intent does matter. Intent, or evidence of intent, can be a really big problem. Let's go at it from the other direction: You have a rifle with all semi parts, but the lower receiver has been drilled to accept the auto sear. I think we can all agree that despite the fact that the rifle will only fire in the semi-auto mode (the parts are all semi) we have clear intent to "create parts designed and intended for use in converting a weapon to shoot automatically."

The BATFE is not composed of gunsmiths with years of experience. They can't handle an AR and in a few seconds determine if it is correctly timed, badly timed, or has been subjected to experimentation to make it into

a machinegun. Nor are the police officers in your local department, or the Sheriff's Deputies or State Police who might be curious about your rifle. In order to make that determination, they'll confiscate it, give you a receipt, turn it over to the experts back in the lab, and await the report. You get to wait, on tenterhooks, until the report that will determine the future course of your life, comes back – and you run the risk that someone along the way will have boxed themselves in a corner: they have to declare your rifle a machinegun, or bad career things will happen to them.

Leave the full-auto fire control parts out! Use an M-16 carrier if you want, but be aware it is an M 16 part and could lead to trouble if someone really, really wants to make trouble for you.

Pistol Grip

The pistol grip of the AR-15, unlike the MP5 for example, allows almost all users to easily and naturally reach the selector lever. What it doesn't do is locate and position the hand for good access to the trigger. The tendency for most shooters is to place the hand too low on the pistol grip, and to drop the elbow and bend the wrist back. To alleviate that, there are a large number of replacement pistol grips available. Avoid pistol grips that add too much bulk to the grip area. The two original grips are the A1 and the A2. Back in the early 1980s, when the M-16 improvement program was going on, the A1 grip was felt to be too skinny. So the A2 is slightly larger and has a finger-hook on the front face. Despite many classes and shooters, we have not yet found someone whose fingers fall perfectly in place for the A2 finger hook. Trying to use the hook places the hand too far down the grip for most shooters. Luckily it is easy to ignore or even remove the finger hook entirely.

Fit and Modification

The pistol grip is held on the lower receiver by means of a screw or bolt inserted through the bottom. Some rifles come with an allen-head bolt in place of a screw. The standard-length allen wrenches found in a toolbox or hardware store are too short to reach that bolt, to remove the pistol grip. You need a special, longer allen wrench to reach. (In a hardware store they are usually on the next set of pegs over.) The standard for most (but not all) of these bolts is a 3/16" size. (Some use a 5/32" allen-head bolt. Why? No one really knows.) The standard mil-spec pistol grip attachment is a slotted for a large screwdriver, and nickel-plated for corrosion resistance. If you buy a rifle with the allen-head bolts, it is prudent to change them for the slotted screwdriver ones. It is possible to find a screwdriver

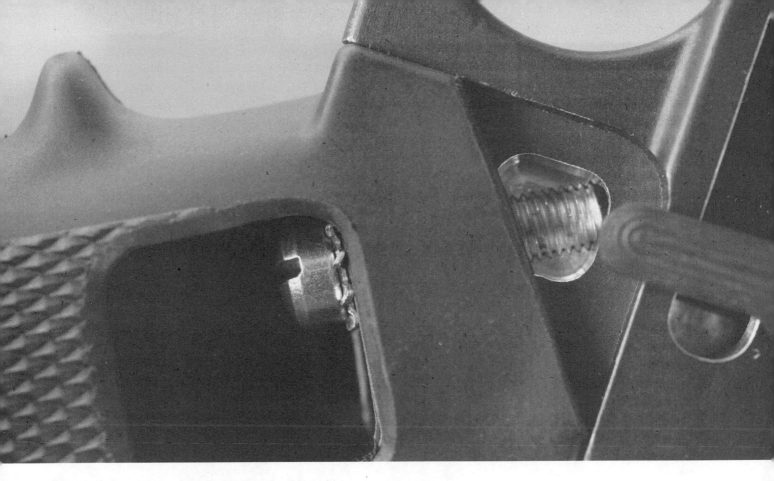

The pistol grip is held on by means of a plain old machine screw.

that will fit almost anywhere. Stopping at a gas station with a service bay will no doubt let you find one. But a long-shank 3/16" allen wrench? Not common even at an auto shop. To make matters worse, the pistol grip screw (as are many firearms parts) is a non-common thread: ¼"X28. If you go to the local hardware store, they'll be able to supply you with (literally) a ton of ¼"X20 screws, in a dizzying variety of lengths. 24 threads to the inch? Not so much. The "28" they'll have to order, if they can find a place to order them from. And finding it with the large head the pistol grip requires? Expect head-scratching and muttering as the counter guy at the hardware store dives into his parts book again, not to be seen for a long time.

Save yourself the hassle and buy the screws (you should have spares on hand) from an AR parts supplier. Slotted-head screws.

You should always use the "star" washer included with the screw. Without it, the screw can (and will) work loose during the vibration of shooting. The pistol grip will get loose, which is not a problem. However, if it gets loose enough it may allow the safety plunger to work loose. The safety plunger (see above) acts as the locating detent for the safety/selector. If the pistol grip comes loose, or you lose the spring, there is nothing to keep the selector located where you left it.

The safety has a groove machined partway around its

perimeter, and that groove has detents drilled into it at each end. The plunger that provides friction for the safety lever, and keeps it in place, rides in that groove and snaps into those detents. The plunger reaches the safety from a hole drilled underneath the receiver, covered by the pistol grip. The pistol grip also holds the spring the pushes on that plunger. When the pistol grip comes loose, either from vibration or being disassembled, the spring and plunger can drop free. To keep the plunger in place, and prevent it binding in the event of corrosion, it should be installed after being dabbed with grease. To keep the spring in place in the pistol grip, tear a small bit of masking tape off the roll and wrap it around the bottom of the spring. You want just enough to keep the spring from falling out when the pistol grip is upended. Not enough to bind the spring in the hole.

The pistol grip fits over a shelf on the lower receiver. If the slot in the pistol grip is too tight, the slot of the grip can be filed to fit. (Always modify the cheaper or more-easily obtained part!)

The pistol grip is a solid moulded piece (not two pieces glued together) with a hollow in the middle for access to the screw. If the finger hook on the A2 is not desired, it can be filed or ground off and the area polished with 600 grit crocus cloth or polishing paper. The pistol grip should fit flush with the shoulders of the lower receiver behind and

The pistol grip contains the safety spring and plunger. Make sure the spring is not kinked when you install the pistol grip.

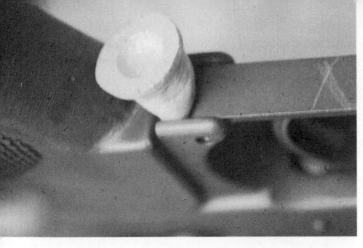

If the gap annoys you, stuff a used earplug into it. There are more-elegant solutions, but that will get you through the match or class.

above the trigger area. There should not be gaps. If there are, the pistol grip needs to be swapped or fitted.

Other Pistol Grips

The basic A1 and A2 serve well. Some shooters object to the sharp edges of the receiver and trigger guard, rubbing their second finger. One solution is to stuff a used foam ear plug into the gap. There are pistol grips that have a shelf or bill that cover that gap; the best-known is called the DuckBill. Both solutions preclude the use of the trigger guard, hinged down, in the winter, with heavy gloves or mittens.

There are also pistol grips that offer storage space for

batteries or a spare bolt assembly. While useful, they do have some downsides. One is the extra gear adds weight. The few ounces aren't much, but it is some weight, and should be considered. (A maxim of backpacking is: "Watch the ounces and the pounds take care of themselves.") If you store batteries there, be sure you keep a schedule for checking battery dates and remaining power. Dead batteries are of no use, except as thrown objects. (Note: Lithium 123 batteries don't weigh enough to be serious weapons when thrown.) A bolt is an expensive object. It also, to be of use. must either be fitted to that particular rifle, or be one of the standard, mil-spec bolts that all your rifles should have. (If all are mil-spec and interchangeable, then the spare bolt stored in the pistol grip will work in any mil-spec chambered rifle.)

A complete bolt (gas rings, extractor, ejector, assembled) can run from $60 to $150. As a portable item, and one easily sold at any gun show, they must be accounted for. Rifles issued with bolt assemblies in the pistol grip must include the bolt as part of the inventory checklist. (Considering the extreme hardness of the bolt steel, it will prove difficult to mark the spare bolt with a departmental identifier.)

Magpul MIAD

The Magpul pistol grip differs from other designs in that it is modular: you can assemble a MIAD pretty much

Some pistol grips, like this Magpul, allow for storage of stuff. In this case, a spare bolt.

any way you want. You can make it as big as possible, by inserting the fat back (which is too much for me, as it changes the angle my hand rests at) and the finger-hooked front. Or you can go to the other extreme and slide the slimmest inserts in. The center of the grip accepts plug-in holders, which (depending on which one you install) will hold a bolt and firing pin, three rounds of ammo, or batteries.

Once you've installed the front and back inserts, you simply bolt it on, as you would any other pistol grip.

Pistol Grip Trick #1

The problem most have in installing the pistol grip is getting the screw to fall into the hole through the grip. Here's how: turn the pistol grip sideways, and slide the screw (with washer) into the grip, so it is lying on the side of the opening. Then place your screwdriver into the screw slot, and gently turn the pistol grip upside down. As you do so, push the screw to the bottom, and you'll have the screw standing on the internal shelf, with the screwdriver holding it in place. You can now tip the pistol grip and slowly turn the screwdriver, and "walk" the screw to the hole.

Pistol Grip Trick #2

Don't press the pistol grip fully onto the frame, and then start turning the screw. You risk cross-threading the hole as you force it. Instead, press the pistol grip onto the frame just enough to let the screw reach, and then begin turning the screwdriver. Let the screw threads catch the receiver threads without forcing them. Once you get the threads "caught" and the screw is smoothly turning in, then you can press the pistol grip on (make sure you have the spring and plunger in for the safety, and the spring isn't kinked) and tighten the screw.

Bolt Catch and Mag Well

The magazine well is created from the aluminum forging of the lower by one of two ways: it is either broached or wire-EDM cut. Both can be very precise methods. If you buy a lower where the magazine well is so tight that your magazines do not drop free, send or take it back. (The best check is to use brand-new USGI magazines fresh from the wrappers.) A too-tight magazine well can be corrected with careful filing and polishing, but it is not easy to determine exactly where the tightness is. Simply opening the whole

The mag well, being broached. This all happens under great hydraulic pressure, and in a few seconds.

magazine well to "correct" the problem is time-consuming and removes the anodizing of the lower. The exposed, soft aluminum will wear faster than the anodized surface you removed.

Send it back and make the manufacturer or supplier make it right.

A broached well has the forging drilled down the magazine well location, and then the drilled forging is placed in a fixture. A long steel bar (seven to eight feet long) looking something like Godzilla's own bench file, is then hydraulically pulled through the forging. The bar has magazine well-shaped steps cut into its surface, each slightly larger than the one that proceeded it through the forging. The last step is the exact size and shape of the finished magazine well. (See the above photo.) Wire EDM uses a wire with a huge electrical charge pumped through it, and the wire is run around the perimeter of the mag well to cut the mag well opening and shaft (exactly like a cheese cutter) and the electrical charge "burns" its way through the aluminum as it travels. Both methods work, and the exact process is left to the company machining the lower receiver. (Unless, of course, it is a real-deal mil-spec manufacturer doing the work, and then they are bound by the requirements of the specs and contract.)

In neither case is the magazine well amenable to post-anodizing fitting and filing. It is what it is, and trying to make it "better" with files, oxide cloth or lapping compound is just a way to waste an afternoon and destroy the usefulness of a lower receiver.

Magazine Catch Installation/Replacement

Behind the magazine well, but forward of the trigger, on the right side, is the magazine button or catch.

The magazine catch is an "L" shaped piece of steel that is spring-loaded to hold the magazine. To install, you'll need the catch, spring and button. A second button makes a useful assembly tool. Insert the magazine catch into the receiver from the left side. Hold it in place, and insert the spring from the right. Press the button into the right side (smooth side in, ridged side out). Use the second button to compress the first button, spring and mag catch. Hold the second button firmly in place, compressing the spring. The magazine catch will protrude from the left side of the receiver. Rotate the mag catch to screw it onto the button that is sandwiched under the button you are pressing. Hold the second button as far in as you can, or as necessary, to allow the spinning mag catch to clear the side of the receiver. Once you have rotated it four times, ease the

button up. Remove the second button. Use a pencil eraser or fingertip to press the button in enough to clear the receiver, and rotate the magazine catch until the tip of the threaded portion is flush with the face of the button.

Ambi-Catch

Norgon makes an ambidextrous magazine catch. It is an assembly that replaces the regular mag catch, and its internal pivot allows you to release a magazine by pressing on the Ambi-Catch from the left side. Lest you refrain from using it on the grounds that "it isn't mil-spec," on August 31, 2007, the USMC authorized all unit commanders to upgrade their rifles and carbines with the Ambi-Catch. The Norgon Ambi-Catch even has a National Stock Number: 1005-01-537-6498, in case you have access to the NSN system. Installation is easy, and Norgon makes it even easier. Simply press the old button in, unscrew the old mag catch, then screw the new catch on. Norgon makes a plastic tool that depresses the magazine button, making unscrewing the old and installing the new a lot easier.

Button Location

Does screwing the button down (actually, the mag catch in, but you get the idea) more increase magazine retention? Maybe, probably not, and you do not need to. As long as the mag catch shaft is flush with the button, you're good to go. I've never seen an AR that would fail to retain a good magazine when the button is properly installed. (Crappy magazines, another story entirely.) The mag catch can't "fit deeper" into the magazine because the receiver is machined to allow only a certain amount of protrusion by the mag catch shelf. Making it tighter does increase spring tension, but not by much, nor is it needed.

So screw it to flush and leave it alone.

Magazine Button Fence

Around the magazine button, there is a protective fence to keep you from inadvertently bumping the button and dropping magazines. The earliest ARs did not have this fence, and those wishing to build a "retro" AR look for lowers lacking a fence. You can buy an old Colt (and pay to wrestle it out of the hands of a Colt collector) or you can go to Nodak Spud and buy a newly-made, pre-A1 configuration lower. You can have no fence at all, a partial fence, or a complete fence.

Match it with an appropriate-era upper (usually an A1, with or without a forward assist) and send the set off to US Anodizing to have them match, and you have a solid base

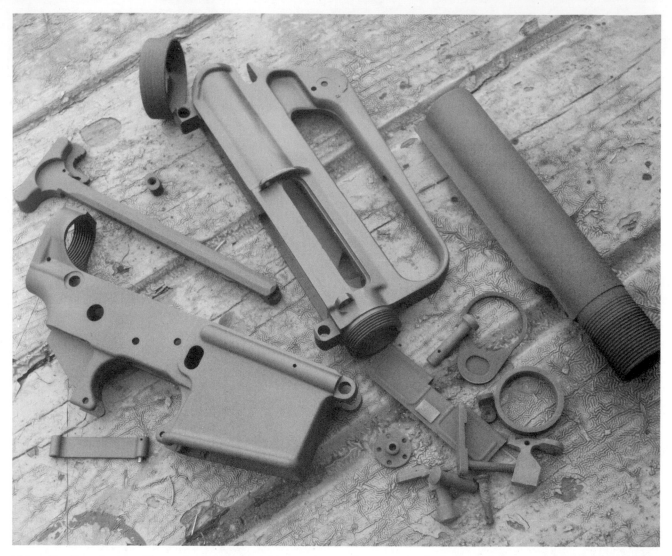

This collection of parts will soon be an XM-177 clone, and an early one. Note the lack of a fence around the magazine button.

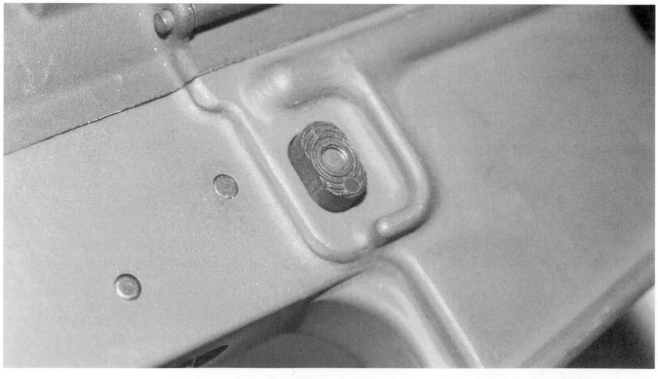

This is a fence on an old cast receiver. Some hate cast receivers, but this one has worked reliably for decades.

to make an M-16 or XM-177 clone, lacking the select-fire option and the $12,000 it takes to get same.

Replacement of Bolt Catch

The bolt stop rides in a slot cut in the lower but protrudes into the top rear of the magazine well. You can see how it works by taking a lower lacking an upper and inserting an empty magazine into the magazine well. Bolt catches cannot malfunction, but they can break. Depending on where they break, the result can either be a rifle that simply doesn't lock open when empty, or a rifle that doesn't work at all.

To replace a broken bolt hold-open you need the special bolt-catch punch. Due to the shape of the left side of the lower receiver, a regular punch will not reach the pin without banging against the side of the receiver. The angle you have to use a standard punch at will foil attempts to drive the pin out. Place the receiver right side down on a padded surface, or use the Cross Tac bench blocks to hold it in place. If you are working horizontally, and there is a stop, or heavy object you can use as a stop, push the front edge of the receiver against that stop. Place the bolt-catch punch against the retaining pin and hit the punch with a hammer to drive the pin most of the way out. Leave the roll pin in place on the other side, to ease re-inserting it. Once the bolt catch or its parts are out, check the spring and plunger that activate the hold-open. Wipe them clean and re-oil them. Check the new bolt catch for fit in the slot. If it doesn't fit, you may find that wire edges from

The busted bolt catch might just fall out, and it might just gum up the works.

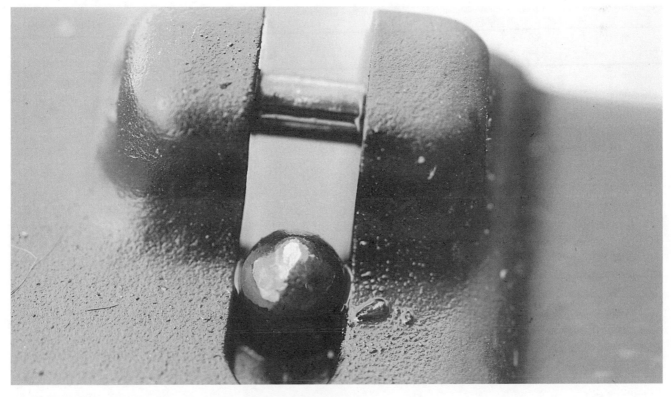

Once the broken parts fall out, you're left with the spring and plunger.

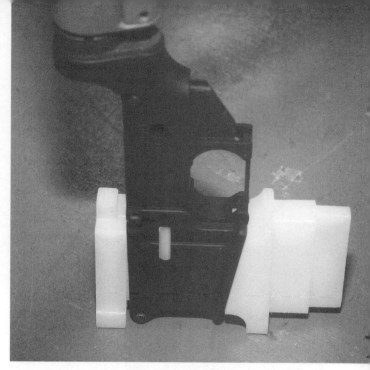

Here you see the thinnest part of the bolt catch, and this one broken.

The Cross Tac blocks, being used to hold the receiver in place for the bolt hold-open pin.

On top of all the other goodies, the Knight's rifle has an ambidextrous bolt catch. Of course, you can't install it; you have to buy the rifle.

machining have made it too wide. Stone or file those edges off. If, however, the cause is that the web of the catch is too thick, you either file it thinner, or send it back for replacement. Do not alter the slot in the lower to make the bolt catch fit. Reassemble. If you left the roll pin in place, tap it back. If not, use a punch as a slave pin, and as you drive the retaining pin back in you'll push the punch out.

Trigger Guard

The trigger guard of the AR-15/M-16 is designed to be hinged down. That allows access to the trigger in extreme cold weather, while wearing mittens. Remember, when the M-16 was being (grudgingly) accepted, there were still plenty of people in the Army and Marines who had had the bracing experience of a cold winter's night in the forest of Germany, or a ridgeline in Korea. And there were lots of people there who wanted them dead. So, the M-16 had to be designed to be used with cold-weather clothing. Hence the pivoting trigger guard. However, the tabs where the trigger guard are attached are perhaps the most fragile parts of the AR lower. One error in installation, or one errant hammer blow, and there is no repairing it or going back. The trigger guard is a plastic bar with a hole in one end and a plunger in the other. The plunger goes up front. Take the trigger guard and compress the plunger. Slide the plunger end into the front, and let the plunger catch in the hole drilled for it, on the right side.

Swing the trigger guard up until the hole in the other end lines up with the hole for the retaining pin. The retaining pin, like so many others on the AR, is a roll pin. Place a backing block under the receiver, at the trigger guard retainer hole. You can use the Brownells barrel block, or the Cross Tac receiver block. A roll of masking tape, on edge, also works if you do not have a lower-specific backing block. Hold the pin with a pair of needlenose pliers. Place the pin against and in the hole, and tap it with your hammer. You only want to get the roll pin started, not driven in on one hit. Once the pin has started, let go with the pliers and pick up a drift punch. Now place the punch against the pin and tap it into place. If you try to beat the pin in or drive it in with the first blow, you'll almost certainly bend or break the tab (or if you're really unlucky, both tabs) and then have a mess.

A busted tab on a lower is a real problem: as the serial-numbered part, it is the firearm according to federal law. Some locales might not want you buying a new AR. Even if you do somehow manage to acquire a new lower with the same serial number as the old, you still have to get it into Kaliforniastan, or wherever else you live. Be gentle; do it right.

Some fill the gap behind the trigger guard with a foam earplug. Perhaps not the most elegant solution, but earplugs are not expensive. You can even stuff the plug in, then shave it flush to make it perhaps a bit less fugly. To make a

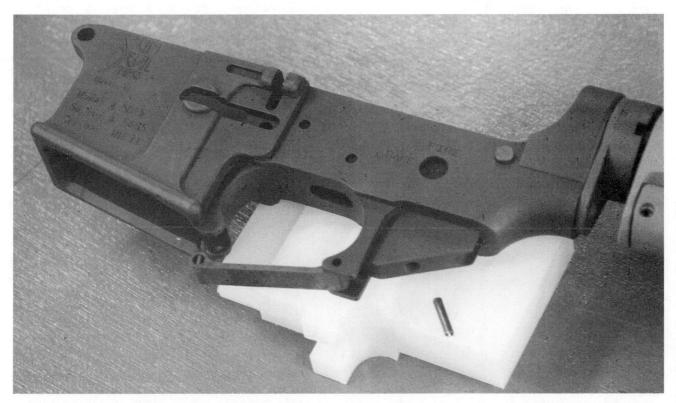

Here the Cross Tac block is being used to hold the receiver while I drive the trigger guard pin in place.

triggerguard large enough to fit a gloved hand, but not have it hinge, Magpul makes the MIAD (a pistol grip assembled from components) and other makers offer trigger guards that are bowed down in the middle. If winter use is an issue, these guards can easily be installed. Remove the old roll pin, and press the locking plunger to remove the old trigger guard. Install the new one as you would a standard guard.

Sharp Edges

Me, I have a different problem. The gap doesn't bother me, but the sharp edge on the outside of the trigger guard does. My shooting grip is a product of the earliest days of IPSC shooting when we were experimenting with grips. I wrangle my hand very high onto the pistol grip, angled so my trigger finger actually reaches down to the trigger. As a result, the edge of the trigger guard, if sharp, can abrade the side of my second finger. So, I simply use a fine-cut file to knock that edge off. A bit of cold blue or a Sharpie pen, and I'm done.

If I've had to do it to a painted AR, then I simply match the paint color as closely as I can and give a spritz.

Fitting the Redi-Mag

The Redi-Mag is a dual mag-well assembly made of sheet steel. It clamps around the lower receiver. On the original design, when you press the magazine release button, both magazines are released. So, to make a quick magazine change, you reach up and grasp both magazines. Press the mag button. Pull both down, shift your hand over to the right, and insert the second magazine. You can drop or pocket the first magazine.

The second model has separate catches for the right and left magazines. So, you press the button to drop the empty magazine, and as you grasp the replacement, your thumb unlocks it from the Redi-Mag.

To install, lower the trigger guard. Press the button on the front of the trigger guard, on the right side, and hinge it down. Carefully spread the Redi-mag clamping "wing." Place the rubber sheeting over your lower, place the Redi-Mag around the lower. The spare magazine part of the Redi-Mag goes on the left side, opposite the ejection port.

Tighten in the screws on the front, trapping the spacer block by passing the screw through it. Now, tightening the screws is not going to be easy. What you'll have to do

The Redi-Mag, ready to go on a rifle.

Once bent and wrapped around the lower (don't forget the rubber sheet insert) you have to press the lips toward each other to start the screws.

Once you've got the threads caught, you can then tighten.

Here is the Redi-Mag, locked on, loaded and ready for business.

is press the wings of the Redi-Mag together enough to get the first screw lined up, through, and catch the threads of the nut. Then, repeat the partial process with the second screw. The screws are not big, but they're plenty big enough to keep the Redi-Mag in place and secure, yet they aren't big enough to close things up. So, squeeze the parts together as you tighten the screw. Once you can't squeeze any more, and the screws won't tighten, you're done.

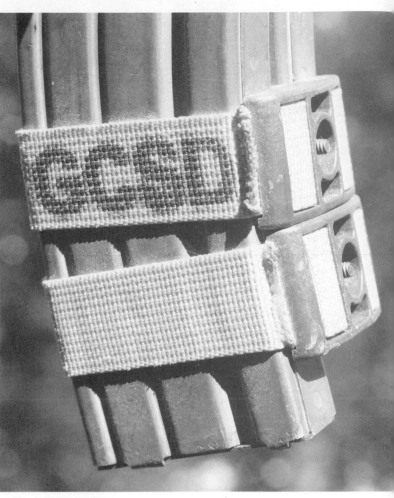

You can always use a coupler to lash two mags together. This one is from MagCinch.

Other Mag Attachment Devices

There are dual-magazine holders that clamp two magazines together. The best of these is the Mag-Cinch. It uses nylon straps and spacers. You must be aware of two things when using the Mag-Cinch or any other dual-magazine holder: 1) The right-hand magazine MUST be held lower than the left-hand magazine. Otherwise, ejecting brass may not clear the right magazine when the left is the one feeding. Also, if they are level, the right magazine may strike the ejection port cover when you're inserting the left magazine, preventing the assembly from locking in place; 2) The top round in the non-feeding magazine may shift forward during firing. If it does, and you don't notice it, it can cause a feeding/reloading malfunction.

The solution to that is simple: when you go to insert the second magazine, you simply roll it in place. That way, the act of inserting the magazine will press the shifted round back into the magazine, and not be a hindrance in loading.

Check the fit of magazines, and if they work fine, paint the screw heads and call it a day. If the magazines don't work as they are supposed to, you've probably pinched something. Check your work, and remove and re-install if needed.

Chapter Fifteen

STOCKS

The stock allows for accurate aiming. Without a stock, a rifle is simply a large, awkward handgun. (The AR-15 can be assembled lawfully as a handgun. However, it is still an awkward handgun, and one that has peculiar legal strictures as to the accessories it can use.) Stock assemblies and lowers are interchangeable, within the limits of fit between various manufacturers. That is, a carbine lower can be fitted with a rifle-barrel configuration upper, and vice-versa, and both combinations will function normally.

Functions

The stock contains the buffer tube, and the stock or stock plate also restrains the rear takedown pin spring from exiting the rear of the rifle. The buffer tube itself also restrains the buffer retainer and spring, as the buffer tube screws forward far enough to capture the retainer and spring. The original M-16A1 and Colt SP1 stocks were made of a plastic not as durable as that formulated for the A2. However, the A2 was made 5/8" longer than the A1, and that creates a problem for some shooters: the stock can be too long. (The original plan was to make the A2 stock in two lengths: the longer one, which the USMC desired for marksmanship reasons, and one the same length as the original A1 stock, for shorter soldiers. However, the line-item for the shorter version of the stock never made it into the paperwork of the proposal, and thus was never approved or adopted.)

The A1 stock, despite it being "less fragile" than the new ones, is sturdy enough for many uses. It is, however, still too long for many shooters, especially if they have to wrestle it out of car racks, or use it while wearing body armor. Thus, telescoping stocks are very useful for use in a defensive situation.

Fixed-Stock Parts

The fixed stock, either A1 or A2, has a pair of screws in the buttplate. The bottom one attaches to the sling swivel. The top one secures the buttstock to the buffer

(Left) If you don't bevel your tele-stock, when you retract the charging handle (especially with the muzzle down) you risk short-stroking the handle.

The fixed stock is attached to the buffer tube by the top screw. The bottom one only holds the sling swivel in place.

tube. The top screw should have a small hole running the length of its axis. This is a drain hole. If the rifle is submerged, it allows trapped water to drain from the buffer tube. Water is what is known in engineering circles as an "incompressible medium." A scuba tank is only a couple of cubic feet in size, but it holds 80 cubic feet of air. Air compresses. If the scuba tank were filled with water, once it was full, no amount of additional pressure would allow the entry of any more water into the tank. Attempting to add more water would increase the pressure, but not put more water into the bottle. Once the pressure rose high enough, the bottle will break.

If the buffer tube has water in it, when the rifle is fired the buffer moves rearward but the water cannot be compressed. If it can't escape fast enough, the buffer will be stopped. The rifle will short-stroke. With enough water present, something might break. The hole in the screw allows water to drain out. (High-speed video of water-testing rifles will show water jetting out through the drain

Carbines have the drain hole, too. Here you can see both the drain hole and the thickness of the end of the tube.

holes for the first few shots. That is residual water not drained, but not providing enough resistance to prevent the rifle cycling when fired.)

You probably won't do much wading through rice paddies, or (at least we hope) won't have to be shooting after falling off a boat or wading ashore, but your rifles should still have the "thru-hole" stock screws.

Replacement

There are two reasons to replace a fixed stock: to install a shorter (from A2 to A1) or to replace the fixed with a telescoping stock. Considering the durability of the fixed stock, it is hard to imagine needing to replace a damaged fixed stock, where the damage didn't also damage part of the rifle.

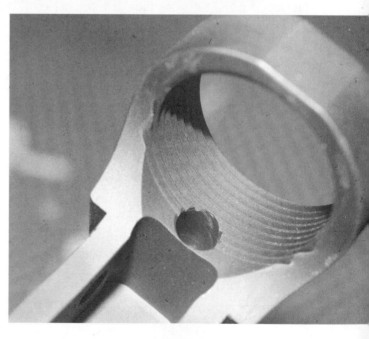

Here you can clearly see the stripped lower, with the buffer tube threads and the buffer retainer hole.

If you are changing from an A2 to an A1, or vice-versa, you'll only need the stock, proper stock screw and filler block. If you are changing form a fixed stock to a tele-stock, you'll need all the new parts from the receiver ring back.

Rifle

Unscrew the top screw in the buttplate. Pull the stock off. Note inside the A2 stock there will be a cylindrical spacer, to fill the gap between the A1 tube and the A2 stock. If you are installing an A1 stock, you will not need the spacer. Also note, the A2 stock screw is longer

Here you see the buffer retainer correctly contained by the buffer tube lip.

than that of the A1. DO NOT use the longer A2 screw to install the A1 stock. Doing so will cause the screw to protrude into the buffer tube, where it may be struck by the buffer and the tube damaged. At the very least the felt recoil will be harsher. At worst, the impact may damage the buffer tube, it will damage the buffer weight, and it may even cause the buffer weight to break, spilling the internal weights into the buffer tube. Generally speaking, parsimony here can lead to an expensive mess to clean up later.

When you lift the stock off, look at the rear of the receiver, where you'll see a small spring protruding, under the buffer tube and on the right. Don't lose that spring. It pushes the detent that keeps the rear takedown pin in place. It is best to pull it out and set it aside to prevent its loss, then re-install it on final assembly.

When installing the new stock, put the small spring back just before you push the stock firmly against the receiver, and then tighten the top buttplate screw.

The rear takedown pin retainer spring, uncovered when you lift the loosened rifle stock.

Assembling a Bare Receiver

You may have occasion (or the urge, or just the curiosity) to build-up a bare receiver from parts. The only lower receiver internals that need be installed when you install the buttstock are the buffer retainer and spring, and the rear takedown pin, detent and spring.

Rifle Stocks

Take the buffer tube and screw it in to the rear of the receiver, to check fit. It should screw in without undue effort. Rifle tubes should snug down flush and evenly. Tele-stock tubes should screw in so the lower fin is straight down and the edge of the tube does not protrude past the front (muzzle end) ring on the receiver. Now back the buffer tube out far enough to clear the buffer spring retainer hole. (That is the one inside the loop, drilled down through the threads.) Place the retainer spring and retainer in the hole. Press them down with the thumb of one hand while screwing the buffer tube in with the other. On rifle tubes the buffer tube shoulder stops against the rear face of the receiver when it is fully installed. Check to make sure the buffer retainer is captured, but stands above the inner diameter of the buffer tube.

Grasp the receiver around the buffer tube ring with one hand, and with your other hand grasp the buffer tube close to the receiver. By hand, tighten the tube as much as possible. The rear of the tube has a square boss, a place for a wrench to tighten the tube. However, hand-wringing the tube on as tightly as possible is sufficient to keep it in place for rifles. Also, the tube is long and hollow, and a wrench provides too much potential leverage. It is too easy to bend the tube or break the receiver, using leverage to over-tighten it.

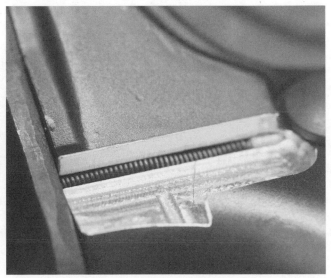

Here you can see the plunger and spring, holding the rear takedown pin in place.

Place the rear takedown pin in the receiver and insert the detent and spring from the rear. Push on the spring just enough to push the detent all the way forward, and move the takedown pin until it is clear the detent is in the slot. Stand the lower on the front on the bench. Slide the buttstock over the tube. (If installing an A2 stock, place the filler cylinder on the end of the tube before placing the stock on.) Slide the buttstock down until it compresses the rear takedown spring, make sure as you press the buttstock in place that the spring is not bent or kinked, but is cleanly compressed into the hole.

Once the stock is flush to the receiver, insert the screw and tighten it. The screw should have a small amount of thread-locking compound already on it. That keeps the screw from working loose when the rifle vibrates from firing. If it lacks that, use a dab or ring of paint around the screw head. Do not apply Loctite to the screw. If you use too much you will have no means of removing the Loctite to take the stock off short of destroying some components of the stock itself.

Carbine

Carbine stocks are those that have a sliding buttstock section, one that allows for several lengths for the shooter. The main problem with the A2 stock is that it is too long. It was designed (for the most part) as a competition stock: with the proper length for someone is a shirt or light jacket, when firing prone or in classic bullseye offhand. For small-statured shooters, or barrel-chested shooters, or those of you wearing body armor, it can be too long. (We

have had instances in the LEO classes where otherwise competent officers were unable to fire a passing score, solely due to the length of the A2 stock. When the A2 stock was exchanged for a tele-stock and adjusted to the proper length, they passed the qualification course easily.)

If you can put up with the slightly greater bulk and length, a rifle stock is less expensive, more durable and entirely acceptable. If you need the adjustments or have to have the fashion, get the tele-stock. I have to confess: I own two ARs with fixed stocks.

Tele-Stock Styles

The original stock was the XM-177. It had a shiny vinyl-coated buttstock, with a sling loop on the top, and only two positions: open or closed. Later "177" stocks were made of polymer. The two-position stock had only "In" and "Out" as settings, which seemed sufficient at the time. However, that proved to be incorrect. Over time, the lower rail, or "spine," gained more stops, until now it is possible to get stocks with six or even seven stops.

The M4 stock deleted the top-mount sling loop. That loop was too often broken in rough handling. (Rather than reinforce it, designers simply removed it.) The M4 stock also gained additional fairings under the curve of the stock, to aid somewhat in a proper cheek weld. While most carbines seen in Iraq and Afghanistan have M4 stocks, a lot of XM-177 style stocks were still in inventory, especially in the Air Force. They show up now and then in photographs from the war zone.

The newest stocks are those with a wedge-shaped

Here you see the result of doing tactical clearance drills with an XM-177 style stock. The impact of the butt hitting the ground broke off the sling loop.

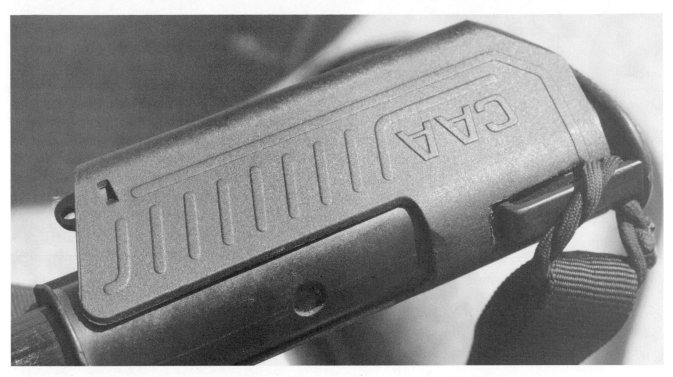

The Command Arms adapter works well to convert old stocks to the more-comfortable design.

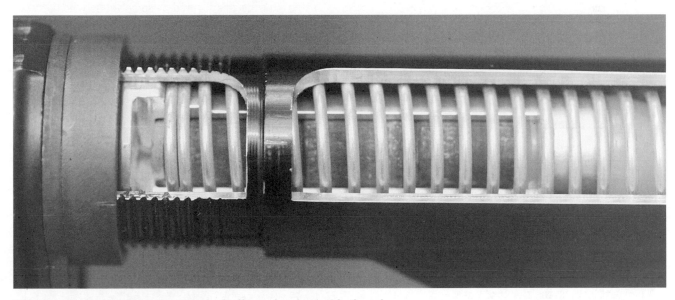

Here is a cutaway carbine, showing the buffer and spring inside the tube.

cross-section. The added material provides a solid cheek weld, and also storage for batteries, an item without which no modern law enforcement or military organization can function.

Command Arms makes a saddle-shaped battery compartment that can be secured to XM-177 or some M4 stocks to provide both battery storage and a good cheek weld. The CAA saddle, at $20, is an extremely useful and cost-effective upgrade to an existing stock, rather than spending the $75+ a replacement buttstock alone can cost. (A tube, buffer, spring and battery-holding new assembly can run $100+.) The CAA saddle also does not care if you have a mil-spec or commercial buffer tube. However, if the

widening ribs under the M4 stock top are too wide, you cannot get the CAA add-on to fit.

Mil-spec vs. Non-Spec Tubes

The buffer tubes of telescoping stocks come in two sizes, one particular, the other general: mil-spec and all the rest. The difference comes from the method of fabrication. The mil-spec tubes are made from forgings. The heated aluminum bars are pounded via large hydraulic presses into the general shape of the buffer tube. (By comparison, the cylindrical rifle buffer tube can be lathe-turned on automatic lathes at an impressive rate.)

The forging is then bored out for the buffer and spring,

reamed to final I.D. and has the forward portion lathe-turned and threaded. (As part of the boring and reaming operations.) Then the rail and cylindrical portion are profiled. Since the rail (or "spine" the slider latches into, and slides along) cannot be turned on a lathe, the profile of the rail and tube are machined in two passes; the part is laid horizontally, and a cutter shaped like that side of the tube is run the length of the soon-to-be-stock tube. Two passes, one on each side, and the tube is done, except for the bottom slot and stock stop holes.

As a forging, the buffer tube is made of 7075-T6 aluminum. When the AR-15/M-15 was being developed, it was meant to be as light as possible. (The first rifles were barely six pounds, the first carbines, five and a half.) So the tube was made as thin as possible and still be strong enough. The sidewalls of the tube are actually machined below the tops of the threads turned on its front. If you look closely at a mil-spec tube, the step down from the thread tops becomes obvious.

Commercial tubes are usually made from 6061 aluminum. As the 6061 is not quite as strong as the 7075-T5, it makes sense to make the sidewall a little thicker. It also makes the machine operation less difficult, and a bit faster. Commercial buffer tubes are machined from bar stock. Thus making the part a bit less expensive. As a result, the outer diameter of the cylindrical portion of a commercial tube is larger than that of a mil-spec tube. As there is no "commercial spec" for the diameter, each manufacturer is free to use whatever dimension works for them.

Internally, they are the same: a nominal one inch in diameter – which makes sense, as there is no alternate standard for spring and buffers. If someone thought they could make a carbine tube less-expensive by making it smaller, they'd run into real problems when the spring and buffer wouldn't fit.

The short form is: the stocks of mil-spec tubes are interchangeable. You can order a new buttstock for a tele-stock, if it has a mil-spec tube, and be sure it will fit. If, however, the tube is a commercial tube, you may or may not be sure a replacement stock will fit unless it is ordered from the same maker as the tube. Since the tube makers do not mark their products (except for the mil-spec ones) then you have no way of knowing.

The makers of mil-spec tubes (as of this writing) are Colt, Stag/CMT, LMT, Vltor. The nominal diameter of the cylindrical portion of a mil-spec tube is 1.140". The commercial tube is roughly (each manufacturer does as he wishes) 1.170". If you have a commercial tube on a carbine, be aware that not all replacement "commercial" sliders will fit properly. Some will be tight, some loose, and some won't

go on at all. And no mil-spec slider will have any chance at all of fitting.

Tele-Stock Installation

Parts and tools: You'll need all the parts from the receiver back: the new stock, tube, buffer weight and spring. You may need a wrench to take the old tube off. You'll need a carbine wrench to tighten the new buffer tube castle nut. You'll also need a staking punch and hammer. If you want to install a single-point sling plate, now is the time.

If you are changing from a fixed stock to a tele-stock, you first must remove the old stock and buffer tube. Unscrew the top buttplate screw. Pull the stock off. Set the rear takedown pin spring aside. Press the buffer retainer down with a small screwdriver or knifepoint, and ease the buffer out. Once it has cleared the retainer, grasp the buffer and spring and pull them out of the tube. Set them aside. (You will use the takedown spring, buffer retainer and retainer spring with the new stock. You will not use the old buffer and spring with the new stock.)

If the old tube was secured by some yahoo who used thread-locking compound, you may have to use penetrating oil and/or heat to break the bond. Be careful, as the threaded loop of the receiver is thin and overheating it will damage it.

Place a thumb over the retainer and begin turning the buffer tube. Unscrew the old tube. When the tube clears the buffer retainer, the retainer will come free. Set it aside. Once unscrewed, place the buffer tube, stock and stock spring (and cylindrical filler, if A2) in a box or bag, labeled and complete.

You have to hold the buffer retainer and its spring down as you screw the tube on, until the tube holds the retainer in place.

If you are building from a bare lower receiver, begin here.

Pull the new buffer and spring out of the buffer tube. Set them aside, you'll be using them in the final steps. The lower is commonly shipped with the backplate and castle nut reversed. Unscrew the castle nut (so called because of the notches cut into it) and pull the backplate off. Compress the stock latch and slide the stock all the way open. You want to work on the stock, starting with a bare tube. So grab the stock latch and pull it away from the slider. You will then be able to remove the buttstock off of the buffer tube.

Take a moment to check the fit of the tube threads to the receiver. It should screw in smoothly, without binding or catching.

Take the castle nut and spin it onto the buffer tube. The large notches go toward the buttplate (or where it will be once again) and the small notches go towards the receiver, or open end of the tube. Rotate it as far back as it will go without forcing it. Slide the retaining plate onto the tube. The ring goes around the tube, and the bottom of the oval retainer has a stamped or machined, raised circle on it. The raised portion goes towards the receiver. The retainer does not screw onto the tube, it slides. It is guided by the slot in the bottom of the tube through the threads, using the raised "key" in the ring of the retainer. Press the retainer all the way back to the castle nut.

For the next step, the process is the same as that of the rifle buffer tube: insert the buffer retainer spring and retainer in the receiver hole and screw the buffer tube on. (The retaining plate turns with the buffer tube, both when screwing the buffer tube in and later, when you're taking it

The parts are usually shipped assembled wrong, to keep them from getting lost. Re-install them correctly, as seen here.

On the telestock, the retaining plate contains the takedown plunger spring.

Here is a tube installed incorrectly. It was not screwed in far enough to trap the buffer retainer, which has escaped into the lower and caused mischief.

off.) However, at the end, you will have to judge the proper tube location. Unlike the rifle tube, the carbine buffer tube does not have a shoulder on it. You will have to rotate the carbine tube until it properly meets two criteria: 1) It locks the buffer retainer in the hole, without binding it or trapping it down in the hole; and by design 2) does not go so far through the lower receiver ring that the buffer tube lip interferes with the upper receiver as it closes.

The best carbine buffer tubes have the top edge of the tube machined back, so you have room to lock down the buffer retainer while still clearing the upper receiver as it closes.

The top edge of the ring of the lower is your guide and adjustment area to the fit of the tube. Screw the tube in until it properly traps the buffer retainer and the rib is straight down. Then look at the top edge. If it is past the lower's ring you have two options. You can unscrew the tube one turn. However, that may allow the buffer retainer to escape, in which case, your second choice is to mark the tube, or measure it for excess protrusion. Then remove it and file the top edge of the tube to provide clearance. (A third option is to send it back with a note on how it didn't match up. However, all tubes from that particular manufacturer are likely to provide the same problem.)

As with so many aspects of the AR, in the old days

we had a lot of problems with buffer tube fit. It wasn't uncommon for half of the carbines that came through the door as parts kits to have fitting problems here. On some, I filed the top of the tube to clear the upper receiver. On others, I filed a semi-circular notch to provide clearance for the buffer retainer. Today, the lower makers and the tube makers pay a lot more attention to "clocking" the threads on their parts.

With the buffer retainer captured and the tube clearing the upper (you can temporarily install the upper as a fit-check) install the rear takedown pin, detent and spring. Put the front edge of the lower against the bench top, and press the retaining plate from the castle nut, down to the receiver. Use it to compress (but not bend or kink) the rear takedown pin spring. Once it is flush to the receiver, spin the castle nut down to it. Tighten the nut by hand.

Hold up the receiver and check the position of the buffer tube. The rail should be directly below the receiver, and vertical. If you have a question you can slip the buttstock on and take a look.

With the tube on and rail properly indexed, you can take two tacks to tightening the castle nut: clamp the tube in a padded vise, or enlist the aid of an assistant. When you clamp it, tilt the tube slightly until the rail binds against the left side (viewed from the shooter's position) of the

An un-staked castle nut is an invitation for it to loosen and create problems.

Here is a good, thorough staking job, one that will not come loose until you want it to.

Ooops, wrong way. Here, the castle nut is on backwards. The wrench can't tighten, and any staking would be pointless. Take it apart and do it over again.

vise jaws. Take the castle nut wrench (also known as the carbine buffer tube wrench) and tighten the castle nut. The castle nut is subject to a great deal of vibration, and the temptation is to not only make it "very tight" but to gild the lily. Avoid gilding (otherwise known as Loctite).

If you enlist the aid of an assistant, lay the receiver down on its side, with the tube sticking out off the bench. Put it on its left side, so the pistol grip acts as a stop to keep the receiver from rotating as you tighten. Have your assistant lean on the receiver while you tighten the castle nut.

Now check the stock alignment by eye. Turn the receiver upside down and look to see that the stock is vertical with the magazine well. If the stock tilts you'll have to loosen, re-align and tighten again.

Tighten the nut as much as possible using only the leverage of the wrench. Do not add length via a "breaker bar" as that will provide too much leverage and risk damaging or breaking the receiver. Once the nut is tight, take your spring-loaded punch and apply it to the edge of the retaining plate, at one of the small notches. The mil-spec method is to stake, not Loctite. Stake the retaining plate into the notch of the castle nut.

In some very limited circumstances, we may have to break the no-Loctite rule. Some retaining plates are made as sling swivel locations for single-point slings. Some of those plates are made of steel that is far too hard to stake.

Then, and only then, do you Loctite.

Re-install the buttstock. You'll need to pull the latch away from the slider body, to clear the lip of the rail. Press the buffer spring into the tube. Then press the buffer in, until it rides past the buffer retainer and is held in place.

Install the upper.

Stock Travel

The stock on a tele-stock used to be considered just a storage option. To shoot, you'd extend the stock. In military use, the adoption of body armor has made extended stock length not possible. However, not all of us wear body armor to leave the house. (If you must, to live in your city, my suggestion is to move.) If the stock is fully forward and you try to shoot without extending the stock, you may well slam the rear sight assembly into your face or eye. Trust me, this is a bad thing. To prevent that, select the shortest stock length that will allow shouldering the stock without striking your face. Usually, that is the first stop out from fully-closed. Wrap the buffer tube with electrical tape to prevent the stock closing any more than that.

Me, I reflexively extend the stock any time I pick up a rifle, and so I don't worry about it. But if you have not made your habits so ingrained, you might think about it.

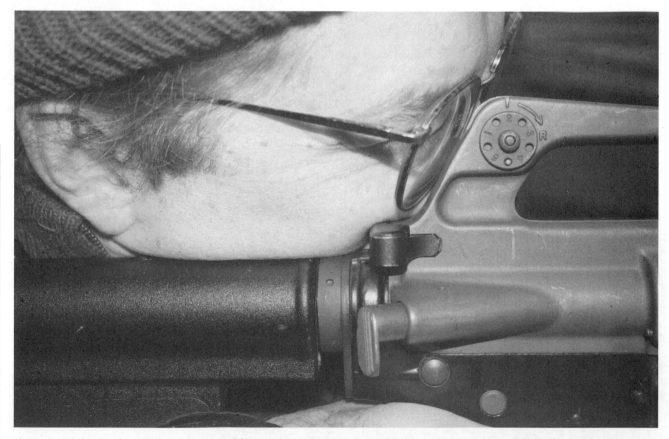

If you crawl the stock, you may have a problem with a tele-stock. In such a case as this, it is prudent to lock the stock out of full forward travel.

Clearance Check

The last check in tele-stock installation is the clearance between the charging handle and the buttstock. Some moulded stock bodies have a raised lip around the front of the buffer tube opening. When fully closed or fully open, the stock will probably not interfere with the charging handle. The charging handle has some play in its fit to the upper. As it is drawn back, it can be lifted or depressed a certain amount. The exact amount differs between various uppers and their charging handles. At the closed position, the handle can't depress enough to hit the stock. At the fully-open stock-length position, the handle may well not reach to the front lip of the slider. However, in between those settings the charging handle can strike the edge of the stock, if the stock lip is too high or the charging handle has too much play in its fit. (Also, if you install a "Gas-buster" charging handle, with the extra lip on the bottom to divert gas, you make the overlap potentially worse.) When there is contact, the operator may well think the handle has been drawn back its full distance, and let go. (The impact may even cause the shooter to lose their grip on the handle, letting it go forward.)

If the handle strikes the stock, the rifle will not be charged. The bolt will not have gone back far enough to strip a round off the magazine, thus leaving the chamber empty. Or worse, the handle goes back just far enough to let the top round tip and then creates a bolt-over-base failure to feed.

The solution is to use a large file, or a belt sander, and bevel the leading upper edge of the stock at the buffer tube hole. (With the slider off the buffer tube, to prevent marring.) Angle down and forward from the top to the buffer tube, so if the charging handle strikes the stock lip, the angle you have filed causes the handle to ride up and over the stock.

Telestock Removal

In the event you need to remove the stock, either to install another or to replace a damaged stock, the staking you so carefully applied will prove troublesome. If the staking is only lightly done, you can clamp the tube (not the receiver) in a padded vise and simply torque the castle nut through the staking. If the staking is heavy, then a dremel tool is the answer. Use a cut-off wheel or grinding wheel and grind off the staked portion of the castle nut and retainer plate. Yes, you'll destroy the nut, and perhaps the plate. But they aren't that expensive. Wrecking the buffer tube is much more expensive, and wrecking the lower receiver (which is what you'll do if you clamp it

The top leading edge of your tele-stock can cause problems, if you don't bevel it to prevent charging-handle impact.

In extreme cases, you may have to do some cutting to remove the old stock.

instead of the buffer tube) is very expensive.

With the staked area ground off, unscrew the castle nut and then the buffer tube. Before you rotate the buffer tube to take it off, pry the retainer plate away from the receiver. Remember, the retainer plate has a recess that locks into the lower receiver. If you try to turn the buffer tube without pulling the plate away from the receiver, the key in the retainer plate will stay in place on the back of the receiver. The centering key on the retaining plate will gouge the threads of the buffer tube. With care, you can wrestle the stock off and still salvage the buffer tube, and even sometimes the retaining plate. Compared to the inexpensive castle nut you had to cut, the buffer tube is relatively costly. If you take care, you can clean the threads and re-use the tube.

MAGAZINES

Why a chapter on magazines in a gunsmithing manual devoted to working on the AR-15/M-16 rifle?

Simple: A repeating rifle without a magazine is a single-shot, and the AR is particularly difficult to use as a single shot. It is also not well-suited for use as a club. The AR magazines come in a variety of capacities (1, 5, 10, 20, 30, 40 and 48 rounds) and materials (aluminum, steel, plastic) and the differences do matter.

Selection

First, capacity. There are single-shot magazines that are meant for long-range target competition, where the cartridges are loaded one at a time as the shooter shoots for record. As the long-range shooters fire 20 rounds in 20 minutes, single-loading is not a hindrance. Also, they may well have loaded their ammo to such an overall length that the rounds simply won't feed through a magazine Five-shot magazines are meant for hunting. There are some few 10-shot magazines available but they are meant for use in jurisdictions where anything larger in capacity is prohibited. The five- and 10-shot magazines are the same size as, and usually constructed from, the shells of 20-shot magazines.

Twenty-shot magazines are the original design, issued when the M-16 was brand new. They are compact, sturdy and amazingly reliable for being shells of aluminum. The design of the feed lips was derived from the magazines of the M-14, which was designed, tuned and refined over more than a decade. The M-14 magazines hardly ever wear out, and the AR-15 20-round magazines are almost as durable. The "20" AR mags do not evidence the feeding peculiarities that some 30-round magazines can show. They are common and inexpensive. They are compact in a pocket,

Here you can clearly see the straight-curved design of the magazine. The design is a kludge, but one we've managed to make work well now for almost five decades.

You can't have too many magazines. You can't have unreliable magazines. This is a carton of Fusil magazines being tested. Each is numbered and tracked.

on the belt, or in the rifle. Twenty rounds is a lot of rifle ammunition in a law enforcement or non-military defensive situation. For the military it wasn't enough, which led to the development of the 30-round magazine. (The military also has troopers packing 6-8-10 magazines on their gear, with extra loaded magazines in the vehicles. I've talked to vets from Iraq who commonly exited their vehicles packing twenty 30-round magazines, between the vest load and the extras bag they grabbed as they jumped out of the Humvee.)

Thirty-round magazines are composed of two co-joined tubes: a curved section and a straight section. Due to the "on-again, off-again" early history of the Colt M-16, each production batch was essentially hand-built. (The earliest M-16s were bought for the Air Force. Colt delivered the contract, then had to set up the tooling again for the next order. And so on, until official adoption and full-scale production.) While the early Colts would all take 20-round

magazines, not all rifles they had made would accept a properly-designed 30-round magazine: that is, one with a constant curve to its shell, top to bottom. Rather than admit to the government that some of the rifles they'd just recently been sold couldn't take the newly-requested magazines, Colt designed the 30-round magazine to be straight on the top and curved below the receiver. They hurried the design and put it into production for the Vietnam War. Once fielded it was years before anyone looked into the matter again.

The 30-round magazines have been made to a much higher standard lately (within the last 10 years or so) and many of the current ones are far from the "jam-a-matic" standards of the old ones. The best USGI mags, CProducts, Okay Industries and Brownells, come with the latest enhancements: an anti-tilt follower and a chrome-silicon alloy spring. They are also manufactured to higher quality standards than older magazines.

The left-hand 20-round magazine has worn through all five coating layers, and still works. The middle one has only worn through two. The right-hand mag is brand new. They all work. I know, because I tested them.

Composition

Magazines come in three materials: aluminum, steel and plastic. Aluminum is the original and is still a good choice. Kept clean and away from abusive experiences, aluminum magazines will last a long time. Steel magazines come in five types: USA-brand magazines, British/Singapore, CProducts, Fusil USA and the HK HRM. USA-brand magazines are made from steel that is not heat-treated after shaping. The feed lips lose their shape, the magazines feed unreliably after that, and bending them back does no good. Avoid them. They can be identified by their bright blue finish, like that of old-time revolvers. The British/Singapore magazines are usually good. Those that are reliable will usually remain so. Those that aren't will soon reveal themselves and can be discarded. They do, however, rust. They are commonly either brushed-blue steel or parkerized, the latter a rough-texture gray/green or black color. Alone of the "surplus" magazines, the British/Singapore magazines are worth rebuilding.

CProducts magazines are made from heat-treated stainless steel. They resist corrosion. We have tested them by standing on a loaded magazine and repeatedly dropping a loaded magazine on the feed lips. We even parked a small SUV (Isuzu Trooper) loaded with gear on one. It not only survived, but fed flawlessly. The HK HRM (High Reliability Magazine) came about from the British government throwing its hands up over the wretched SA-80 rifle. Fed up with unreliable magazines, the Brits handed the rifles and a big cheque to HK, to make it all work. One of the things HK did was to make the magazines far more reliable, and soon after just made new ones themselves instead of overhauling the old British mags. You can recognize the HK mags by the HK logo and the price tag: two to three times what an aluminum AR mag runs.

Fusil mags are all-steel, and properly designed to fit, feed and function. They are made in the US, and those we have tested have proven durable and reliable. One thing to note about steel mags is that the CProducts, Brit and Fusil mags take standard followers and springs, so you can rebuild

Stomping this CProducts magazine did nothing to effect its reliability.

You should be so lucky as to find cartons of brand-new 20 round magazines, sitting on a shelf. If you do, snap them up.

This PMag 30 is getting stomped with all of my 235 pounds (25 of that is gear, thank you very much). It survived with a few scratches and works fine to this day.

Mark your mags! That way you'll be sure the ones you get back at the end of a match, or class, are yours.

them if you want. The USA mags are not worth the effort, and the HK uses non-standard (but engineered to German specifications) springs and followers.

Steel magazines, while durable, have a shortcoming that cannot be avoided: weight. If you do plan on having a full-up tactical vest, ready for the zombies or The End Of The World As We Know It, that vest will be a couple of pounds heavier due to the steel.

All-polymer magazines come in three ages. The earliest (made by Eaton) are made of a brittle polymer, usually a smoke-color and/or slightly translucent, and are useful only as training magazines until they break. I have an Easton that has lasted 20+ years, but it is the last of a bunch I started with. The second are Orlite and the Thermold magazines. The Orlites hail from Israel, and while useful, they have a severe problem: they were made from two different moulds, and those from one of the moulds won't fit many non-Colt rifles. The magazine body has a rib around it to fit against the opening of the mag well. The rib was meant to keep out dust. However, the Israeli maker made the rib fit Colt rifles. Many other rifles will not accept the Orlites, as the rib is too high and thick for those other rifles. Best to keep these as training magazines, too.

The Thermolds come from Canada. While better-fitting than the Orlites, the Thermolds apparently were just a bit prone to failing when in a hot weapon, thus gaining them the Canadian nickname of "Thermelts." They are decent training magazines but should not be used as duty/defensive magazines.

Last of the all-polymers is the Magpul P-Mag30. It has been manufactured with all the shortcomings of earlier magazines designed out, and it is cheap, reliable, dependable and corrosion-proof. Some very early pre-production and production mags will not drop free of their own weight from some few rifles. That is more a training matter than a functional matter. And Magpul is very good about exchanging old mags for new, if the old ones are in any way defective. The PMag30 covers are to be used only in storage, when storing loaded magazines. The latest generation of PMags have "fitting pads" on them. If your rifle is a tight fit, you can sand/file the fitting pads to allow more clearance for the mags. Do not do this as a routine, but only if you have a particular rifle that the PMags are a tight fit in. Magpul has also begun making 20-round Pmags, for those who want the compact size of the shorter mags.

A composite magazine, the Lancer L5, is a magazine with steel inserts to reinforce the feed lips but a polymer (and translucent) smoke-colored body. You can see how many rounds remain. Also, Lancer makes a 48-round

Accurate. Deadly.

A really harsh test is full-auto. Of course, it is beyond extravagant to spend $12,000 on a select-fire AR just to "properly" test magazines.

magazine, where they have an aluminum clamshell that clamps two tubes together. While it can be useful in competition (at least, where it is allowed) it is not something you'd want in a defensive rifle.

Inspection

Magazines should be inspected regularly, as well as the ammunition in them. Inspect the top rounds for corrosion. If using softpoints, check to see if the tips have "riveted," that is, the soft exposed lead has banged against the front wall of the magazine until it has upset into a mushroom-shaped head. Such bullets will not feed, and must be removed from the magazine and disposed of. Check for accumulated lint, dust, fabric and other debris, and if present, remove them.

Check the feed lips. Are they smooth and straight? Are the rear sections free of cracks?

Check the magazine floorplate. Are the ribs intact? If they have some sort of "pull-cord" or other aid to extract them from a mag pouch, is it secure?

It is prudent for you to mark your magazines in some way. Cities do it: departmental property must be tracked and personal magazines (if that is departmental policy) kept out of the supply system. Ideally, magazines would be tracked both as individual items, and issued-with-a-rifle items. Adhesive property tags work, as long as the tags are not applied where they will interfere with insertion into the rifle. Paint also works. Something as

simple as the last three digits of the rifle serial number, along with an "A through however many" painted stencil code will do. For those of you with personal rifles (and no department to answer to) a simple numbering or letter code system will do. If you want to go to the trouble of testing and "assigning" magazines to a particular rifle, work up whatever code system works for you.

Marked magazines also prevent exchanges of magazines in classes or in matches. Especially with older magazines, a magazine that is 100% reliable in one rifle may not be so reliable in another. Having gone to the trouble to test and verify that the magazines you own work in the rifle or rifles you own, it seems wasteful to then inadvertently trade magazines with someone you met just earlier that day.

How Long Loaded?

The question comes up on a regular basis: how long do loaded magazine remain reliable? The answer is unknown, but I do have some experiences that give us guidelines. First, springs wear from cycles, not compression. As long as a spring has not been stressed past its design limits, it will lose strength directly proportional to the number of times it has been flexed. (The loss of flexion capacity over time is utterly inconsequential on the human scale.) Loading and unloading a magazine to "rest" the springs is actually worse on the springs than leaving a magazine loaded. We have personally seen AR-15 (20-round) magazines left loaded for three years that worked 100% and 1911, Browning Hi-Power and 15-

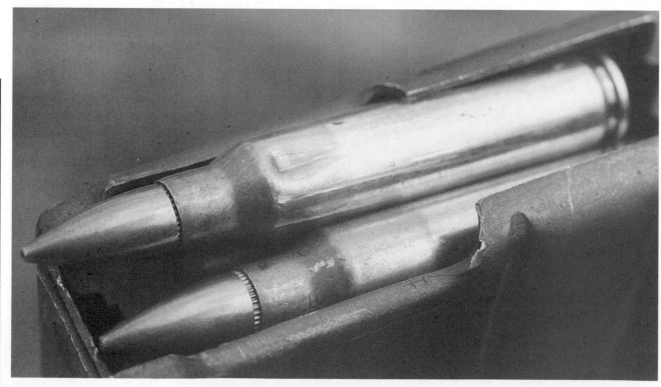

Here is a bolt-over-base failure, indicative of a magazine that could benefit from rebuilding.

Each magazine doesn't cost that much, but get a bunch together and they represent an investment. Once tested and proven, mark them. Here, a $5 paint pen and ten minutes has marked two dozen PMag30s.

round M1 Carbine magazines left loaded for more than 17 years that worked without fail.

The limit is more the ammunition than the magazines. Exposed to heat and cold, condensation from air conditioning and humid days, ammunition kept loaded for defensive use should be rotated every six months just to ensure it isn't crusty, corroded or otherwise unsuited for use.

Fired for practice, qualification and verification of zero and function, magazines compressed and relaxed twice a year will last more than an officer's career. If they are reliable to start with, that is. Ideally, each rifle you own should have a set of magazines assigned to it, and so marked. Then, those magazines should be used in the duty-check before you depend on them for defense. If any prove unreliable, they should be immediately replaced there and then. Kept clean and in good repair, the set you've paired with each rifle will last at least as long as the barrel will, and probably longer. At the current cost of some $11 per magazine, a new set of USGI or other reliable source magazines for each rifle, when that rifle gets a new barrel and bolt, is money well-spent. (The math again for rebuilding a rifle after each 10,000 rounds? Ammunition

cost: $3,000+. Barrel and bolt: $500 at most. Five magazines: $55. Peace of mind: priceless.)

Upgrade/Replacement

Some recommend rebuilding magazines. While it can be prudent to upgrade the internals of some magazines, it isn't always needed. The cost of a new spring, follower and baseplate is about half the cost of a new magazine. The new magazine probably already has the new and improved spring and follower design already installed. If given the choice, buy new, better-quality magazines rather than rebuild old ones. Upgrade kits can be used to enhance the performance of marginal magazines if the problem is spring or follower related. However, if the source of the problem is not merely a weak spring or a cracked or warped follower, but instead bent feed lips or dented tube, installing a new spring and follower won't help much or at all. Rebuilt magazines should be considered training and practice magazines only. In the scheme of things, magazines are cheap, durable, common and easily-replaced. Buy the best and throw them away if they give you any problems. With the exception of the steel

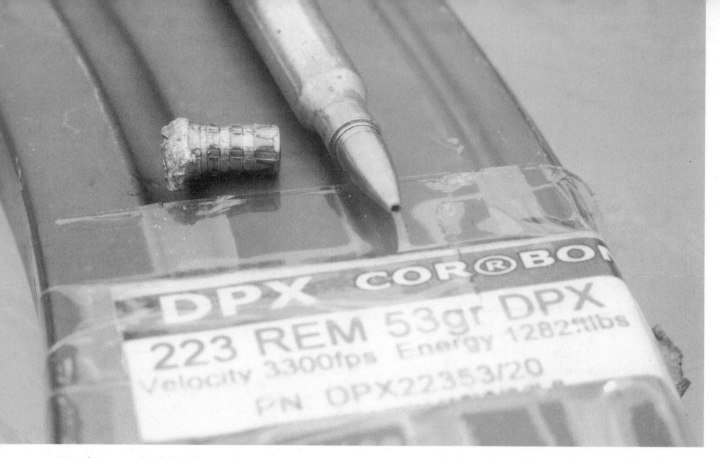

Here is a magazine labeled as to the ammo, ready for use on duty.

magazines of quality, rebuilding AR magazines is usually a waste of time and money.

Testing

The testing for a magazine involves shooting. No amount of simply pushing the follower down with your fingertips will disclose the operational status of a magazine. Before you even get to the range do some testing. Does the magazine insert cleanly into a magazine well? Does it drop free of its own weight when the magazine button is pressed? Does it lock the bolt back when you cycle the action? If it fails in any of those tests, you must determine why. In checking newly-purchased magazines, you should use the rifle you own with the tightest magazine well.

The first step in checking live-fire is to load five rounds only, and fire drills or fire for zero. One common magazine malfunction is a weak or dragging spring, or tilting follower, and they result in a "bolt-over-base failure." The round in a magazine with a weak spring will have risen tilted, nose-up, and the bolt struck it in the case body. The bolt lugs will be driven into and have creased the case. (DO NOT attempt to re-use a round so damaged. Dispose of it safely.)

If a magazine works through a number of iterations of the five-shot test, then test it fully loaded. Load to capacity and fire a five-shot string. Stop, remove the magazine and re-load it to replace the five fired rounds. A weak spring will fail to rise quickly enough, lifting the "stack," and the top round will fail to feed. If the bolt closes in an empty chamber (and the rifle is clean, lubricated and has a tight gas key) then the problem is a weak spring. If the top round is nose-down, with the base pushed by the bolt, and the nose in the feed ramp or magazine body, the follower is tilting.

Weak springs and tilting followers can be replaced, and should be.

If, however, the failures include two rounds being fed at once, or a loose round in the feedway while another is trying to get into the chamber, the feed lips are probably the culprits. Those cannot be fixed with new springs or followers. It is rare to need a source of followers, spring and baseplates, but if you have a magazine with defective feed lips (and you can't return them) then strip out the parts and destroy the tube. If you save the tube, someone, sometime, will attempt to "tune" the feed lips and "restore" reliability. It rarely works, it takes a large amount of time, effort and ammunition to prove that the "fix" has been successfully done (or not done) and the far easier solution is to replace the magazine with a new one.

I love the guys at Brownells like brothers. They offer an AR magazine feed lip tuning tool. If there is anything in the Brownells catalog I would not buy, it would be that. Any magazine I've ever had that had damaged feed lips, I discarded without a moment's thought and didn't miss it.

Then again, I have enough magazines to fill a footlocker, so I can be brutal. However, when it comes to your own safety, you should be, even if you own but two or three magazines.

Magazine Labels

There is no such thing as ammunition that "does it all." You cannot have a barrier-penetrating round that pierces vehicles without it also efficiently piercing buildings. Commonly, a department will issue one type, and officers will have to adapt. However, some departments will issue differing loads for different uses. The entry teams might get more-frangible softpoints or hollowpoints, the highway officers get barrier penetrating rounds and everyone else gets plain old XM-193. Inevitably, people will find themselves in a predicament where they need the other ammo. You, as a non-sworn (not "civilian," as even police officers are civilians) citizen, are not restricted to only type of ammo unless, of course, state law restricts you. Using paint, marking tape, or even the labels off the boxes of the ammo, you can mark your magazines as to their contents. Especially if you have a Redi-mag on your rifle, you can quickly swap from one load to the other.

If you are going to do it, you should be using a consistent marking method. Ideally, the marking system would be visible at night, or the differing loads could be told by touch. One method is to have magazine loaded with the frangible or FMJ load left clean (but painted with departmental identifiers) and the barrier-penetrating ammo in magazines with the end flap of the box taped to it. Even with gloves, the taped-on box flap will make it possible to identify the magazine containing the barrier-penetrating ammo. (Tape the flap onto the magazine below where the magazine enters the receiver.)

Ammo Inspection

While inspecting magazines, also pay attention to the ammunition in them. It is possible for the ammunition to suffer from exposure or rough handling, but the magazines are fine. One thing to check for is to see that bullets with large amounts of lead exposed have not "riveted." The noses bang against the front interior of the magazine tube, and the lead can be bent back. Bent enough, and it will not feed.

Such ammunition should be properly disposed of. While it won't feed from the magazine, you can hand-feed it individually into the chamber to start a practice string. It won't be as consistent as your other ammo, so don't expect it to be on-zero on the 600 yard line. But for a 25 yard drill on paper targets, it will do fine.

Ammo in which the bullet has been set back into the case should not be fired, ever.

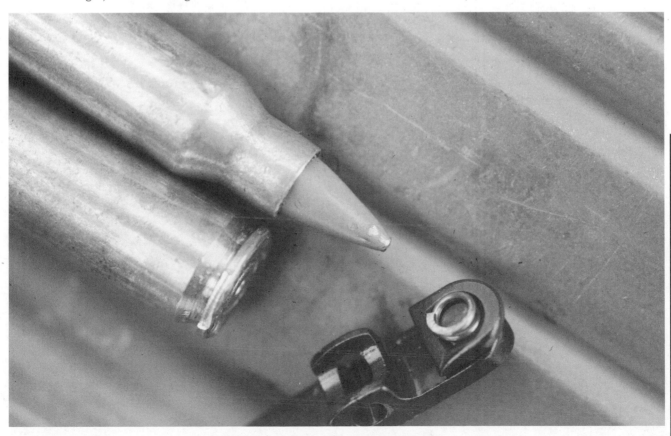

Inspect your ammo. Even a D-Fender isn't going to make this round feed properly.

Chapter Seventeen

SLINGS

No one uses a handgun without a holster. To do so is obviously unsafe. Without a sling, you never really have an option to use both hands and must always keep a hand on the rifle. That, or put it down, which really isn't an option. I had one person argue the point, saying they could put their rifle down for a moment to do an essential task. OK, my reply: you've just arrived in New Orleans after Katrina. Everything is ankle-deep in the most disgusting gunk you've ever seen. Where are you going to put your rifle down, that you'd be willing to pick it up again?

However, a sling is like a holster only in limited ways. It does not cover the triggerguard, and as a result the rifle trigger can be engaged by chance objects, even your own gear. The sling does not secure the rifle to your person like a holster does a handgun. There are no security devices on a sling as there are on Level II and Level III holsters. Rifles should not hang loosely from your person, secured only by the sling, unless you are in the act of carrying someone or some thing, attending medically to a person or holding someone else's rifle. While you wear it, even though you have a sling, you should have your hands on the rifle.

Selection

For non-tactical personal, simpler is better. The plain old military carry strap is better than nothing.

A complicated sling that requires a bit of training and practice is more than anyone needs, when the task is simply to keep the rifle off the ground and away from

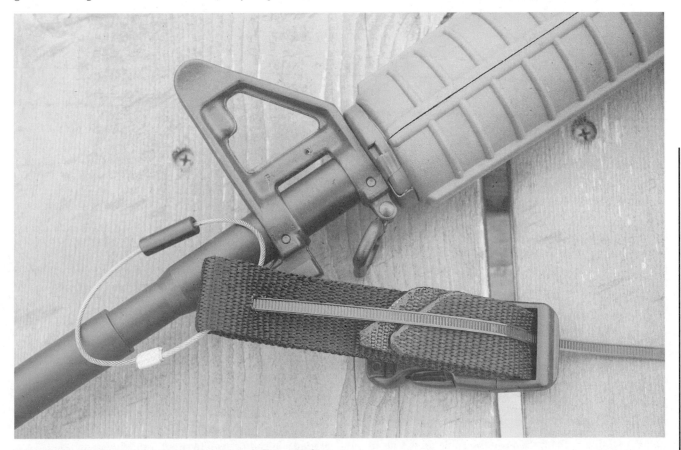

The M-guns Unslinger is a quick and universal sling attachment.

Loop the wire around your gas tube, then run the Unslinger through the loop.

Pull the Unslinger tight, then use the cable tie to snug it down and keep it tight.

A good sling allows you to shoot from either shoulder.

Here is a universal single point attachment plate, on the rear of a carbine.

others. The simplest is a single strap looped from front to back, the Simple Sling. On the front, a coated wire loop or double-wrap of 550 cord, and on the rear a multi-wrap loop of 550 cord are your attachment points.

The wire loop goes through the front sight housing. If the rifle is to be used by both right and left-handed shooters, loop the wire through the larger opening. If only a right or left-handed shooter will use it, loop the wire though the gap between the barrel and the gas tube housing. Then the sling will stay to one side or the other. Ned Christiansen of Michiguns makes the wire loops, and he also makes his "UNslinger" which has the loop and a web strap section holding a fastex buckle. With the Unslinger you can quick-detach from your self-made sling, an important consideration if you work around water.

On the rear, the 550 cord differs between rifle types. With a fixed-stock rifle, first make a fist-sized four or five-loop 550 cord circle. Then, lash that to the top of the stock by using the bottom sling swivel as the anchor, and connect the smaller loop on top. Tie the lashing down, knot tightly, cable-tie it to secure it and then melt the loose ends. Basically, it will look like a figure-8, with the stock through and attached to the lower loop.

On a tele-stock, either loop your fist-sized 550 cord loop through the top sling swivel slot on an XM-177/CAR type stock, or through the sling slot on an M4 stock.

Now, connect a simple, looped one-slider sling (Uncle Mike's would be one example) between the front and rear loops, or buckle it to the Unslinger.

Other Attachment Options

One choice on the front is the Colt M4 side-sling swivel. It attaches around the barrel inside the front sight housing. To attach, press one roll pin through the attachment anchor. Press the sling swivel assembly over the barrel from one side or the other. Hook the roll pin on the lower end of the sling housing, and pivot it to clamp the barrel.

Now drift the second roll pin through the anchor, trapping the other arm of the housing around the barrel. Paint-in the roll pins so if the move you'll see.

Midwest Industries makes a front ring that clamps onto the side rail of a railed handguard. The big advantage there is the ability to lock the MI sling ring on at any point along the rail.

In the rear, you can use the rear attachment of the Simple Sling, above. Or a rear side attachment like the Midwest Industries attachment, which bolts through the slot in the M4 or similar slider on a carbine stock.

Single Point Slings

Single point slings are much-enamored in some circles. Me, I have found few that work well for me, but then I'm an old fart who grew up and learned to shoot back when slings were still made of leather. Most use a plate that replaces the rear retaining plate of the telestock. To install it you have to remove the stock assembly (as in the stock chapter) replace the plate and re-install everything. Or, use an "Agency" sling anchor. Many police departments forbid end-users from installing anything that requires the use of a tool other than a screwdriver or allen wrench. Many of you might be loathe to be wrenching on the stock of your rifle, perfectly content that it is secure and just the way you like it. The Agency sling ring is just the thing. Remove the slider, loosen the clamping screws on the Agency sling and slide it over the buffer tube. Press it up against the receiver and tighten the clamping screws. Re-install the buttstock. Install the sling. The Midwest Industries agency sling hardware shown is aluminum, lightweight and clamps down securely. Other companies make a similar product. (Don't forget to remove the allen wrench before installing the sling.)

Here is a QD single point Agency sling adapter from Midwest Industries. Bolt on, adjust your sling, and go.

The Magpul single-point plate uses a bar, which allows your single-point sling to go either way.

More Options

One of the problems I have with single point slings are the rings themselves. They sit right at the receiver where my firing hand has to work. The bigger and easier they are to use as sling locations, the worse they are for my shooting hand. One option is to go with a central-mount hookup. The sling stud here is drilled and tapped directly into the rear of the retainer plate (while it is off the rifle, please) and gives you a sling latch that works for both right and left-handed shooters. And gets the sling ring out of the way.

Another option is the Magpul single point plate, the ASAP, has a steel rod underneath the buffer tube, similar to the carbine sling attachment rod on cavalry carbines of the US Army in the period after the Civil War. Your sling simply slides side-to-side as needed, and the idea of left or right handedness becomes moot. If you have to have a single-point sling, and the usual plates are a pain, this is the way to go. Heck, it's a cool way to go anyway.

Another approach is to go with certain stocks and railed handguards, which have built-in quick detach sockets. The sling swivels themselves have a spring-loaded plunger and four ball bearings in them. Press the central button, and you can insert or remove the sling. Now, you have to buy and install the stock and or rails to do it, but since a lot of you are going to be doing that anyway, buying ones with the sockets is a smart move.

As a final trump card on this, Kinght's Armament machines their receivers to have the sling swivel sockets right in the rear of the receiver itself. If you have a stock and forearm with sockets (the Knight's does) and the Knight's receiver, you'd have more sockets than you could possibly deal with. You'd need a semester of math just to figure the possible combinations and a lifetime of range testing just to try them all.

Ditch the Rifle?

Why all this emphasis on a quick-disconnect from your emergency tool, your rifle? Simple: if you go into the drink, there is no rifle light enough to aid you in floating. In fact, they are all anchors. The USMC feels strongly enough about this that they have special training simulators to allow Marines to practice exiting overturned and submerged vehicles or aircraft: all slings must have QD fasteners, and each Marine is instructed to use the fastener each and every time he takes off the weapon. That way, they are in the habit of unsnapping rather than untangling.

Now, if you live in a desert, and your only daily introduction to water is your shower, it won't matter much. For the rest of us, leaving a rifle at the bottom of the lake (where the dive team can recover it) or the river is preferable to going down with it. And it makes it a whole lot easier to take off even on dry land.

The Knight SR-15 has QD sockets machined right into the receiver and the rails.

OPTICS

Optics allow for a more precise aim, and in some cases offer magnification to allow for better target identification. However, as with all things in life, nothing is free. Magnification is a good thing at distance but can be a problem at close range. Optics, while having become much more durable of late, are still less durable than iron sights. If they use batteries the batteries can die. Even if they don't, dust, rain or snow can cover the glass to make it more difficult to aim. Simply putting optics on rifles does not make the rifle more accurate, and it does not make you a better shot. Only training and practice will do that.

Selection

Optics can be had one of two ways: magnifying and non-magnifiying. The non-magnifying optics are primarily the "red-dot" sights. They use batteries and a reflector inside the housing to project the image of a red dot. The big advantage of these sights is that they are parallax-free. That means wherever the dot is, that is where the shot goes, assuming a properly-zeroed rifle. It doesn't matter where in the viewscreen the dot appears, that's where the bullet will hit. The disadvantages are these: if the battery quits, the sight stops working, and rain, snow frost and condensation

The two bases are simply held onto the scope (a most excellent Trijicon here) by bolts on the bottom.

Optics have become common on standard rifles, something unheard of a generation ago. (Thank IPSC shooters for that.)
U.S. Army photo by Staff Sgt. Russell Basset.

can cloud the view. (The latter disavantage is shared with all optics.) The government has bought hundreds of thousands of the Aimpoint M2 or M3 or M4 sights, calling all of them the M-68 CCO (Close Combat Optic). One can hardly look at a photo from Iraq or Afghanistan without seeing a rifle, and even belt-fed machine guns, with an M-68 mounted. One type of optic keeps working despite battery expiration, for it doesn't use batteries. And another keeps working despite rain, snow and condensation. The no-battery lighted optics are the Trijicons, which use a light-gathering bar on top to add light to the Tritium-powered reticle.

The EOTech Holosight does not need an entirely clear view though the scope. If there is enough of the side facing the shooter to reflect the reticle, then the shooter sees a reticle. But unlike the Trijicon, if the battery of the EOTech dies, it ceases being a useful aiming aid.

Magnification can be a good or bad thing, depending on what you need at the moment. The Marines in Iraq are finding that while a 3.5X scope is often useful, it has limits: at long range it isn't enough, and across a room it is too much. As neither you nor the police are highly unlikely to be trading shots at distances further than a medium-

An EOTech, on a gooseneck mount.

sized parking lot, 3X might be a useful upper limit. If the department insists on magnifying optics, they should try to keep the magnification on issue scopes as low as possible.

Attachment

Avoid optics attachments that use the carry handle, unless they are the "gooseneck" mounts that extend over the handguards and are as low as possible. Ideally, optics would be mounted on the top rail of an M4 upper, or on the top rail of a railed handguard.

The locking screws of the mount must be painted-in once the rifle is zeroed. While the quick-detachable mounts are very cool (and the good ones return to zero well) the hazards are great, and the cost can be significant. The temptation to show off: "Hey, my scope comes off and goes right back on again" is more likely to be, "Hey, my scope comes off and . . . oops!" Before changing to the purchase only of flat-top rifles and carbines, the Armed Forces invested in a great many gooseneck mounts. Those may be available surplus, if you search the internet and gun shows, and if you wish to put optics on rifles or carbines with regular carry handles.

The knobs are OK, but nothing beats a quick-detach system. Here, we're going to swap out the one base for a LaRue.

This Insight optic is mounted just forward of the BUIS, so the irons can be flipped up when needed.

Here's the Trijicon with the LaRue base attached, ready to go on a flat-top rifle.

Can you mount too much stuff? How about a magnifying optic, a thermal imager, and a video panel display?

A non-magnifying optic is plenty good to 300 meters, as this NG trooper is demonstrating. However, it doesn't help much in target ID.

The GG&G Accu-cam quick mount makes it a snap to put optics on or off your rifle.

Checking zero at 100 yards, with a Leupold C/QT. Which zero you use is less important than knowing what the one you have will do.

Easy-On, Easy-Off

Having a scope or other optic that can be quickly removed is nice. It can even be useful. Some come that way. Those that don't, you get mounts for. A.R.M.S. makes a mount for the Aimpoint, as do Midwest Industries, GG&G and LaRue. When you mount it, make sure the mounted scope does not interfere with the folding BUIS you've installed. (You do have back-up iron sights on your rifle, don't you?) That way, if your batteries die, you can flip up the irons and keep going, If the optics block the rear sight, you first have to pry the optics off before you can use the irons.

GG&G makes their Accu-cam, a single-lever mount. It works the same for all optics: once you have a location, you test-fit the mount. If it is loose (you want it to take some force, but not too much to clamp on and off) you adjust the

fit. One thing to note: the EOTech uses a rather small-diameter bolt to clamp the sight on. The Accu-cam replaces that bolt with the bolt of the Accu-cam. If the bolt breaks, your sight falls off. We've done some experimenting to make the shaft bigger, but it requires drilling and re-tapping the hole, a definite non-warranty task that could mean you have an expensive paperweight. This is not to indict EOTech, as their optics are otherwise bomb-proof (almost literally) and many shooters, myself included, are very happy with them.

Co-Witness

The big advantage to red-dot sights and a folding BUIS is that the optics are handy, and if they quit, the iron sights are but a moment away. Plus, they can be used to verify zero. The zero method is the same for both, and must be

This Trijicon ACOG will let you see your target and place shots precisely out to 300 yards. But you still have to zero it, and know your trajectory.

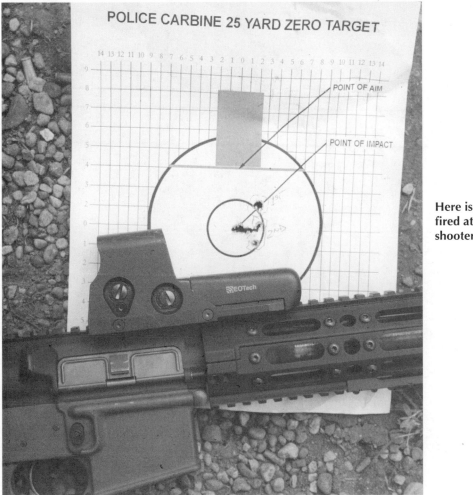

Here is a last-step 100-yard zero target, fired at 25 yards. Two clicks left and this shooter is finished with his zeroing task.

done with both. But once done, it can easily be checked, one against the other. In almost all instances, the red dot, on a properly-zeroed rifle, will coincide with the irons. To check, turn on the dot. Flip up the irons, and aim the iron sights as if you were dry-firing. (Need we remind you again the rifle must be unloaded when you do this?) With the irons properly aimed, the dot should appear to be perched on the top-center of the front sight blade. Once a proper zero of both is done, the sights can be checked any time. If, in checking the co-witness, the irons and dot no longer coincide, then one of them has changed. Granted, knowing that one of them is wrong, but not knowing which, can be frustrating. But not knowing at all that the single sighting system on other rifles (optics without BUIS, or irons without optics) is correctly zeroed and undamaged is worse.

If the BUIS and the optics do not agree, find out what happened. If your rifle just fell, and there's a big crease in your scope, you've got what those in law enforcement call a "clue."

The M-guns Ballisticker gives you a quick reference to recall bullet drop. Know the range, have a zeroed rifle, you can get hits quickly.

The Leupold Prismatic gives you a 1X, with a lighted reticle. Very fast, very solid, and with its own base included.

If you do your job properly, the zero will not change between 1X and 3X (this magnifier added to the Aimpoint). If it does, the problem is usually the shooter.

A scope is an aid, not a replacement for good technique. You still have to do the work of zeroing.

M-guns also makes a sticker to sort out your EOTech adjustments. If you have an EOTech and zeroing is a hassle, you need this.

Boresight and Zero Check

Boresighting is simple, and the modular design of the AR-15/M-16 makes it easy. Simply remove the upper from the lower. Remove the bolt/carrier group and charging handle from the upper. Now place the upper in a cradle, rest, or solidly-supported position. Look through the bore and center the bore on an object 25-50 yards away. Now look at the sights as if aiming. Are the sights close to the object you used as a bore-sighting target? If it is, then boresighting is complete. Any shots fired when zeroing the rifle will be close enough to hit paper, be observed, and can then be corrected.

If not, then the barrel might be bent, the sights adjusted far from the mechanical zero, or the front sight housing might be tilted. Inspect and correct.

You can also use a laser aiming device to boresight. The process is backwards, but the results are the same. Take the upper, minus bolt and carrier, and place it in a vise, cradle or solid rest. Insert the laser in the muzzle, and turn it on. Aim with the sights until the sights are correctly aligned on the target, then look for the dot. (Either walk downrange or use binoculars.) The dot indicates where the bore is pointed. If the dot is on paper, you're good to move on to the firing portion. If not, find out why.

A rifle must be zeroed for it to be useful. Trying to aim at a target using "Kentucky windage" is not a reliable method. But the problems can be quite involved. The bullet travels on an arc when it is fired. If it were not "pitched up" when fired, it would immediately begin dropping below the barrel. The sights of the AR-15/M-16 are 2.6 inches above the center of the bore. The bullet is directed upwards, and will cross over the line of sight at some short distance. (Known as the zero distance, or first intersection.) After that it will travel above the line of sight for quite a distance, before gravity and air drag bring it back down to the line of sight. (The second intersection.) Then it continues to pitch downwards to the ground until it comes to rest. Where should that initial Zero distance be?

Military Zero

The military, having firm ideas about engagement distances, has settled on (in the case of the A1 sight system) two "first crossing" distances: 25 and 42 meters. The latter is the short-range sight. On the "short-range" zero setting the bullet travels above the line of sight until it gets out to 250 meters. The long-range zero uses a closer initial crossing, which creates a greater upward angle of fire. The 25 meter zero has as its second line-of-sight crossing a target at 375 meters. I think we can all agree that 375 meters is beyond all normal distances for engagement in a self-defense or law enforcement setting. In fact, most incidents will be well inside of 100 yards. The problem with either military zero is that inside of 25 yards (or 42) the bullet strikes below the line of sight, while beyond 25 (or again, 42) it strikes above the line of sight. Since the large majority of defensive rifle shootings will be inside of 100 yards, the question then becomes a tricky one: is the target at a distance where the shooter needs to hold over or under the desired impact point on the target? And once you've determined if the offset is over or under, then the question is: How much?

There is an easier way.

100-Yard Zero

Despite referring to it as the 100 yard zero, the initial shooting for sight adjustment is done at 25 yards.

By sighting the rifles to impact 1.5 inches low at 25 yards, the bullet does not rise to the line of sight until it has reached 100 yards. It then rises a small amount above the line of sight, and then drops again just before it get to 200 yards. At 200 yards, the distance it drops is easy to remember: 2.23 inches. Out at 300 yards, the bullet has dropped a foot, but treating the shooting problem as if it were a head shot accounts for that trajectory drop. So, with a rifle zeroed using the NEMRT 1.5 inches below the target, a shooter need not worry about line of sight issues. Inside of 25 yards his problem is the same as everyone else's: the sights are 2.6 inches high, so hold for a lower point of impact. At 25 yards on out to any reasonable engagement distance, the bullet will not be more than an inch or two away from the line of sight.

To aid in keeping track of the distances hold-overs with the 100-yard zero, Michiguns has produced a rifle sticker. If you sight-in rifles according to the 100-yard zero, the label will provide the offsets needed for target engagement to any reasonable distance. Across a small room, the bullet will obviously strike the target 2 to 2.5 inches below the line of sight. Some law enforcement situations are different. Entry Teams must be (and usually are) familiar with this problem. Beyond the distance of a small room, the difference between line of sight and bullet impact becomes small., At 25 yards, it is 1.5 inches (bullet low); at 50 it is 0.7 inches. At 100

yards, the difference is zero. So, at very short distances, the shooter must hold over. Entry teams are well-aware of that, spending all their time in the "10 yards and in" zone. They have all had to learn to hold over their target, as inside of 25 yards, it matters with the AR. Beyond that the difference between sight line and trajectory is not much larger than the group size the shooter can accomplish. Beyond that, the chart provides hold-overs. Adhesive-backed, simply find a location on your rifle where it will be easy to use, degrease, apply and you're done. (Except for the practicing.)

"Entry" Zero?

The thought comes up from time to time, to zero rifles at the usual engagement distance, and for entry teams that means across a room. That usually means seven yards. With a seven-yard zero, you wouldn't have the same hold-over problem. (Well, you would, but it would exist only from the range of zero to two yards, or so.) However, it won't work. The bore starts out 2.6 inches below the line of sight. If, at seven yards the bullet and sight lines meet, then simple geometry tells us that at 14 yards the bullet will be 2.6 inches high. At 28 yards, 5.1 inches high. At 100 yards, more than a foot and a half high. In balance, a bad idea, and one mechanically impossible, as the front and rear sights cannot even be moved far enough to get the rifle zeroed at seven yards.

The Zero Process

Getting rifles zeroed is a simple process to describe, and appears to be an easy task to accomplish. It typically is not. One method used by some police departments is for the armorer or one of the firearms instructors to zero each rifle before it is issued. If the department has only five to 10 rifles, they could all be zeroed in an afternoon. However, with 20 or more, it becomes real work. And the officers to whom the rifles are issued will still have to familiarize themselves with the operation and check the zero for themselves. Having the officers do the zero under supervision both familiarizes them with the rifles (and the zero process) and provides a quick function test as well. You, the guy who isn't in a department, has to do it for himself. (And ladies, I'm not being sexist here. You own a rifle, you'll have to zero it yourself, even if it is pink.)

However, despite that we all consider ourselves competent, not all officers have an initial skill level up to the task of zeroing a rifle quickly. It may take several iterations of the process: Shoot from a solid rest, unload and show clear, walk down to the target, determine the group

center and the adjustments needed, walk back, make the adjustments, re-load and fire again. As each cycle can take five minutes or more, range time quickly gets consumed just with zeroing rifles.

I've zeroed rifles using just six rounds (not bragging, I didn't have any time to do it except quickly) firing two three-shot groups. But that is the exception, not the norm.

If when you go to zero you shoot a group more than an inch in size at 25 yards, locating the group center becomes problematic. Even an average rifle should be capable of shooting a group at 25 yards that has two or three of the five shots touching. A good shooter, with an above-average rifle and good ammunition, should be able to put all five shots in a group through one ragged hole at 25 yards, time and again.

The smaller the group, the easier it is to determine the actual zero of the rifle, and the smaller the group the easier it is to calculate and crank in the corrections needed.

The good news is, once your rifle is zeroed it is zeroed. You don't have to go and re-do it every time you change ammunition. Now, theoretically, each batch, brand or production lot of ammo you use would call for a re-zero. And if you were shooting across-the-course, head to head with someone like David Tubb, yes you'd want to re-zero if you made any change in ammo. But realistically, you don't. As an example, I took one of my rifles and bolted a 3.5-10 Leupold scope on it. At 10X, using several different brands of ammo loaded with the same bullet weight on 100-yard targets, I had changes in the point of impact that came to over half an inch.

A half-inch change in zero, to a sniper, is cause for an attack of the vapors. For the rest of us, it doesn't matter, especially as such a shift could have as easily been due to me as to any other cause.

You do not, however, want to be changing bullet weights without checking zero. The point of impact of a 55 grain bullet and a 77 grain bullet may not coincide at 100 yards. Best to check, and be sure.

AR PISTOLS

O K, let's take this subject head-on. The building of an AR handgun is complicated in two areas: the mechanical and the legal.

Building an AR Pistol

The mechanics of it are severely constrained. On the front end, you have an ultra-short barrel, with a very small operating window for port size, gas flow, extraction and ejection dynamics, etc. Obviously, you could make that easier by using a 14.5-inch M4 barrel, with its gas system already tuned. But, a "handgun" with a 14.5-inch barrel is, to be kind; an odd duck. On the back end, your gas system headaches are complicated by the need to make the buffer as compact as possible. Again, you could go with a standard-length buffer tube (but not a standard buffer tube) – but why?

At the extreme, if you went with a 14.5-inch barrel, and a standard carbine-length buffer tube, you would not have a "handgun" much, if at all, shorter than a regular carbine with the stock collapsed.

So, you have the unenviable task of assembling and tuning an AR with a 7-inch barrel, and a shorter than normal buffer tube (and thus shorter and lighter buffer weight) as your handgun. The usual result is a loud, hard to control handgun in .223 that works when it wants to.

It is, however, something a bunch of people want to do and have done.

The pistol AR has to use a pistol-only buffer tube. It can't be a regular tube without a stock.

Without a stock, aiming the AR pistol becomes more work.

Legalities

The legal aspects of building an AR pistol are considerably more complex than the mechanical, and much more arbitrary. First, how to get a handgun AR? There, the advocates fall into two camps, both arguing the law, and both or neither right/correct/legal/wrong until it is decided in a court of law.

Side A

Here, we have those following the outlines of the court decision involving Thompson/Center. T/C makes receivers that can be handguns or rifles, depending on the stocks and barrels you install. The court decided that the receivers could be whatever the owner wanted, as long as the owner took care to not assemble an unlawful combination. So, T/C receiver, long and short barrels, pistol grip and stock. As long as the receiver never had on it the short barrel/stock combo, it was kosher.

Following that logic, an AR can be either a handgun or a rifle, depending on several things under the control of the owners: First, that it be a "virgin" receiver. That is, it came to the owner as a bare receiver, never having been assembled, and never being declared on any paperwork as a rifle. Second, that the owner build it first as a pistol, and once done, can then re-build it to a rifle and back again, AS LONG AS it is never in the configuration of short barrel and rifle stocked lower.

An aside here: the BATFE is particularly suspicious of "unassigned lowers." That is, you want AR handguns and rifles in your safe, have them all assembled, and not have spares of each lying about. An example: you own a M4-gery (carbine, fully-assembled) a pistol, (short barrel, fully assembled) a spare M4-gery upper, and a spare carbine lower. Cool, the spares come together as another carbine. However, make that collection: M4-gery, pistol, spare pistol upper, spare carbine lower, and you could be in trouble.

The unassigned lower, combined with the spare pistol upper, becomes an SBR, a no-no. So, be aware that spares can be dangerous combinations.

Side A has, to buttress its argument, numerous letters, issued as opinions by the relevant (and authorized) BATFE officer, saying exactly the above. However, letters of opinion are just that: opinions. If the legal branch or the top brass decide otherwise, all those letters are for naught.

Side B

Here, the advocates are reading actual regulation, and the requirement by manufacturers that they declare each and every firearm they manufacture as a long-gun or a handgun. By this reading, unless the manufacturer declares it a handgun, it is a de-facto rifle, and you cannot make a pistol out of a rifle. Thus, you must find a lower that is made as, marked as, and sold as, a handgun. Once made into a handgun, you can then (following the logic of the T/C case) re-build it as a rifle. But once a rifle, you can't go back.

The "virgin" status of the receiver means naught. The manufacturer makes it as a rifle, and ships it off. The FFL you get it from is a Dealer, not a Manufacturer, and he/she has no legal authority to change it from a rifle to a handgun. And technically, if they were a manufacturer, they could make it an SBR, which trumps handgun, but isn't a handgun.

Can the regulation requiring manufactures to declare each firearm as a long or short gun, be squared with the opinion letters? No.

Both sides are logical, and have clear and obvious reasoning behind them. They are also contradictory. The BATFE has not settled this, as it is a very arcane point of law and regulation (even by the arcane standards of firearms regs and law) and it is not likely to be settled until someone ends up in court or until the issue gets pushed to a decision by the BATFE.

Where am I in this? Of both minds. I can see the logic in each. I cannot reconcile them, and I'm not in a legal position to do so. (Were I, I would not be writing firearms books, and my solution would be decidedly unsettling to many.)

Some Extras

There are some things you can't do to your AR pistol, regardless of Side A or B. You cannot gain extra control by installing a vertical foregrip. Doing so makes your AR pistol into a firearm in the category known as "Any Other Weapon." Now, you can, if you live in a State that allows it, file the appropriate paperwork and have it lawful to make your pistol into an AOW. That is, fill out a Form 1, include your $200 tax payment, and wait for approval. Once you get approval, knock yourself out. But just slapping on the foregrip without approval, as far as the BATFE are concerned, is the same as putting on a stock, or making it a machinegun.

If the $200 tax is too much, you could also find an NFA Manufacturer willing to do the "work" for you. Ship them your gun, they apply for the approval, install the vertical foregrip after you pay your $5 transfer, and it's yours.

Regardless of which side is correct, A or B, you cannot take an existing rifle and turn it into a handgun. Only if (and this is a relatively gray-ish area) you built it yourself as a handgun and then made it a rifle, and then want to make it a handgun again. Maybe.

Just when the "unassigned lowers" headaches seemed they could not get worse, you have to consider the timeline of building your AR pistol. If you plan to build one, the first thing, the absolute first thing you buy is an AR pistol lower, and you immediately slap on a (correct) pistol buffer tube. Otherwise, you have the potential of building non-allowed combinations. Now, if you don't own any ARs at all, you can do as you please. But if you own rifles, you must walk with care.

The biggest trip is the barrel. You want a pistol, you have rifles, you see a deal on a pistol barrel, and you buy it. Ooops, you now have the parts to build an SBR, and you could be in trouble. Yes, people have gone to jail over just this. Why slap a pistol buffer on your pistol receiver asap? Again, if you have spare rifle stock parts, that receiver could just as easily be assembled with rifle stock and handgun barrel, and viola, you have an SBR.

If you're going to do this, you have to carefully dance the dance of avoiding things that would look bad, even if there is no intent of bad in your heart.

Weaseling Out

Well, what some might consider weaseling out: just buy one. Yes, it does sort of defeat the whole purpose of a book on gunsmithing, to just buy something. But it does completely sidestep two issues: the legal one, and the working one. If you buy a complete AR pistol and it has functioning problems, you have someone to turn to. You also have a pattern, and sample to compare, when you build your own.

And let's be truthful here: no one reading this book is going to be content with just one AR, are they? If you're like the rest of the shooters I know, you'll end up with three or four at a minimum.

Chapter Twenty

PISTON SYSTEMS

The hot new thing is piston systems for the AR. The idea is simple: you don't want all that hot, nasty abrasive, dirty gas being pumped back into your receiver. The good news is, there are plenty of piston systems to pick from. The bad news is, not all are user-installed. A lot of them are factory-only. You want an LMT, HK, S&W or Ruger piston AR, you buy the rifle or the upper. But there are some that can be had, and some that you can have retrofitted.

One retrofit is the PWS from Primary Weapon Systems. Send them your upper and they will install their piston, which consists of a new gas block, a rod that replaces your carrier key, and the guide parts to keep the rod in line. The rod also acts to avoid carrier tilt, a problem that appeared

with piston systems once they began to leave the R&D benches and appear on the ranges.

There are some that you can install, but first a few things to note about piston conversions. First, they will cost. Early in the evolution, we all thought we could simply replace the carrier key with a thrust pad, and have the new piston push there. After an epidemic of shorn screws, it became clear that a piston conversion would require a new carrier, one with the thrust shoulder machined as an integral part of the carrier. That adds cost. Also, the carrier had to be re-designed at the rear, to mitigate the effects of carrier tilt. When the rod hits or pushes the carrier, it tilts it down in the back. That can wear at the buffer tube.

The PWS piston is something they will install. Make sure you read the list of what handguards it will fit under.

The PWS piston conversion uses a long rod attached to the carrier, which prevents carrier tilt.

Here are the Adams kit parts, plus the barrel it will go on.

The Adams thrust shoulder replaces the carrier key on older conversions. Adams now offers a new carrier as part of the kit.

Take off the old front sight housing and bolt on the Adams gas block.

Piston systems solve some problems while creating others. The gas doesn't get directed back into the receiver, but it doesn't go away. Instead of there, it gets vented up front. That means your piston gets grubby, and your front block gets hot. Shoot enough without cleaning, and you'll need oil-soaking and big pliers to get your gas system apart.

If you want to build a piston system, it is best to do it to a barreled upper, and not convert one with carrier and bolt in it. Otherwise, you're simply setting aside the carrier, a costly part of the upper. If you want to do it, let's walk you though it:

Piston Conversion

The ones you can install are the Adams, the CMMG and the Bushmaster. (Bushmaster makes a different one for their factory-built piston guns.) I'll use the Adams, as it is much the same as the CMMG in installation. The Bushmaster we'll cover at the end.

Strip the upper down to the upper and barrel: take out the bolt and carrier, remove the flash hider, front sight housing and gas tube, handguards and any other extras like optics. If you plan on using a railed, or free-float handguard, now is the time to either remove the barrel and take those parts off or cut them off.

The Adams system replaces the carrier key, but unlike earlier designs (not Adams) it does not rely on the bolts to take the thrust. The new key has a thrust stud and a hole for the locking bolt. Remove your old carrier key and screws. Degrease and scrub the key slot. Place the new thrust shoulder on the carrier, with the holes lined up, and press the thrust stud down into the gas flow hole in the carrier. Install the screws, to make sure things are aligned. Next, you need to press-fit the new shoulder on the carrier. I just clamp it in a padded vise and slowly squeeze it in. then tighten the screws. Given the vibration the system takes, Loctite would not be a bad idea. Adams strongly urges Loctite and lists the screw torque as 72 in-lbs. Me, I just used a long-handled allen wrench and made sure it was tight. Several thousand rounds later, mine is still tight.

Scrub the upper (if you've ever shot it) in the gas tube entry area. Take the rod guide bushing, and press it into place in the receiver. Then, place the upper against your bench, barrel straight down, and using the bushing rod, tap the bushing into place. Use a bit of oil or grease to ease its journey, and tap it in flush.

If you're going to go back to an M4 type rifle, slide the front handguard retainer on. If not, leave it off.

Now take the stripped gas block and slide it onto the barrel. Assemble the piston, spring and plug. If you have a flat-top upper, you can use a flat surface to align things. Just turn it upside down and make it all align. If not, slide the gas block until it lines up with the port, and gently tighten the screws. Now check it by eye, and see that the piston slides back and forth without shifting direction.

Once it is all lined up, tighten the gas block screws. Oh, one last thing: before you reassemble, take the gas rings off the bolt. You don't need them anymore, and they'd just cause extra friction and problems.

Reassemble and head to the range. If you have a front sight you're going to use, bolt it on. Take your allen wrenches with you, of the gas block screw size. You may find that a little tweaking is necessary to get the front sight top dead center. The plug is your adjustment. Top is full gas, one o'clock is lower gas, for you lucky suppressor users. 3 o'clock is off.

The CMMG installation is much the same.

The Bushmaster conversion is the old ARES system, but with the last of the engineering done to make it work reliably. It does not replace your existing gas block or front sight tower. Instead, you drive out the gas tube pin and remove the gas tube. (Obviously, you do this after you've taken the upper off the lower and removed the handguards.)

Then slide the gas piston block into the gas tube hole and drive in the new gas tube pin. (I'd use a new one here; no point in being cheap.) Drive in the new piston bushing on

Once everything's lined up, I use a bench vise to press the thrust shoulder into the carrier.

Here is the thrust shoulder on, bolted in place, Loctited and ready to go.

Adjust the gas block so the sight is vertical, and the piston rides freely into and out of the upper receiver.

the upper receiver. Assemble the system, and then install the piston guide holding clamp. This is the figure-eight gizmo that clamps on the barrel and holds the piston guide in place. Without it, you're asking the tiny roll pin in the front sight housing to keep things aligned, an impossible task.

Slide on the new handguards, install your bolt (no gas rings, again) into the new carrier, and head off to the range. The big advantage to the Bushmaster is for those of you who do not have any interest in a folding front sight. You use the one you've used all along.

Will piston systems take over? Will they replace the direct impingement system on the AR? Time will tell, but I doubt it. If the government changes, they'll change to a whole new rifle, not an overhaul of the existing system. That means for a long time, the millions of existing ARs will still be direct-impingement guns, and that means a lot of satisfied customers who are happy with the way things are.

The Adams arms piston has an adjustable gas setting. Up is full, offset is less, and to the side is no gas.

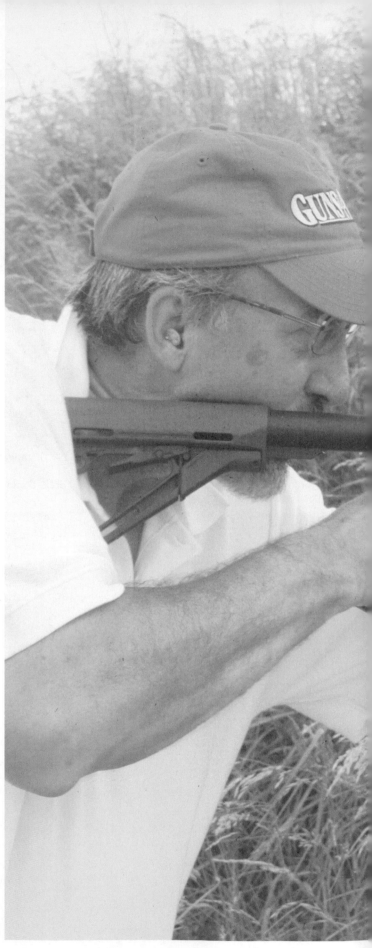

Yes, being a gun writer is fun. Here I'm thrashing a CMMG piston-conversion on a select-fire carbine. Yes, it worked flawlessly. Yes, it was tons of fun.

FIELD MALFUNCTION CLEARANCE

Field malfunction drills are done in a combative situation. The imperative there is to get the rifle running again, or determine that it cannot be fixed in time, and thus transition to a sidearm or another long gun. There are many elaborate flow charts, methods of problem solving and acronyms developed for the AR. Having gone through various classes, taught a bunch, and observed malfunctions on the range and in matches, I feel that the best is the simplest, and that is to treat each problem as if it were the worst, to do simple steps first and then the full corrective process if necessary;

The simplest and fastest solution to an un-firing rifle is to safe it and drop it on its sling, draw your sidearm and continue solving the problem. However, that is not always an option if the rifle is your sole weapon, if dropping it without a sling will cause its loss in deep mud, water, or damage from heights, if dropping it (sling or no) will make it available for use to your opponent, or if the fight is of such range that a handgun will not be very useful. In these and similar situations, you may have no choice but to solve the rifle mystery.

Your Checklist and Order

In the event the rifle fails to fire, check the selector. Has it been pushed to FIRE? If not, push and repeat your attempt to fire. In many instances, shooters unfamiliar with the AR (or who have not kept current in their practice) will miss pushing the selector completely with

(Left) A malfunction we never saw in the old days. Here, the bolt has broken at the cam pin hole, stopping the rifle.

their thumb, or fail at all to engage it. Assuming the rifle then fails to fire, the following procedure will correct it, if it is at all correctable:

Remove the magazine. If you have another, you'll replace the first magazine with the spare, but retain the original magazine. Grasp the charging handle and pull back, locking the bolt open. Insert your fingers into the magazine well to dislodge anything blocking function. (A double-feed often will not fall free of its own weight. You must push the cartridges to dislodge them.) Cycle the bolt repeatedly. Insert the magazine, push it in and attempt to pull it out, to make sure it is seated. Work the charging handle again.

If the charging handle moves, the magazine is in place, and the selector is on FIRE, the rifle should work.

If the charging handle will not move, hold it back with tension, kneel or crouch, and strike the butt of the weapon on the ground. The strike will usually provide enough impetus to unlock the bolt. If it does not, repeat. If that fails, the rifle is inoperative and the shooter should transition to another weapon.

For those who wish to engage in the firearms equivalent of discussing religious doctrine, the various classes of malfunctions are listed in Appendix B, along with their causes and solutions. On the range there is plenty of time to analyze, test and correct problems. On the street, the rifle must be gotten working again as quickly as possible. If you're like the rest of us, you're unlikely to have memorized the flowchart of malfunction classes and their corrective actions. The above method clears all solvable problems.

The 30-Second AR Check

From nationally-known 1911 custom gunsmith Ned Christiansen, who is also a stellar AR-15 'smith and operator:

"They're almost upon us, grab one of these rifles and get ready": the 30-second prioritized AR15 checklist. Items are prioritized factoring in criticality, ease of checking, sequence and likelihood.

If you have half a minute, you can confirm that:

1) *Hammer and trigger pins are flush to receiver sides and not hanging out.* A trigger pin sticking out almost certainly means the hammer spring is improperly installed and is not detenting the trigger pin in place. The result will almost certainly be sporadic or continuous misfires, burst fire, shut-down. A hammer pin sticking out probably just means it was not pushed in far enough. It is detented by the "J" spring, which is simply a length of spring wire that is permanently staked into the hammer. These practically never fail or come loose.

2. *Hammer spring is correctly installed* with both legs horizontal, spread out against inside wall of receiver, and laying on top of trigger pin properly in that pin's outboard groove, acting as a detent for same. A hammer spring installed backwards will give a light primer strike causing misfires, and although it may appear to be laying on and detenting the trigger pin, it in fact will not. This will lead to the trigger pin walking out and causing failures to fire, or doubling/burst fire. Hammer springs not installed backwards can still be improperly installed, with legs either under the trigger pin resting on the floor of the receiver, or inboard of the receiver wall and thus not laying in the detention groove of the trigger pin. In either case the above trigger-pin-walking problems will be the eventual result, plus, when the legs are under the trigger pin instead of on top of it, the blow to the firing pin is reduced somewhat as the spring is not as "wound up" as it would be when properly installed.

3. *Carrier key is not loose.* Simply hold the carrier in one hand and try to wriggle the carrier key with the other. This is almost certainly the number one cause of AR-15 malfunctions. Carrier keys come loose, allowing gas to escape from between the carrier and key. Then there is not enough gas to operated the bolt. The immediate, field expedient fix would be to simply tighten the screws (9/64, and sometimes 1/8, Allen wrench). A better fix would be to remove the screws, clean them and dry them, apply red Loctite, and tighten. Better yet, when time allows, is to do the above and then stake the screws in, displacing carrier key metal over them. This is supposed to be done at the factory but most manufacturers are doing it poorly and some are doing it not at all. Even staked, screws have been known to come loose and although they cannot separate from the carrier key due to the stakes, they will actually turn and lift the key off the carrier. One final bit of insurance after staking and Loctiting can be had by counter-staking the screws, just to the clockwise side of the stakes in the carrier key. This way, if the screw ever did try to turn, the outwardly displaced metal of the screw will hit the inwardly displaced metal of the carrier key, preventing the screw from turning.

4. *Firing pin retaining pin (cotter pin) not blocking the firing pin.* Simply slap the carrier's back end into your palm to make sure the firing pin cannot come out. Also, with the bolt pushed into the carrier, you can press the firing pin forward and check that it protrudes from the bolt face. With this check you have checked two things: that the firing pin is free to travel fully forward and that the firing pin tip is present (although I have never, ever heard of one breaking). Note that the firing pin will not protrude if the bolt is extended forward.

If you have another 90 seconds before the mob is upon you:

5. *Remove bolt and check for presence and condition of gas rings and check barrel for obstructions.* With the firing pin and cam pin removed, if the bolt will drop from the carrier of its own weight, the gas rings are overdue to be replaced (although the gun may well still be working as long as they are present). It is not critical that the gaps in the three rings be staggered, but it doesn't hurt, either. With new-condition gas rings, the bolt carrier will not telescope onto the bolt under its own weight, that is, if you set the assembled bolt group on a

table bolt-down, with the bolt first having been pulled to its forward position, the carrier will not "settle" on the bolt. If it does, but the bolt will not drop free of its own weight as above, you are in the "time to find some new ones but probably OK for the next gunfight" zone. Gas rings are a perishable item and are dirt cheap.

6. *Remove and inspect extractor.* Check that the hook is sharp and undamaged, and that the extractor body is not bent or otherwise deformed. Check for presence of extractor spring and inner "buffer"; these can be white, OD, red, blue or black. Hope for at least a blue one (next to latest), preferably a black one (latest and strongest). If the extractor spring has a "D" ring over it, you are completely good to go. This is a highly recommended part (www. http://www.mgimilitary.com or Brownells). It simply drops over the existing extractor spring and boosts extractor tension. In our experience it has eliminated extraction problems, lasts for 20K-plus rounds, and does not appear to have a down side.

This is something your check will reveal only if you remove the buffer and spring. If you have time, do it. Otherwise, you'll just have to depend on having purchased quality parts.

7. *Check for sufficient lube, re-assemble bolt group with special attention to #4 above, and visually confirm that the extractor is on the right-hand side.* AR-15 bolts are staked or peened on one side of the cam pin hole to prevent the bolt from being assembled backwards. Some bolts lack this feature and the bolt can be installed backwards. This would result in a rifle trying to eject the first fired case out the left side where there is no ejection port.

8. *Check trigger group / safety function:* confirm that the safety works by cycling the rifle to make sure it is unloaded and to cock the hammer, then apply the safety and pull the trigger. Obviously the hammer must not fall. Check that the disconnector properly releases the hammer to the sear – some guns will fire again when the trigger is released because of worn or poorly installed parts. To test this, take off safe, pull trigger to drop hammer and manually cycle the bolt while still holding the trigger back. Release trigger slowly; a click will be heard as hammer falls from disconnector to sear; pull trigger again and hammer should drop. If it does not, it means it dropped as you released the trigger and that the rifle is unsafe. This is not as common as it once was but has occurred in new, out-of-the-box rifles.

If you have another 20 seconds:

9. *Loose barrel-to-upper receiver fit.* Grasp muzzle and upper receiver and twist back and forth to check for looseness. It is not uncommon to find it and it is very detrimental to accuracy, to the tune of 8"-10" at 100 yards. This is caused by the barrel nut being loose; special tools are required. Also check for a loose front sight base by again grasping the muzzle, and twisting the front sight base. There should be no movement. Shake between the upper and lower receivers is absolutely OK. Standard hand guards can also be expected to have movement- - again, no problem.

10. *Check for loose stock and pistol grip* by twisting them whole holding the lower receiver. Looseness in the moving part of a telescoping stock is to be expected.

These checks aren't just for the above, improbable scenario. Go through them every time you clean or otherwise maintain your rifle, and your chances of a nasty surprise at the wrong time will be greatly reduced.

TOOLS

Tool Kit, Basic

Brownells Parts Number	Description
827-530-320	Taper pin starter
827-525-800	1/8" punch
827-525-840	1/4" punch
827-512-820	5/32" center punch
080-216-011	Pivot pin install tool
739-000-010	M4 stock wrench
080-216-012	Bolt catch pin punch

Cleaning Kit, Basic

Rod
Patches
Brushes
Lubricant
Bore solvent
Shop towel
Hand wipes
Nitrile gloves (useful)
Safety glasses

Tool Kit, Advanced

Brownells Parts Number	Description
702-003-015	Peace River action block
702-004-015	Lower receiver vise block
080-000-252	Front sight bench block
795-015-100	Barrel vise jaws
531-460-000	Snap ring pliers
769-100-223	Broken shell extractor
080-000-079	A2 rear sight spring tool
851-115-001	Bbl nut wrench
939-000-003	Bolt ejector tool
513-100-240	Headspace gauge, GO, 223
513-100-241	Headspace gauge, NO-GO

Other Tools

CAT M4 tool
MOACKS
Gunsmith vise
Barrel blocks
Receiver fixtures
Chambering reamers

MANUFACTURERS

Armalite
P.O. Box 299
Geneseo, IL 61254
309-944-6949
www.armalite.com

AR15 Barrels
P.O. Box 66821
Mar Vista, CA 90066
www.ar15barrels.com

Badger Ordnance
1209 Swift Street
North Kansas City, MO 64116
816-421-4956
www.badgerordnance.com

Brownells
200 South Front Street
Montezuma, IA 50171
641-623-5401
www.brownells.com

Bushmaster
999 Roosevelt Trail
Windham, ME 04062
800-998-7928
www.bushmaster.com

CAT M4
www.catm4.com

Colt
P.O. Box 118
Hartford, CT 06141
800-241-2485
www.colt.com

CProducts LLC
28 Harvard St.
New Britain, CT 06051
866-274-0247
www.cproductsllc.com

Lewis Machine & Tool
1305 11th St. West
Milan, IL 61264
309-787-7151
www.lewismachine.net

M&A Parts
1298 Ensell Rd.
Lake Zurich, IL 60047
847-550-8246
www.m-aparts.com

Magpul
P.O. Box 17697
Longmont, CO 80308
303-828-3460
www.magpul.com

Midwest Industries
833 West College Ave.
Wausheska, WI 53186
262-896-6780
www.midwestindustries.com

MGI
102 Cottage Street
Bangor, ME 04401
207-945-5441
www.mgimilitary.com

Michiguns (M-Guns)
55017 Flatbush
Three Rivers, MI 49093
www.m-guns.com

PRI
710 Streine Dr.
New Bremen, OH 45869
419-729-2603
www.pri-mounts.com

Rock River Arms
1042 Cleveland Rd.
Colona, IL 61241
309-792-5780
www.rockriverarms.com

Specialized Armament Warehouse
P.O. Box 6310
Chandler, AZ 85246
480-940-7397
www.specializedarmament.com

Stag Arms
515 John Downey Dr.
New Britain, CT 06051
860-229-9994
www.stagarms.com

Vltor
(no showroom)
520-408-1944
www.vltor.com

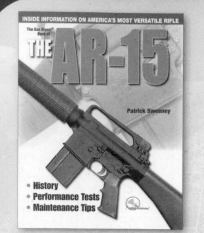
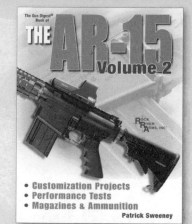

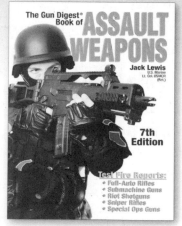
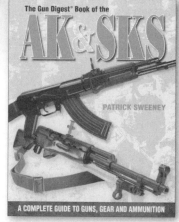